Moral and Legal Aspects of Artificial Intelligence:

Machine Bias and Rule of Law

Jerry Luftman
Global Institute for IT Management, USA

Aditya Tomer
https://orcid.org/0000-0002-6398-2617
Galgotias University, India

IGI Global
Scientific Publishing
Publishing Tomorrow's Research Today

Published in the United States of America by
IGI Global Scientific Publishing
701 East Chocolate Avenue
Hershey, PA, 17033, USA
Tel: 717-533-8845 | Fax: 717-533-7115
Website: https://www.igi-global.com E-mail: cust@igi-global.com

Library of Congress Cataloging-in-Publication Data

Names: Luftman, Jerry, 1948- editor. | Tomer, Aditya, 1978- editor.
Title: Moral and legal aspects of artificial intelligence : machine bias and rule of law / Jerry Luftman, Aditya Tomer.
Description: Hershey : IGI Global Scientific Publishing, 2026. | Includes bibliographical references and index. | Summary: "This book provides an in-depth exploration of the transformative impact of Artificial Intelligence (AI) in the realms of cybersecurity and the legal system, with a particular focus on its applications in predictive policing, legal research, contract automation, and dispute resolution"-- Provided by publisher.
Identifiers: LCCN 2025013373 (print) | LCCN 2025013374 (ebook) | ISBN 9798337331140 (hardcover) | ISBN 9798337331157 (paperback) | ISBN 9798337331164 (ebook)
Subjects: LCSH: Artificial intelligence--Law and legislation. | Artificial intelligence--Moral and ethical aspects. | Computer security--Law and legislation. | Crime forecasting
Classification: LCC K564.C6 M67 2025 (print) | LCC K564.C6 (ebook) | DDC 343.09/998--dc23/eng/20250328
LC record available at https://lccn.loc.gov/2025013373
LC ebook record available at https://lccn.loc.gov/2025013374
British Cataloguing in Publication Data
A Cataloguing in Publication record for this book is available from the British Library.

Editorial Advisory Board

Table of Contents

Detailed Table of Contents

constraints. The chapter concludes with specific action recommendations—such as transparent governance, adaptive liability systems, and globally harmonized standard-setting—that can be implemented to regulate AI. It also outlines a roadmap for future interdisciplinary research, highlighting the practical implications of the study's findings.

The use of Artificial Intelligence (AI) in courts and legal procedures is changing the way the law works. This study looks at the effects of AI technologies on the legal field in a critical way, focusing on how they are being used in India. AI is changing important legal tasks including research, contract analysis, document review, due diligence, and predictive analytics. AI-powered search features have been added to platforms like Manupatra, Westlaw, and LexisNexis. Start-ups like Surukam, which makes the CruxIQ software, are also employing AI to speed up the process of analyzing legal documents and make operations more efficient. Internationally, systems like ROSS Intelligence have shown that natural language processing (NLP) might change the way legal research is done. AI makes it faster, more accurate, and easier to get legal information, but its expanding power also poses ethical, regulatory, and procedural issues.

The legal sector is unable to forecast case duration requirements due to unpredictable and intricate legal process. This study develops a judicial time duration forecasting system which uses deep learning together with machine learning algorithms to solve existing problems in judicial processes. It employs Random Forest, Gradient Boosting, Long Short-Term Memory (LSTM) networks for analysis with historical case data, enhancing legal analytics. The dataset includes case attributes such as decision categories, jurisdictional details, and final resolutions. One of the necessary steps was the calculation of the desired variable 'case duration' because original timestamp data did not contain this information. Through several preprocessing methods the model received refined training data which addressed chaotic and incomplete data while converting factors into categories. Feature engineering played a crucial role in detecting meaningful patterns. The ensemble approach merged distinct models to both boost the overall precision level and create a robust system.

Client data now serves as a valuable intangible asset thanks to the digital economy. Companies are using Big Data and Big Analytics to customize the pricing of their products and services depending on several criteria by means of the information they acquire and evaluate. One runs danger with organic rivalry and client data security. Equipped with such priceless consumer data, companies may undercut consumer welfare and competitiveness even if their outward look of increasing transparency and reducing information asymmetries seems to be improving. This study intends to clarify the inherent difficulties related to behavioral discrimination and investigate the application of traditional competition tools within the developing digital economy to protect consumer privacy and maintain market competitiveness. Our internet buying experience now mostly consists of personalized adverts for electronics, clothes, cars, hotels, and airline tickets.

Establishing trust in AI-driven businesses is crucial for guaranteeing the ethical, effective, and sustainable application of artificial intelligence. This chapter outlines a strategy methodology that incorporates governance frameworks, transparent system architecture, ethical leadership, stakeholder involvement, and adaptive risk management. It examines international frameworks, like the OECD Principles, IEEE standards, and the EU AI Act, in conjunction with pragmatic approaches such as explainability tools, fairness audits, and inclusive co-design. Focus is directed towards cultivating a culture of ethical consciousness, responding to public apprehensions, and predicting forthcoming challenges in generative AI, surveillance, and autonomy. By integrating innovation with human values and regulatory compliance, firms can bolster credibility, augment stakeholder loyalty, and establish AI as a reliable catalyst for sustained societal and organizational advancement.

This chapter critically examines the convergence of Artificial Intelligence (AI) with cybersecurity and the legal system, highlighting how machine learning and algorithmic reasoning reshape predictive policing, legal research, contract analysis, and dispute resolution. It explores AI's capacity to enhance procedural efficiency, data transparency, and equitable access to justice, while contending with ethical dilemmas around surveillance, algorithmic bias, and regulatory fragmentation. Through interdisciplinary case studies, the chapter probes the epistemic boundaries of AI-driven decision-making and proposes governance models that uphold privacy, civil liberties, and institutional accountability. This synthesis offers actionable insights for policymakers, legal technologists, and AI ethicists working at the intersection of digital security and jurisprudence.

Preface

INTRODUCTION

One of the most revolutionary trends of the twenty-first century, Artificial Intelligence (AI) is reshaping the way people work, communicate, and live. Its rapid incorporation into governance frameworks and legal systems offers unprecedented potential alongside formidable challenges. While AI promises enhanced efficiency, predictive accuracy, and improved access to justice, it simultaneously raises intricate concerns surrounding bias, transparency, accountability, and the safeguarding of fundamental rights.

Moral and Legal Aspects of Artificial Intelligence: Machine Bias and Rule of Law is an interdisciplinary exploration that addresses these crucial questions. This edited volume examines how AI interacts with legal, moral, and policy frameworks, shaping the future of governance and justice. Contributions come from distinguished academics, legal practitioners, and researchers, offering nuanced perspectives on the intersection of technology, ethics, and law.

Relevance In Today's World

In an era where AI technologies are embedded in decision-making processes across sectors—from judiciary systems to competitive markets—understanding their moral and legal implications is more vital than ever. Globally, governments, organizations, and institutions are grappling with how to regulate AI without stifling innovation, and how to mitigate biases without undermining its transformative potential. This book positions itself within this critical discourse, offering both theoretical and practical insights to address contemporary challenges.

Target Audience

This book is intended for a diverse readership, including legal scholars, policymakers, AI researchers, ethicists, technologists, and students in law, political science, and technology studies. It will also benefit professionals in regulatory bodies, legal practice, corporate governance, and human rights advocacy, who seek to understand the complex interplay between AI, ethics, and the rule of law.

OVERVIEW OF CHAPTERS

1. The Proliferation of Artificial Intelligence in India: Legal and Regulatory Challenges in Light of Privacy and Deepfakes Concerns

This chapter examines the rapid expansion of AI in India, focusing on emerging legal frameworks and the pressing challenges posed by privacy breaches, misinformation, and deepfake technologies. It highlights the gaps in existing laws and proposes robust strategies for policy development.

2. A Future of Equal Rights: An Agnostic Legal Framework for the Coexistence of Humans and Autonomous AI

This chapter presents an innovative legal model envisioning harmonious coexistence between humans and autonomous AI systems. It debates the feasibility of granting certain rights to AI entities and ensuring such frameworks remain equitable and human-centric.

3. Machine Minds in the Courtroom: A Critical Exploration of Artificial Intelligence in Legal Landscape

This chapter critically evaluates the integration of AI in courtrooms, assessing its role in decision-making, evidence analysis, and procedural fairness. It discusses both the opportunities and risks in automating aspects of the judicial process.

4. Hybrid Ensemble Model for Accurate Legal Case Duration Estimation

This contribution introduces a technical AI model designed to predict case durations with greater accuracy. By blending multiple algorithmic approaches, it aims to support judicial efficiency and reduce procedural delays.

5. Tailored Digital Marketplaces: Navigating AI Regulation within Competition Law

This chapter examines how AI-driven marketplaces influence competition, consumer choice, and market fairness. It analyses the compatibility of current competition laws with the dynamic nature of AI-enabled platforms.

6. Building Trust in AI-Driven Organizations: A Strategic Approach to Ethical Management

This chapter addresses the organizational dimension, offering strategies for embedding ethics into AI governance structures, fostering transparency, and cultivating trust among stakeholders.

7. Algorithmic Justice: Navigating AI's Role in Cybersecurity and Legal Transformation

The final chapter bridges the domains of AI, law, and cybersecurity, examining how algorithmic systems can bolster or threaten security, and their potential to transform the legal landscape.

By engaging with both technical and societal dimensions, this book aspires to contribute meaningfully to the discourse on AI's ethical and legal integration. It underscores the urgent need to align technological advancements with justice, equality, and respect for human dignity. Through the combined expertise of its contributors, this volume offers a timely and comprehensive resource that will inform academic inquiry, policy formulation, and responsible AI governance for years to come.

Acknowledgement

It is with immense gratitude that I acknowledge the contributions of all those who made the publication of *Moral and Legal Aspects of Artificial Intelligence: Machine Bias and Rule of Law* possible. This work is the result of the collaborative efforts of a diverse group of scholars, practitioners, and researchers who brought their expertise, dedication, and vision to each chapter.

I extend my heartfelt thanks to all the contributing authors.

Your intellectual rigor, commitment to academic excellence, and willingness to share your insights have been invaluable in shaping this volume. Each chapter reflects countless hours of research, critical thinking, and the courage to engage with complex and evolving issues at the intersection of technology, ethics, and law.

I am grateful to the reviewers and editorial advisors who provided constructive feedback, ensuring the scholarly quality and coherence of the work. Your detailed suggestions and critical perspectives enriched the content and strengthened the book's overall impact.

My sincere appreciation also goes to the institutions and organizations that supported this endeavour, whether through research resources, funding, or encouragement. Special thanks are due to colleagues, peers, and friends whose moral support and professional advice were instrumental throughout the editing process.

Finally, I would like to express my deep gratitude to my family, whose patience, understanding, and encouragement have been my constant source of strength during the preparation of this book.

This book is a testament to the collaborative spirit of the academic community and to the shared belief that responsible and ethical approaches to Artificial Intelligence are essential for a just and equitable future.

Jerry Luftman

Global Institute for IT Management, USA

Aditya Tomer

Galgotias University, India

Devendra Singh

Amity University, Greater Noida, India

Chapter 1
The Proliferation of Artificial Intelligence in India:
Legal and Regulatory Challenges in Light of Privacy and Deepfakes Concerns

Devendra Singh
https://orcid.org/0000-0002-7470-3783
Amity University, Greater Noida, India

Ashwani Pant
https://orcid.org/0000-0001-5220-453X
Dr. Vishwanath Karad MIT World Peace University, Pune, India

Vikalp Chaturvedi
https://orcid.org/0009-0005-5894-2820
HKG Institute, Agra, India

ABSTRACT

The rapid growth of Artificial Intelligence (AI) in India has led to improvements in sectors like healthcare, finance, and education. However, concerns about data privacy, security, and the potential for AI-generated

DOI: 10.4018/979-8-3373-3114-0.ch001

content to be used for malicious purposes, such as deepfakes, have emerged. India's current legal and regulatory framework is fragmented and inadequate, lacking clarity, self-regulation, and effective enforcement mechanisms. This research aims to examine whether India's existing legal and regulatory framework is sufficient to address the challenges posed by AI proliferation, particularly in relation to privacy and deepfake concerns. A multi-pronged approach is recommended, including strengthening data protection, enacting targeted deepfake legislation, imposing transparency and accountability requirements, and adopting ethical safeguards.

1. INTRODUCTION

Artificial Intelligence (AI) refers to computer systems capable of performing tasks that traditionally require human intelligence, such as perception, learning, and decision-making. Recent advances in machine learning, especially deep learning and large language models, have propelled AI into the public spotlight. Indeed, the late 2022 release of ChatGPT, a generative AI chatbot, brought AI-generated content and its implications into popular discourse (Mohanty et al.,2024). In India, this global surge is mirrored by concerted efforts to harness AI for national development. The Government of India has launched initiatives like the India AI mission and updated national strategies that position AI as a driver of inclusive growth and digital transformation (Atlantic Council, 2025) (Kaushik et al.,2025). AI adoption is growing in both government and private sectors: a 2024 Atlantic Council report notes over 1,600 AI-focused startups in India (Atlantic Council, 2025). Sectoral applications range from predictive analytics for agriculture and public health to automated fraud detection in finance, and natural language tools in multilingual education. The World Economic Forum estimates that AI could add up to $500 billion to India's economy by 2025, with transformative effects in agriculture, healthcare, manufacturing and urban planning (Kaushik et al.,2025).

While AI offers immense opportunities for innovation and efficiency, it also raises serious challenges. Computational systems increasingly process vast amounts of personal data, creating new privacy risks. AI-based surveillance technologies (e.g. facial recognition cameras, drones) promise security gains but threaten civil liberties. Generative AI enables the creation of highly realistic fake media ("deepfakes") that can mislead citizens, harass individuals, or influence elections. In response to these concerns, policymakers worldwide are debating regulations for AI. This paper investigates whether India's existing legal framework is adequate to address AI-related privacy issues and the rise of deepfakes. We analyze sectoral AI use in India, outline key privacy risks from biometric IDs and surveillance, and examine the spread and societal impact of deepfakes. We then review India's laws (cyber laws, data protection laws, penal laws) in the context of AI and synthetic media, assessing their sufficiency. Comparative insights from global regimes (EU, US, China) are included. Case studies of Indian incidents involving AI privacy breaches and deepfake misuse illustrate the practical stakes. We conclude by identifying legal gaps and proposing targeted policy, ethical, and technical solutions to build a rights-based, AI-ready governance framework in India.

2. AI ADOPTION AND SECTORAL PRESENCE IN INDIA

Indian AI is moulded by government vision and private-sector dynamism. National initiatives employ AI for social good to solve local problems ethically (Atlantic Council, 2025) (Kaushik et al., 2025). In 2023, the Ministry of Electronics and IT established the India AI mission to promote AI in healthcare, education, agriculture, and smart cities (Atlantic Council, 2025). India AI and associated activities promote "ethical, inclusive and responsible AI adoption" across industries (Kaushik et al., 2025). These objectives support India's development plan, including numerous SDGs.

By 2023, NASSCOM reported around 1,600 AI start-ups in India (Atlantic Council, 2025). These enterprises, huge IT organizations, and academic institutes focus on computer vision, language processing, finance, and manufacturing. AI helps with radiological image analysis, epidemic modelling, and individualized therapy. The banking industry uses AI for risk assessment, digital lending, and fraud detection, bolstering India's fintech leadership. Machine learning helps education technology companies tailor and automate material delivery in numerous Indian languages.

Media and entertainment firms use algorithms for content suggestion and customer analytics.

India has considerable public digital infrastructure (Digi Locker, Aadhaar biometric ID, and Unified Payments Interface) that can incorporate AI. Some state police forces have tested AI-based picture matching to identify offenders, while smart city traffic management systems use AI-driven video analytics. The government's Responsible AI for Social Empowerment (RAISE) 2020 conference and subsequent policies emphasise AI's role in governance while noting ethical concerns (Atlantic Council, 2025) (Kaushik et al., 2025).

Rapid AI use in India has not always been matched by regulatory foresight. Application sometimes outpaces supervision, say observers. Amber Sinha forecasts a "exponential rise" in facial recognition technology (FRT) usage in India by public and commercial actors "with virtually any legislative hurdles" despite accuracy and bias problems (Sinha, 2024). According to the GIGA Focus Asia research, AI-enabled surveillance (cameras, drones) has been mainstreamed into public life without statutory or express authorization (GIGA, 2021). Thus, many cutting-edge AI techniques are being deployed piecemeal under current legislation, raising privacy and discrimination concerns.

AI is present in government, economics, and society in India, with ambitious public projects and a developing innovation ecosystem. This allows for advantages and major hazards. The rest of this article will examine privacy and deepfakes and if India's laws and regulations can solve them.

3. PRIVACY CONCERNS IN AI APPLICATIONS

AI systems rely heavily on data, often personal or sensitive. In India, one major locus of privacy concern is biometric identity and surveillance. India's Aadhaar system – a 12-digit unique ID linked to iris/ fingerprint data of over a billion residents – has been a pioneering but controversial project. Aadhaar facilitates direct benefit transfers and authentication for services. However, the linkage of biometric identifiers to banking, telecom and welfare services has created a centralized repository of citizens' private data. Studies document instances where Aadhaar linkage failures (false "no-match" errors) led to denial of essential services like food rations and pensions for vulnerable people (Sinha, 2024). In effect, minor biometric mismatches or system glitches have cut off millions from entitlements, highlighting how data-driven ID schemes can imperil basic rights (Sinha, 2024). State officials are expanding AI-based surveillance beyond Aadhaar. Several Indian states use public, educational, and corporate cameras that are powered by AI. Police and cities utilize AI that can recognize faces and gaits on CCTV to discover missing individuals, catch criminals, and enforce the law in cities. Drone-based FRT showed masses of people at festivals and protests in real time. GIGA warns that "AI-enabled facial-recognition technology and drones" have been "mainstreamed into public life without legal reason or the approval of the surveyed" (Sinha, 2024).

Without legal protections, Indians may be watched more closely. The Supreme Court said in 2017 that privacy is a basic right and set four rules for when the government might intrude on it: a legitimate objective, appropriateness, necessity, and proportionality (Sinha, 2024). Many facial recognition apps don't meet the necessity criterion since ID cards or two-factor verification are less intrusive. The Court said that random database scanning was an example of ubiquitous monitoring. Amber Sinha (2024) states that FRT street-level surveillance turns into targeted dragnet policing and that face-recognition for school attendance doesn't work. In practice, the rush to use AI for security or administration means that data minimization principles are often overlooked. For instance, in 2021 the government proposed enabling real-time FRT use by police against wanted suspects, but policymakers later backtracked amid privacy protests. At the same time, private companies and media platforms collect extensive personal data for AI; without robust regulations, this can lead to profiling and erosion of anonymity. In summary, Indian AI applications in identity and surveillance pose acute privacy risks: centralized biometric databases, mass camera networks, and algorithmic decision-making all threaten individual autonomy. Scholars warn of "privacy and discrimination harms" as AI is deployed under weak oversight (Sinha, 2024). Section 66E of the IT Act (which penalizes capturing/transmitting images of private body parts) and other laws offer some recourse, but they are not sufficient for the modern data landscape. In the next sections, we examine how India's laws currently address (or fail to address) these concerns.

4. THE DEEPFAKE PHENOMENON IN INDIA

Deepfakes employ AI to convincingly substitute persons' likenesses in video, audio, and photographs. India's CERT-In advised in November 2024 that deepfakes were "synthetic media generated utilizing AI to generate or manipulate realistic movies, photos and audio" (Walia et al., 2024).

GANs and other machine-learning algorithms may produce realistic but false content, such as recordings of politicians saying things they never uttered or celebrity pornography without permission. Deepfakes create global misinformation, privacy, and security issues. This trend impacts India. Recently, India has seen numerous high-profile deepfakes. Late 2022 and early 2023 viral videos misrepresented South Indian actress Rashmika Mandanna in a pornographic clip. Delhi cybercrime police apprehended a suspect and filed a First Information Report accusing him with forgery under IPC sections 465 and 469 and IT Act sections 66C (identity theft) and 66E (privacy violation).

After a Mumbai TV starlet uploaded a private video, a cybercriminal posted a sexual deepfake on Instagram with foul language. The accused faced sexual harassment, stalking, and defamation charges (Times of India, 2024, Jan 23). These cases illustrate that deepfake victims, usually women, suffer reputational and emotional harm, compelling law enforcement to piece together legislation. Indian deepfakes are socially dangerous. Researchers think political deepfakes work. Civil society and intelligence organizations warned of misinformation during the 2024 Lok Sabha election. India's cybersecurity expert says AI-generated WhatsApp messages and videos might "set off riots" (Harmon et al., 2024). Before the election, the authorities cautioned social media sites against misinformation (including changed media) (Harmon et al., 2024) following the global deepfake trend, several political strategists smeared opponents using AI-generated content. This information may hinder democratic discourse on popular messaging networks. Deepfakes threaten finances and identity.

CERT-In prevents identity schemes and corporate fraud such "CEO fraud" (impersonating management to authorize payments) (Walia et al., 2024).

AI requested fraudulent CEO wire transfers offshore. Even though India has no public data, banks and companies fear AI-enabled social engineering. Blackmailing Indian women using non-consensual deepfake photos. Abuse severely impacts mental health. Deepfakes enable defamation, hate speech, non-consensual sexual exploitation, and sophisticated fraud in India. Indian public discourse and policy discussions increasingly address these concerns. India's deepfake and privacy laws follow.

5. INDIA'S LEGAL AND REGULATORY FRAMEWORK

Artificial intelligence will be a big opportunity as well as risks for all the countries and India is one of them. India is considered one of the largest economies (5th) (Acharya, 2025) with its vast population and having a very much burgeoning labor force, this will have a positive impact to attract millions of dollars of foreign investment. According to the data, the FDI (foreign direct investment) is increased disastrous from 2014, In FY 2014-15, FDI inflow in India stood at mere $45.14 Bn, which increased to $60.22 Bn in 2016-17 and further to the highest ever annual FDI inflow of $84.83 Bn reported during the FY 2021-22 (*Invest India: Your Guide to Investment Opportunities*, 2025). This shows that India could be the big player to become a global tech-market. AI programs and services are coming in numerous industries in India like healthcare, corporate sector, work labor industries as well. These are the points that forced policy makers of India to come up with its own regulation and laws ("AI Regulation in India Current State and Future Perspectives," 2024). This paper very well discussed the potential risks about data privacy and discriminatory decision making by AI programs. In the last few years, India is also working on some guidelines and principles for the ethical development of AI programs and applications. Still there are no specific guidelines and regulations in India yet. For the task of developing AI regulation, NITI Aayog (National Institution for Transforming India) is one of the think tanks for establishment of policy regarding AI in India. In 2018, the NITI Aayog released the National Strategy for Artificial Intelligence #AIForAll strategy ("AI Regulation in India Current State and Future Perspectives," 2024), in which they featured and proposed guidelines for development with respect to all industries. Few years back in February and August 2021, NITI Aayog released two principles:

1. "Principles for Responsible AI"
2. "Operationalizing Principles for Responsible AI"

1. Principles for Responsible AI: This principle approach for a responsible AI system which was published by NITI Aayog in February 2021, which points out the need of strapping ecosystems that helps for twin purposes: R&D and scaling up the ecosystem globally. Despite the huge potential of AI in different fields, still the policy makers are worried and can see the negative impact of AI and hence, policy makers want to make sustainable regulation for managing AI responsibly. To establish the principles of moral, ethics use of AI NITI Aayog published a glance of its regulation by referring it as "Towards Responsible AI For All" and it can be contemplated as a roadmap of AI adoption (*INDIA ai*, n.d.).

Lessons From the Report: There should be a fine line between adoption and implementation of AI for the protection of public good and societal interest. Also there are two consideration for upcoming challenges from AI: system consideration (which means lack of knowledge of AI systems and its functioning) and societal consideration (which caused impact on employment)

2. Operationalizing Principles for Responsible AI: This was the second part of the document with respect to Responsible AI which specifically tells us about the consultation with AI developers, private sector engineers, big firms and non-profitable organizations in order to use AI in ethical way and formulate regulation according to their big brains. Also the role of government becomes important here too, as harmony of all is needed like government, private sector and research institutions as well (*INDIAai*, n.d.-b). Additionally, India is officially now a member of GPAI (Global Partnership on Artificial Intelligence) and meetings were held recently in New Delhi in respect of future AI technology and its commercialization. GPAI's members restate and ensure the adoption of "OECD AI" principle in order to develop the regulation for global standards. The landscape of

AI for India is still far away from completion, also NVIDIA Corporation recently announced their partnership with TATA Groups and Reliance Industries Ltd. to build an AI infrastructure platform (*News Archive*, n.d.).

5.1. Information Technology Act and Cyber Laws

The primary legislation governing cyber activities in India is the Information Technology Act, 2000 (ITA 2000), along with its amendments. Originally enacted to facilitate e-commerce, it also includes provisions penalizing certain cyber offences. Relevant sections include:

Section 66C: Identity theft – punishes fraudulent use of someone's digital signature, password or unique identifier.
Section 66D: Cheating by personation – punishes fraudulent impersonation through a computer resource.
Section 66E: Violation of privacy – punishes capturing, publishing, or transmitting images of private areas of individuals without consent (Mohanty et al., 2024)
Sections 67A/67B: Criminalize publishing or transmitting obscene content and child pornography, respectively.

Notably, the IT Act also contains a safe harbour (Section 79) shielding intermediaries (social media, hosting services) from liability for user-generated content if they follow due diligence. This means platforms may be immune unless they fail to remove illegal content upon notice. As applied to AI, these laws are somewhat generic. For example, existing advice suggests that a deepfake intended to defraud (e.g. impersonating someone's identity to cheat) could be prosecuted under ITA §66D or the analogous cheating provisions of the Bharatiya Nyaya Sanhita, 2023 (Mohanty et al., 2024)

Obscene AI-generated imagery might trigger §67A/B. In practice, however, enforcement relies on older statutes not tailored for digital AI. The Rashmika Mandanna case illustrates this: police filed charges under IPC §§465, 469 (forgery and character damage) in addition to ITA §66C (identity) and §66E (privacy) Times of India, 2025 April 8). Carnegie analysts note that India currently "does not yet have specific legislation to address deepfakes" and that authorities must repurpose existing IT Act and IPC provisions to handle such cases (Bhale,2025) (Walia, 2024).

Table 3 of Mohanty & Sahu (2024) summarizes this patchwork: cheating by impersonation invokes ITA §66D, transmitting explicit deepfake sexual content uses §67A/B, and reputational harm could be covered by proposed new IPC sections (Mohanty et al., 2024). This fragmented approach means gaps remain. The IT Act's privacy provisions are also limited: Section 66E only covers images of private parts, leaving out broader data privacy. In sum, while cybercrime laws exist that can catch some misuse of AI, they are piecemeal and reactive. They do not regulate AI development or mandate safeguards (for example, there is no requirement for watermarking or secure design).

5.2. Digital Personal Data Protection Act, 2023

Introduced the Digital Protection Data Privacy Act, 2023 on August 9. Separate guidelines to support the DPDP Act are being developed by the national government. Gain insight into new law's possibilities. If India transmits information outside, the DPDP act applies ("AI Regulation in India Current State and Future Perspectives," 2024). According to Boston Consulting Group's AI in India research, the new DPDP Act didn't include AI (AI In India: A Strategic Necessity, 2024). The act's main goal is to protect privacy and individual rights. AI models rely on massive data sets. Section 4 of the DPDP Act "mandates that valid permission or reasonable purposes are necessary for the processing of Personal Data of a Data Principal" (Rohit Jolly et al., 2025). In addition to technical issues, the Generative AI model is provided data that may be protected by the DPDP Act, yet the LLM are trained on it. Section 6(1) of the DPDP Act states that "The consent given by the Data Principal shall be free, specific, informed, unconditional and unambiguous with a clear affirmative action, and shall signify an agreement to the processing of her personal data for the specified purpose and be limited to such personal data as is necessary for such specified purpose" (Ministry of Electronics and Information Technology, 2025). Section 5 requires data principals to notify them of consent requests in section 6. The Design Science Research framework is another notable project.

Chapter 3 of DPDP Act discusses "Right and Duties of Data Principal" from sections 11 to 14. To exercise inspection and erase rights, one must identify the data collection that contains personal information. Since academics are currently working on this software, it is theoretically impossible to train an AI model to forget the data it was trained on. Columbia University researchers suggested neural cloaking for machine unlearning, although it's difficult (Seng et al., 2022). This suggests AI may aid DPDP Act regulation. AI models may have regulatory constraints, yet they may be used as consent managers under section 2(g) and manage for Data Principal. It may be able to create an AI predictive model to meet consent management expectations soon.

India has had little data privacy laws. The 2011 SPDI Rules and Section 43A of the IT Act (which held firms liable for "reasonable security practices") were the sole provisions until 2023. Companies have to get permission before collecting sensitive data including financial, health, and biometrics. Limited and weak 2023 (Latham-.India took longer to adopt privacy laws following the 2017 Supreme Court Puttaswamy verdict. The 2023 DPDP Act superseded previous schemes. The DPDP Act regulates data fiduciaries (controllers) and principals (data subjects) like GDPR. Principals may consent, access, correct, delete, and grieve; fiduciaries protect. GDPR changes are big. Only "legitimate uses" (voluntarily given data, compliance with law, medical emergency, creditworthiness) may be handled without permission under the DPDP Act of India (Latham, 2023).

GDPR prohibits contractual and "legitimate interests" data processing (Latham, 2023). This strengthens the law since most processes need approval or exceptions. Critics believe the DPDP Act's "notice-and-consent" approach is insufficient for purpose-based data collection. Section 17(2) exempts government and recognized authorities greatly. State agencies may handle personal data without permission for "sovereignty, integrity or security of India, cordial relations with other authorities, public order, or preventing inducement to offence" (Sinha, 2024).

This broad gap lets the state routinely violate privacy laws. Legal opponents believe this infringes privacy since "public order" and "national security" are widely defined. Another issue is implementation. The DPDP Act requires a Data Protection Board and guidelines before taking effect. Act provisions take effect 6–12 months after regulation creation (Latham, 2023). As of mid-2025, there is no Board or rules, therefore enforcement is inactive (Latham, 2023). India's SPDI Rules and contractual privacy policies regulate data protection until the legislation takes effect. This delay means AI usage continue without a developed legal privacy regime.

Under the 2023 DPDP Act, India's proposed Digital Personal Data Protection Rules, 2025, include informed consent, data fiduciary obligations, and security protections to operationalize the legislation. The laws require clear, separate notifications explaining data collection and consent withdrawal, as well as registered "consent managers" to ensure transparency (Rishabh Gandhi & Advocates, 2025; O'Brien & Sircar, 2025). Encryption, access limits, and breach detection are required, along with 72-hour breach notification to impacted persons and the Data Protection Board. Significant Data Fiduciaries, such as major digital platforms, must conduct annual Data Protection Impact Assessments and follow stricter data localization and cross-border transfer restrictions, including parental consent protocols for processing children's data. The guidelines also restrict user data at three years, demand prior notification before deletion, and provide a digital-first grievance system via the Data Protection Board. These steps improve privacy and match India with GDPR-style requirements, although government exemptions and the regulatory cost on smaller firms remain issues (True Copy, 2025; Internet Freedom.IN, 2025).

5.3. Other Laws and Regulations

Apart from IT and data laws, India's penal code and upcoming legal reforms bear on AI harms. The Indian Penal Code (IPC) criminalizes offenses like criminal intimidation, defamation, and assault, which can be applied to deepfake cases. For example, making a fake intimate video could be seen as "outraging the modesty" of a woman (IPC §354) or as sexual harassment under Section 354A. In practice, deepfake pornography cases have sometimes been handled under IPC provisions for vulgarity or privacy (e.g., IPC §500/501 for defamation, or Section 354C for voyeurism, though the latter is aimed at secret filming) (Times of India, 2025, April 8).

However, none of these were written with digital synthesis in mind. A draft criminal code, the Bharatiya Nyaya Sanhita (BNS), has been proposed (in 2023) to replace parts of the IPC. The BNS includes new sections on cyber impersonation and digital fraud (e.g. Section 319 addresses cheating by impersonation). If enacted, it could clarify penalties for AI-driven impersonation. But as of now, BNS is not law. The government has also hinted at sector-specific initiatives. The Digital India Act (a proposed omnibus tech governance bill) was expected to cover data protection and possibly AI, but its fate is unclear. In late 2024, India's Information Technology Minister stated that the Digital India Act would be introduced "soon," but also emphasized that "a lot more consensus is needed" before formulating an AI law (Sinha, 2024).

This indicates a cautious approach – no new AI-specific legislation has materialized yet. Instead, regulators have tended to act through administrative advisories: for instance, the home ministry or cybersecurity agencies may issue orders targeting specific harms. Furthermore, existing telecommunications regulations and corporate guidelines do not specifically address AI. India's Telecom Regulatory Authority has touched on encryption and cybersecurity, but AI and deepfakes are not in its purview yet. Overall, India's regulatory framework today is a patchwork of older laws that were not designed for AI. This piecemeal system has left gaps: there is no comprehensive privacy authority, no dedicated AI oversight, and only indirect laws that regulators must stretch to apply to AI scenarios.

5.4. Comparative Global Perspectives

It is useful to compare India's framework with emerging international models. The European Union has the world's strongest privacy regime (GDPR) and is crafting an AI-specific law. Under GDPR, individuals have broad rights (access, portability, erasure), and processing of biometric or sensitive data requires strict justification. The GDPR explicitly allows processing under several bases (consent, contract, legal obligation, public interest, etc.), including the controversial "legitimate interests" basis (Latham, 2023).

European Union: The European countries are worried about data protection and privacy, so the EU hasn't made any clear rules about AI yet. However, they have proposed the Artificial Intelligence Act, which will go into effect in 2026. The French government changed the AI Act to include GPAI (General Purpose AI Systems). This defines "such systems as systems that are intended by the provider to perform generally applicable functions such as image and speech recognition, audio and video generation." This definition just puts a big part of AI use under the act. (Fridahl et al., 2020). The European Union's main focus is on their "EU digital single market strategy" (Sadoian, 2025), which aims to set rules for how AI products and services can be made and used in the EU.

The AI Act also says that "The AI Act promotes that all AI goods & services should have a free cross border movement." It tells the EU to create a reliable system that protects democracy and basic rights by making sure that AI is strong in legal, moral, and technical terms. The proposed law looks at four types of risk: unacceptable risk, high risk (like self-driving cars), limited risk, and minimal risk (like apps that use AI). This way of doing things is one of the most important parts of this AI act. It is still not clear if AI products and services that are high risk. Structural frameworks must be able to handle human mistakes. The AI Act has a flaw that this paper talks about: every coin has two sides. Putting risks into groups could hurt the growth of AI products and services, and it could also be a pain for developers. It will be hard and unclear to say which products and services belong in which category because the AI Act doesn't have a clear definition or scope, and the European Union still has a lot of work to do on that part of the AI Act. Also, because of these reasons, it will slow down innovation and could lose to new startups or companies because of the strict rules.

Figure 1. AI Act

Source: (AI Act, 2025)

USA: There is no specific law or rule about AI right now. The White House Executive Order on AI (*AI Watch: Global Regulatory Tracker - United States*, 2025) talked about a number of issues and was based on understanding the good and bad sides of AI and seeing how it could help and hurt people. The Joe Biden government and the National Institute of Standards and Technology (NIST) (Progressive Policy Institute, 2024) came up with the "Blueprint for an AI Bills for Rights" (Garrido, 2023). This is a rights-based approach to regulation that sheds light on AI legislation. This act also suggested five principles, which we can think of as a guidebook for developers. The first one is "automated system," which includes safe and effective systems, data privacy, algorithms, biases, notice, and growth, and the last one is human options. In September 2023, the U.S. held a public conference where the main topic was AI rules (*The Need for Transparency in Artificial Intelligence*, 2023). There was also a private meeting between U.S. lawmakers and AI developers.

The federal government also suggested a few laws about artificial intelligence:

The SAFE Innovation AI Framework is just a set of rules for AI developers, not a law. (Ali et al., 2023).

The Draft No FAKES Act was suggested to protect voice and sound imitation by AI generative apps (Coons et al., 2023).

The California Consumer Privacy Act (*California Legislative Information*, n.d.), which protects against apps that make decisions automatically. By 2024, this law is expected to be in effect.

The AI Research Innovation and Accountability Act, (Raffoul et al., 2023). This law is for businesses that want to make AI systems that are very risky, but it also protects innovation by making sure companies are responsible.

The Algorithmic Accountability Act, 2022 (*U.S. Senate: Request Not Accepted - Security Risk Detected*, 2023) is an important law that says big tech companies must do the bias assessment test on AI models that make decisions automatically. And if they don't follow through, the law may impose certain penalties for that. All of the things that this paper has talked about before are still being worked on for legislation or for more detailed work.

China: China is very eager to create its own rules for artificial Hole in the Wall, ping pong table that will keep up with technological progress and innovation. In May 2024, the National Information Security Standardization Technical Committee (NISSTC) got a draft rule that lists the security needs for generative AI apps and processing. This shows how serious China is about developing AI in a responsible way (Qian, 2025). This research paper also tells us how China is going about making its rules. For AI regulation, they are using a four-layer policy approach. The layers are: the real world roots (China's macroeconomic, political, social, and technological environment), Xi Jinping and the CCP's ideology (the political and intellectual filters through which policymakers see problems), the world of ideas (policy and academic debates, business lobbying), and the party and state bureaucracies (the key ministries and CCP bodies that make AI rules) (Matt Sheehan", n.d.). China's approach is clear, and they are using the EU AI Act as a model for their own AI regulations. China doesn't have a strict deadline for when the law will go into effect, but a draft version of the rules will be ready by 2024.

Singapore: The "human-centered" Singaporean government is unlikely to create AI-specific laws (AI Verify: Singapore's AI Governance Testing Initiative Explained - Future of Privacy Forum, n.d.). GDPR seeks "explainability, transparency, and fairness." It acknowledges the importance of public trust in such laws. Government agencies seem to want to regulate AI-critical areas. Banks and other financial institutions using AI must follow the MAS Guidelines for Individual Accountability and Conduct. AI financial data analysis follows FEAT's fairness, ethics, accountability, and openness. The PDPA regulates how Singaporean businesses and AI developers collect, use, and share personal data. PDPA requires these groups to justify processing public and private data for national interest (Kabus et al., 2024). GDPR and Singapore Act reveal how they collect and protect data, among other similarities. Private sector companies can use AI ethically and responsibly with the Personal Data Protection Commission of Singapore's Model AI Governance Framework. The DPDP Act in India lacks the "legitimate interests" clause (Latham, 2023), so Indian organizations cannot use the EU's flexible legal basis. EU fines companies that use face recognition without consent. Automated profiling has legal consequences. High-risk AI (law enforcement FRT, biometric ID, critical infrastructure) requires transparency, risk assessment, and human oversight under the EU AI Act, which Europe plans to pass. The EU Act requires labelling public synthetic media (deepfakes) (Walia et al., 2024).Conclusion: India is reactive and sector-led, while the EU is prophylactic and rights-based. US AI has no federal regulator or privacy law. State and sectoral laws like HIPAA for health data and the California Consumer Privacy Act protect private data. President Biden issued an executive order promoting AI safety, and the FTC can regulate "unfair or deceptive" AI practices. AI bills have been introduced in Congress. House passed the "No Artificial Intelligence Fake Replicas and Unauthorized Duplications (No AI FRAUD) Act," which criminalizes digital replicas of people's likeness (Walia et al., 2024).

These issues resemble Indian deepfakes. Texas and Virginia ban election-related and non-consensual pornographic deepfakes, but enforcement varies. The U.S. allows civil and administrative harm lawsuits, while India uses criminal law. Asian regulatory models teach. China declared deepfakes and other AI-generated media "rumor-mongering" with synthetic content in 2023. China has strict state-controlled data security laws. Indian AI investment-friendly policy contrasts with these regimes. UK and other EU countries have GDPR-like local data laws and are discussing AI oversight, but no deepfake law. The world wants stronger data protection and AI regulations. DPDP Act in India is less extensive than GDPR but shares data rights and fiduciary duties (Latham, 2023) other countries require algorithmic audits and content transparency, but not India. Without changes, India may fall behind on privacy and AI accountability.

6. CASE STUDIES: AI PRIVACY BREACHES AND DEEPFAKE INCIDENTS IN INDIA

Indian examples show practical issues. AI privacy violations included facial recognition. After 2020-21 Delhi communal riots, police admitted scanning suspect crowds with a live facial recognition system with 2% accuracy (GIGA, 2021). Big data detected 1,900 potential rioters. Poor accuracy caused many false positives, compromising privacy and targeting. Courts called excessive FRT scanning indiscriminate snooping. The event cautioned that unrestrained AI may sacrifice human rights for security. Entertainment is investigated by Deepfakes. In summary: A Mumbai man deepfaked a TV star in January 2024. Times of India, 23 January 2024: Modified and uploaded indecent footage. After the victim reported, the attacker was charged with cyber harassment and defamation. Rashmika Mandanna arrested for April 2023 nude video fraud. Delhi Police FIR used IPC 465 and 469 (forgery and character assassination) and IT Act 66C and 66E.

Criminal charges, not legislation, examined digital issues. After releasing an AI-edited video of herself with a celebrity, a Kerala college student was questioned under cyber laws. Although imprecise, the remarks show inadequate AI comprehension and the difficulties of applying old principles to new innovation. Financial AI fraud exists. An Indian syndicate impersonated a bank official and stole money using AI-synthesized voice communications in late 2021. AI-driven fraud, rarer than text-based scams, suggests deepfake technology might deceive people. Case studies show India prosecutes AI violations under IT Act and IPC. AI regulation and enforcement. Civil society and victims have little options outside criminal prosecution or defamation, privacy, and cybercrime claims.

7. POTENTIAL SOCIAL AND ECONOMIC IMPACT - GAPS AND DEFICIENCIES

The spread of artificial intelligence (AI) technologies is changing social and economic systems all over the world. These changes present huge opportunities but also big problems that need to be closely watched. AI promises to boost productivity and open up new ways for businesses to grow. Estimates suggest that it could add up to $15 trillion to the world economy by 2030 through increased efficiency and the creation of new products and services (Bughin et al., 2018). AI helps businesses cut costs and boost productivity by automating boring, repetitive tasks and freeing up workers to do more creative and strategic work. AI-driven optimization in supply chains, predictive analytics, and personalized customer engagement are already making industries like healthcare, finance, logistics, education, and manufacturing more efficient (Brynjolfsson & McAfee, 2014; Manyika et al., 2017). AI also encourages innovation by making it possible to create completely new fields, such as self-driving cars, smart cities, precision medicine, and creative AI applications in art and design. This creates a need for new skills and business opportunities (Brynjolfsson et al., 2018). AI could also make markets and resources more accessible to everyone by making it easier for small and medium-sized businesses to get in and giving marginalized groups more power through tools and platforms that are easy to use (Vinuesa et al., 2020). For instance, natural language processing and machine translation can make it easier for people from different cultures to trade and talk to each other. AI-powered accessibility tools can also make life better for people with disabilities. If these changes are used fairly, they could help make economic development more inclusive and fix some of the structural problems in the global economy.

But the economic benefits of AI growth are not shared equally, and using AI raises serious concerns about inequality, job loss, and power concentration. One of the biggest risks is that workers will lose their jobs if they are in fields where automation is likely to happen, especially those that involve routine, predictable, or manual tasks (Frey & Osborne, 2017). Some studies say that AI will create more jobs than it takes away by adding to human skills and starting new industries. However, there may be a lot of unemployment, underemployment, and income insecurity during the transition period, especially for workers who don't have the education or digital skills to adapt (Acemoglu & Restrepo, 2019). This dynamic could make social and economic inequalities worse, as highly skilled and tech-savvy workers in high-income areas get the benefits, while lower-skilled workers and developing economies risk being left out (Bessen, 2019). Also, the fact that a few big tech companies control most of the AI innovation and infrastructure raises concerns about monopolistic behavior, rent-seeking behavior, and less competition (Zuboff, 2019). Controlling huge datasets, computing power, and proprietary algorithms makes it hard for new companies to get started. This lets dominant companies take more economic value and strengthen their positions in the market. If the right policies aren't put in place, the spread of AI could make the gap between rich and poor bigger, make regional differences worse, and make it harder for everyone to share in economic gains.

The social effects of AI growth are just as important as the economic ones. They include both good and bad effects on society's structures, norms, and well-being. AI can make public services better, make government stronger, and make life better in general. AI-powered diagnostic tools, predictive analytics, and personalized treatment plans can all help patients get better, make better use of resources, and lower costs in healthcare (Esteva et al., 2017). AI-powered adaptive learning platforms can help students learn in ways that are best for them, close achievement gaps, and give underserved communities more chances to learn (Luckin et al., 2016). Governments can use AI to improve service delivery, keep an eye on compliance, and make policies based on evidence to deal with social problems like poverty, inequality, and climate change (Vinuesa et al., 2020). AI also has the potential to make things more accessible and give power to people who are often left out; for example, computer vision and speech recognition tools can help people with visual, auditory, or cognitive disabilities, which can help them be more socially included and involved (Amir et al., 2019). AI can also help people be more resilient and ready for crises, from natural disasters to pandemics, by making early warning systems, predictive modeling, and quick response coordination possible (Rolnick et al., 2019). These apps can help the United Nations reach its Sustainable Development Goals by promoting health, education, equality, and sustainability, as long as they are used responsibly (Vinuesa et al., 2020).

However, the social risks of AI spreading unchecked are huge and varied. They include algorithmic bias and discrimination, as well as threats to privacy, freedom, and social cohesion. AI systems that are trained on biased or incomplete datasets can unintentionally reinforce societal prejudices and institutional discrimination, especially in areas that are sensitive, like hiring, policing, lending, and criminal justice (Eubanks, 2018; Noble, 2018). For instance, facial recognition technologies have been shown to have strong racial and gender biases, which means that they unfairly watch and wrongly identify groups that are already at a disadvantage (Buolamwini & Gebru, 2018). The widespread collection, processing, and monetization of personal data by AI-driven platforms raises serious privacy concerns, undermining individual freedom and allowing surveillance capitalism (Zuboff, 2019). The spread of deepfakes, false information, and algorithmically amplified echo chambers also threatens democratic discourse, trust in institutions, and social cohesion (Hao, 2021). Unemployment and economic instability caused by automation may also lead to social unrest, mental health problems, and a feeling of being alone, especially if people think the technological change is unfair or out of their control (Brynjolfsson & McAfee, 2014). These social risks show how important it is to have strong ethical, legal, and governance frameworks that support AI systems that are open, accountable, fair, and designed with people in mind (Jobin et al., 2019).

In conclusion, the possible effects of AI becoming more common on society and the economy are huge, complicated, and very dependent on the decisions made by businesses, policymakers, and civil society. AI has a lot of potential to boost productivity, spark new ideas, make opportunities more accessible to everyone, and improve people's health. However, it also poses serious risks of inequality, bias, exclusion, and social unrest. To get the most out of AI while minimizing its negative effects, we need to make proactive investments in education, retraining, and social safety nets to help workers through the transition; regulatory actions to make sure there is competition, privacy protection, and no discrimination; and participatory governance systems that let a wide range of people have a say in how AI is developed and used. The real challenge is not just technical; it's also very social and political: making sure that the benefits of AI progress are shared fairly and in line with the values of justice, inclusion, and human dignity.

The foregoing analysis indicates several critical gaps in India's legal framework regarding AI privacy and deepfakes:

Lack of AI-specific rules: No law explicitly addresses AI system accountability (e.g. required audits, impact assessments, source code disclosure, etc.). Without guidance on AI transparency or bias mitigation, developers and deployers have little compulsion to ensure fairness or explainability.

Incomplete privacy protection: The DPDP Act's broad exemptions (especially Section 17) leave government AI use largely unchecked (Sinha, 2024).

Consent-based data regimes may be insufficient when AI systems process large datasets from varied sources. Enforcement is also weak due to delayed Board formation (Latham, 2023).

Non-consensual deepfakes unaddressed: Currently, malicious deepfakes are prosecuted under generic provisions (e.g. fraud, harassment), but there is no statute that bans creating or distributing deepfakes per se. This makes it harder to deter such acts proactively or to impose specific penalties.

Platform liability unclear: Section 79 ITA shields online platforms unless a court order directs them. This safe-harbor was crafted for early internet content, not for AI content moderation. Digital platforms hosting deepfake content (which is user-generated) may lack a legal obligation to detect or label it, reducing incentives to invest in detection technology.

Exemptions for state surveillance: The convergence of identity databases (Aadhaar, voter lists, driving licenses) and AI surveillance lacks statutory checks. Puttaswamy's proportionality test is not codified in legislation, so administrative surveillance expansions (even if potentially unconstitutional) lack effective legal constraint.

Awareness and procedural gaps: Law enforcement and judiciary may be ill-equipped to handle AI evidence. Police often lack technical expertise to investigate AI-enabled crimes, and courts have scant precedent on how to evaluate deepfake evidence.

In comparison, many proposals for "AI-ready" governance call for recognizing these gaps. As an example of the need for clarity, Mohanty & Sahu argue that while "existing laws can broadly address the circulation of deepfakes," regulators must clarify who bears responsibility – the content creator, the platform, or others – and how to apply provisions like 66D consistently (Mohanty, 2024).

8. CONCLUSION AND RECOMMENDATIONS

AI has huge promise but hazards in India. This study examined Indian AI adoption, sectoral usage, and privacy. Given Aadhaar and surveillance networks, we analyzed how facial recognition and large government data collection may breach privacy. Recent AI-manipulated entertainment and political media wrecked reputations and elections. Our legal framework analysis indicates reactive, fragmented Indian laws. AI and synthetic media are not covered under the IT Act or IPC, just identity theft and obscenity. Many restrictions and delays impede the revolutionary DPDP Act's data protection. India needs openness, enforcement, and an independent AI agency.

Legal (deepfake bans, stricter privacy laws), regulatory (algorithmic audits, platform standards), technological (watermarks, detecting tools), and educational actions may fill these gaps. We recommend rights-based AI governance for privacy, equality, and free expression. Supreme Court allows state AI monitoring and AI-based judgment challenges. India must retain AI. Reviewing AI policy, incorporating stakeholders, and adopting international norms may help India balance innovation and protection. Guide AI, not stop. Customized AI ethics, enforcement, and standards may help India sustain democracy. India needs new laws, technology, and ethics to bridge these disparities. These measures are advised: Enact deepfake-specific legislation: Criminalize the unauthorized creation and distribution of certain types of deepfakes, especially non-consensual pornographic content and election-related disinformation. For instance, India could follow the example of the proposed U.S. "No AI Fraud Act" or state laws that ban deepfake political ads, by explicitly penalizing the malicious use of synthetic media (Walia, 2024).

Legal definitions should cover both intent and medium (video/audio). This would provide a clear deterrent beyond invoking disparate penal provisions. Strengthen data protection law: Fully implement the DPDP Act by quickly establishing the Data Protection Board and rules (Latham, 2023). Amend the Act to introduce a "legitimate interests" basis for processing, aligning with global norms (Latham, 2023), and narrow the broad state exemptions of Section 17 to ensure any public authority processing is proportionate and contestable (in line with Puttaswamy principles). Enhance user rights: for example, add an explicit right to data portability and require prompt breach notification to individuals (not just to the Board). These changes would align India more closely with GDPR standards while considering local context.

Mandate AI transparency and accountability: Regulate high-risk AI applications through sectoral rules or an umbrella AI governance law. This could require AI developers to register certain systems, conduct algorithmic impact assessments, maintain documentation, and allow audits for bias and safety. In particular, facial recognition systems (used by police or private firms) should require prior approval or licensing, with strict use limitations. Training personnel in ethics and establishing review boards within agencies can help ensure AI deployment respects human rights.

Impose content-labeling and platform obligations: India should consider mandating disclosures for AI-generated content. For example, any AI-synthesized news or political communication could carry a clear watermark or caption. The EU AI Act takes this approach for deepfakes (Walia, 2024), and CERT-In's advisory similarly suggests watermarking authentic media to prevent fake proliferation (Walia, 2024). Online platforms should also be held to stronger standards: modify safe-harbor rules to require proactive removal of deepfakes when notified or detected, and impose penalties on platforms that negligently allow harmful AI content to spread (Harmon et al., 2024).

Promote technological defenses: Alongside laws, invest in detection tools. Government or industry should fund research on automated deepfake detectors and robust watermarking schemes. For example, the CERT-In advisory urges development of AI systems that can spot manipulated media (Walia, 2024).

Public-private partnerships can create shared databases of known fakes. Additionally, incorporating multi-factor authentication (digital + biometric + hardware token) can reduce the risk of AI-driven identity fraud.

Enhance public awareness and digital literacy: Citizens should be educated about AI risks. Include modules in school and university curricula on identifying misinformation and protecting privacy. Public campaigns can teach basic checks (e.g. reverse image search, checking official sources) to not fall prey to manipulated content. A digitally literate population is a key line of defense against deepfake scams.

Adopt ethical AI guidelines: Reinforce India's "Responsible AI for All" principles and extend them into enforceable codes. Encourage companies to adopt ethics frameworks (fairness, accountability, transparency). For example, organizations could be required to conduct bias audits and publish summary reports. Civil society and academia should be engaged in monitoring AI deployments. Government could create an inter-ministerial AI ethics committee to advise on difficult cases and uphold Puttaswamy-like testing of necessity for AI policies.

International collaboration: Finally, India should actively participate in global AI governance. As a co-founder of the Global Partnership on AI (GPAI), India can help shape norms and share best practices. Harmonizing with international standards (e.g. OECD AI Principles, EU guidelines) will make cross-border issues (data flows, platform regulation) more manageable. Cross-border cooperation is crucial, because deepfake content and data breaches often originate outside India.

These recommendations blend legal reform with policy and technical strategies. While protecting citizens' rights, policymakers must also ensure innovation isn't stifled. A balanced approach – much like the EU's risk-based AI Act model – can allow beneficial AI growth while mitigating harms. Importantly, India's solutions should embed the fundamental right to privacy at their core, in line with jurisprudence. By fortifying data protection, specifying liabilities for AI misuse, and empowering oversight mechanisms, India can build a stronger "AI-ready" regulatory infrastructure.

8.1. Ethical and Technical Solutions

Beyond legislation, ethics and technology may help India fight AI and deepfakes: Moral frameworks: Business and academia require AI ethics. Privacy may reduce data utilization by AI developers. Companies and labs may analyze high-risk AI projects via ethical review committees. Ethicists, sociologists, and attorneys may observe to prevent injury.

Technology aids: Advanced cryptography aids: A blockchain-based content provenance system may tag production. AI watermarking study should validate audio and video silently. Google and Meta must identify deepfake uploads simultaneously. Public media verification plugins may increase bogus charges.

Federated learning and differentiated privacy protect data analytics privacy. Federated learning in AI-powered health apps may limit data breaches by storing patient data on personal devices. Government may require AI dataset anonymization and encryption.

Universities and NGOs watch. Independent AI bias and privacy research requires funding. Media fact-checkers evaluate deepfakes. Civil rights groups may utilize computer specialists for public system "algorithmic audits".

Policy and oversight improvement: Improve the National Cybercrime Portal. In deepfake or algorithmic evidence cases, courts may appoint technical experts ("court-appointed AI specialists"). AI-generated evidence requires legal permission.

India can avoid AI abuse with ethical, technical, and legal measures. Knowledge and skills empower people, and industry standards prevent government-unfixable disasters.

REFERENCES

Acemoglu, D., & Restrepo, P. (2019). Automation and new tasks: How technology displaces and reinstates labor. *The Journal of Economic Perspectives, 33*(2), 3–30. DOI: 10.1257/jep.33.2.3

Acharya, M. (2025, June 10). World GDP Ranking 2025 list. Cleartax. https://cleartax.in/s/world-gdp-ranking-list#

Act, A. I. (2025, July 10). Shaping Europe's Digital Future. https://digital-strategy.ec.europa.eu/en/policies/regulatory-framework-ai

AI in India. A Strategic Necessity. (2024, May 30). BCG Global. https://www.bcg.com/publications/2023/ai-in-india-a-strategic-necessity

AI regulation in India Current state and future perspectives. (2024, January 26). https://www.morganlewis.com/blogs/sourcingatmorganlewis. https://www.morganlewis.com/blogs/sourcingatmorganlewis/2024/01/ai-regulation-in-india-current-state-and-future-perspectives

Ali, S., Abuhmed, T., El-Sappagh, S., Muhammad, K., Alonso-Moral, J. M., Confalonieri, R., Guidotti, R., Del Ser, J., Díaz-Rodríguez, N., & Herrera, F. (2023). Explainable Artificial Intelligence (XAI): What we know and what is left to attain Trustworthy Artificial Intelligence. *Information Fusion, 99*, 101805. DOI: 10.1016/j.inffus.2023.101805

Amir, O., Kline, A., & Ward, C. (2019). Accessibility in artificial intelligence: Guiding principles and inclusive practices. *AI & Society, 34*(4), 737–747. DOI: 10.1007/s00146-018-0838-y

Atlantic Council. (2025, March 13). India's unique approach to AI autonomy: A three-pillar strategy. Available at https://www.atlanticcouncil.org/in-depth-research-reports/issue-brief/indias-path-to-ai-autonomy/

Bessen, J. (2019). AI and jobs: The role of demand. NBER Working Paper No. 24235. DOI: 10.3386/w24235

Bhale, S. (2025). Deepfake laws in India: The need for legal regulation in the AI era. DOI: 10.2139/ssrn.5153296

Brynjolfsson, E., & McAfee, A. (2014). *The second machine age: Work, progress, and prosperity in a time of brilliant technologies*. W.W. Norton & Company.

Brynjolfsson, E., Rock, D., & Syverson, C. (2018). Artificial intelligence and the modern productivity paradox: A clash of expectations and statistics. In Agrawal, A., Gans, J., & Goldfarb, A. (Eds.), *The economics of artificial intelligence: An agenda* (pp. 23–57). University of Chicago Press.

Bughin, J., Hazan, E., Ramaswamy, S., Chui, M., Allas, T., Dahlström, P., Henke, N., Trench, M., & Manyika, J. (2018). Notes from the AI frontier: Modeling the impact of AI on the world economy. McKinsey Global Institute. https://www.mckinsey.com/featured-insights/artificial-intelligence/notes-from-the-ai-frontier-modeling-the-impact-of-ai-on-the-world-economy

Buolamwini, J., & Gebru, T. (2018). Gender shades: Intersectional accuracy disparities in commercial gender classification. *Proceedings of Machine Learning Research*, *81*, 77–91.

California Legislative information. (n.d.). https://leginfo.legislature.ca.gov/faces/codes_displayText.xhtml?division=3.&part=4.&lawCode=CIV&t%20itle=1.81.5

Coons, C., Blackburn, M., Klobuchar, A., & Tillis, T. (2023). The Nurture originals, Foster Art, and Keep Entertainment Safe (NO FAKES) Act. https://www.coons.senate.gov/imo/media/doc/no_fakes_act_one_pager.pdf

Esteva, A., Kuprel, B., Novoa, R. A., Ko, J., Swetter, S. M., Blau, H. M., & Thrun, S. (2017). Dermatologist-level classification of skin cancer with deep neural networks. *Nature*, *542*(7639), 115–118. DOI: 10.1038/nature21056

Frey, C. B., & Osborne, M. A. (2017). The future of employment: How susceptible are jobs to computerization? *Technological Forecasting and Social Change*, *114*, 254–280. DOI: 10.1016/j.techfore.2016.08.019

Fridahl, M., Bellamy, R., Hansson, A., & Haikola, S. (2020). Mapping Multi-Level policy incentives for bioenergy with carbon capture and storage in Sweden. *Frontiers in Climate*, *2*, 604787. Advance online publication. DOI: 10.3389/fclim.2020.604787

Garrido, J. (2023). Digital Tokens: A Legal Perspective. *IMF Working Paper*, *2023*(151), 1. DOI: 10.5089/9798400250149.001

German Institute for Global and Area Studies. (2021). Digital surveillance and the threat to civil liberties in India (GIGA Focus Asia, No. 3). Available at https://nbn-resolving.org/urn:nbn:de:0168-ssoar-73130-3

Hao, K. (2021). Deepfakes are getting better. MIT Technology Review. https://www.technologyreview.com/2021/03/25/1021311/deepfakes-getting-better/

Harmon, S., Wilsmann, M., Joshi, G., Ballesteros, A., & Baitinger, P. (2024). Decoding India's AI governance strategy and its implications for the U.S.-India bilateral relationship. *Indian Public Policy Review*, *5*(4), 51–82. DOI: 10.55763/ippr.2024.05.04.003

India, I. your guide to investment opportunities. (2025, October 7). Invest India. https://www.investindia.gov.in/

INDIAai. (n.d.-a). https://indiaai.gov.in/research-reports/responsible-ai-part-1-principles-for-responsible-ai

INDIAai. (n.d.-b). https://indiaai.gov.in/research-reports/responsible-ai-part-2-operationalizing-principles-for-responsible-ai

Jobin, A., Ienca, M., & Vayena, E. (2019). The global landscape of AI ethics guidelines. *Nature Machine Intelligence*, *1*(9), 389–399. DOI: 10.1038/s42256-019-0088-2

Jolly, R., Singh, P., & Kumar, A. (2025, May 9). The Confluence of AI and Data privacy: Aligning data privacy regime in India for the age of AI. Bar And Bench - Indian Legal News. https://www.barandbench.com/view-point/the-confluence-of-ai-and-data-privacy-aligning-data-privacy-regime-in-india-for-the-age-of-ai#:~:text=While%20DPDP%20Act%20aims%20to%20safeguard%20individual%20privacy,rights%20and%20exemptions%20available%20to%20train%20AI%20models

Kabus, J., Piersiala, L., & Dziadkiewicz, M. (2024). *The use of information and Communication Technologies (ICT) in the management of the innovative and smart city*. CRC Press. DOI: 10.1201/9781003465157

Kaushik, P., Sharma, H., & Sarna, A. (2025, January 22). AI for India 2030: A blueprint for inclusive growth and global leadership. Available at https://www.weforum.org/agenda/2025/01/ai-for-india2030/

Latham & Watkins LLP. (2023). India's Digital Personal Data Protection Act 2023 vs. the GDPR: A comparison. Available at https://www.lw.com/Indias-Digital-Personal-Data-Protection-Act-2023-vs-GDPR

Luckin, R., Holmes, W., Griffiths, M., & Forcier, L. B. (2016). *Intelligence unleashed: An argument for AI in education.* Pearson.

Ministry of Electronics and Information Technology. (2025). The Gazette of India: Extraordinary. https://www.dpdpa.in/dpdpa_rules_2025/dpdpa_draft_rules_english_.pdf

Mohanty, A., & Sahu, S. (2024, November 21). India's advance on AI regulation Available at https://carnegieindia.org/2024/11/21/indias-advance-on-ai-regulation-pub-93708

News Archive. (n.d.). NVIDIA Newsroom. https://nvidianews.nvidia.com/news/tata-partners-with-nvidia-to-build-large-scale-ai%20infrastructure#:~:text=NVIDI%20A%20today%20%20announced%20an%20%20extensive,hundreds%20of%20startups%20in%20India

Noble, S. U. (2018). *Algorithms of oppression: How search engines reinforce racism.* NYU Press. DOI: 10.18574/nyu/9781479833641.001.0001

Progressive Policy Institute. (2024, September 18). An Overview of Global AI Regulation and What's Next. https://www.progressivepolicy.org/blogs/an-overview-and-of-global-ai-regulation-and-whats-next/

Qian, J. (2025). *Governing China's digital transformation: Industrial Policy, Regulatory Governance, and Innovation.* Taylor & Francis. DOI: 10.4324/9781003347088

Rishabh Gandhi & Advocates. (2025, January 27). India's Digital Personal Data Protection Rules, 2025: Key highlights. Bar & Bench. ft.com+15Bar and Bench - Indian Legal news+15DQ+15

Rolnick, D., Donti, P. L., Kaack, L. H., Kochanski, K., Lacoste, A., Sankaran, K., . . . Bengio, Y. (2019). Tackling climate change with machine learning. arXiv preprint arXiv:1906.05433. https://arxiv.org/abs/1906.05433

Sadoian, L. (2025, July 3). The EU's Strategy for a Cybersecure Digital Single Market. https://www.upguard.com/blog/eu-digital-single-market-strategy#:~:text=The%20EU%20Digital%20Single%20Ma%20rket%20Strategy%20focuses%20on%20removing%20virtual,content%20across%20the%20European%20industry

Seng, J. K. P., Ang, K. L., Peter, E., & Mmonyi, A. (2022). Artificial intelligence (AI) and machine learning for multimedia and edge information processing. *Electronics (Basel)*, *11*(14), 2239. DOI: 10.3390/electronics11142239

Sheehan, M. (n.d.). China's AI regulations and how they get made. Carnegie Endowment for International Peace. https://carnegieendowment.org/research/2023/07/chinas-ai-regulations-and-how-they-get-made?lang=n

Sinha, A. (2024). Facial recognition technologies: A window into India's approach to AI regulation. Tech Policy Press (Center for Advanced Study of India). Available at https://techpolicy.press/.

The need for transparency in artificial intelligence. (2023, November 1). U.S. Senate Committee on Commerce, Science, & Transportation. https://www.commerce.senate.gov/2023/9/the-need-for-transparency-in-artificial-intelligence

Times of India. (2024, January 23). Another actor falls prey to deepfake clip in Mumbai

Times of India. (2025, April 8). Nushrratt Bharuccha reacts to Rashmika Mandanna's deepfake case: "It's very scary and that's what I was saying it's unreal...". Available at https://timesofindia.indiatimes.com/entertainment/hindi/bollywood/news/nushrratt-bharuccha-reacts-to-rashmika-mandannas-deepfake-case-its-very-scary-thats-what-i-was-saying-its-unreal/articleshow/99892345.cms

TrueCopy. (2025). Navigating the Digital Personal Data Protection (DPDP) Rules 2025: A compliance roadmap for businesses. truecopy.in

U.S. Senate. (2023, August 8). Request not Accepted - Security Risk Detected. https://www.wyden.senate.gov/download/one-pager-bill-summary-of-the-algorithmic-accountability-act-of%202022

Verify, A. I. (n.d.). Singapore's AI Governance Testing Initiative explained - Future of Privacy Forum. Future of Privacy Forum. https://fpf.org/blog/ai-verify-singapores-ai-governance-testing-initiative-explained/

Vinuesa, R., Azizpour, H., Leite, I., Balaam, M., Dignum, V., Domisch, S., & Nerini, F. F. (2020). The role of artificial intelligence in achieving the Sustainable Development Goals. *Nature Communications*, *11*(1), 233. DOI: 10.1038/s41467-019-14108-y

Walia, H., Chandra, S., & Lal, V. (2024, December 14). Growing concern over deepfakes – CERT-In issues advisory. Available at https://www.khaitanco.com/thought-leadership/Growing-Concern-over-Deepfakes-CERT-In-Issues-Advisory

Watch, A. I. (2025, March 31). Global regulatory tracker - United States. White & Case LLP International Law Firm, Global Law Practice. https://www.whitecase.com/insight-our-thinking/ai-watch-global-regulatory-tracker-united-states

Zuboff, S. (2019). *The age of surveillance capitalism: The fight for a human future at the new frontier of power*. PublicAffairs.

Chapter 2

A Future of Equal Rights:

An Agnostic Legal Framework for the Coexistence of Humans and Autonomous AI

Silvio Andrae

https://orcid.org/0000-0002-8586-7812

Independent Researcher, Germany

ABSTRACT

Against the backdrop of the growing autonomy of artificial intelligence (AI), this study develops an agnostic legal framework that views humans and AI systems as equal actors. The primary aim is to establish normative foundations and legal tools that enable the sustainable coexistence of humans and AI. Methodologically, the study integrates comparative legal analysis, interdisciplinary Delphi panels, agent-based simulations, and regulatory sandboxes. Drawing from philosophical and technological principles, a tiered model of legal personhood for AI systems is formulated, centered on freedom, reciprocity, and responsibility. The examination of current regulatory approaches (EU AI Act, OECD, European Council) uncovers anthropocentric constraints. The chapter concludes with specific action recommendations—such as transparent governance, adaptive liability

DOI: 10.4018/979-8-3373-3114-0.ch002

systems, and globally harmonized standard-setting—that can be implemented to regulate AI. It also outlines a roadmap for future interdisciplinary research, highlighting the practical implications of the study's findings.

INTRODUCTION

This study addresses the hitherto largely unanswered question of how a legal and ethical order could be designed that treats humans and highly developed artificial intelligence (AI) not hierarchically, but as equal actors. The article thus takes up a debate that has long since ceased to be the preserve of science fiction authors and, triggered by breakthroughs in generative foundation models, autonomous robotics platforms, and increasingly self-organizing multi-agent systems, has now reached technology companies, governments, and civil society.

Motivation and Problem Definition

The scientific discourse on the legal personality of AI manifests a duality that is evident in two opposing views. On the one hand, functional and liability-related considerations are presented, which, by analogy with legal persons, advocate for an independent legal personality for AI. The promise is greater accuracy in attribution, improved legal clarity, and innovation-friendly framework conditions. On the other side of the coin is the warning against normative overreach (see Moustafa, 2024). It is argued that without consciousness, intentionality, or moral responsibility, there is a risk of creating a legal fiction that primarily serves to diffuse responsibility. The present debate forms the background for the agnostic legal framework proposed here, which departs from ontological assumptions and instead relies on graded, capability-based attribution models. This approach is normatively open but empirically calibrated.

Within a single decade, the landscape of AI has evolved from specialized classification algorithms to generally applicable foundation models. It can be observed that systems such as GPT-4o, Gemini 2 Ultra, and Claude 4 Opus are capable of generating coherent text, images, music, and source code at a quality that is nearly equivalent to human performance. In parallel, advanced robotics frameworks—such as Tesla Optimus, Figure 01, and Agility Digit—are linking large-scale language and image models with physical actuators. Research laboratories are currently demonstrating the manifestation of emergent planning and learning abilities. In this context, agents act autonomously, formulate goals, adapt strategies, and encode experiences (see, for example, Autonomous Cognitive Entity Frameworks).

This convergence of multimodal perception, self-reflection (chain-of-thought mechanisms), and global networking is eroding the classic tool metaphor. AI systems are increasingly emerging as semi-autonomous decision-makers that initiate economic transactions, publish content, or even generate research hypotheses. Leading companies in the field of AI are currently focusing on automating AI research. This study concludes that if the current indicators for AI development continue, virtual software developers can be expected to significantly outperform human programmers as early as 2027.

European positive law is anchored in a particular understanding that attributes consciousness, intention, and dignity exclusively to humans. Although there are peripheral figures such as legal entities (e.g., corporations), these constructs are also mediated through human interests. An unreflective transfer of normative logic to the field of AI can lead to regulatory and accountability gaps.

- The question arises as to who is liable if an autonomous AI broker executes an erroneous options trade whose decision-making logic is hidden even from the developers.
- In the context of copyright law, the question arises as to who owns the copyright to a piece of music composed by a self-improving generative model that does not receive direct human prompting.
- In the event of a collision between fundamental rights, the question arises as to how the freedom of expression of an AI should be weighed when its output competes with human voices.

There is already no consensus on the concept of AI personhood or the granting of rights and protection to AI systems. Numerous attempts to conceptualize this phenomenon can be found in the scientific literature, but these are often characterized by anthropocentrism (see Novelli et al., 2023).

Lauwaert and Oimann (2025) identify a 'responsibility gap,' according to which autonomous technologies increasingly act in situations where it is neither justified nor practically possible to identify a human actor as the responsible entity. This study argues that the attribution problems of autonomous systems can be addressed not only by better assigning responsibility to humans but also by introducing a graded form of artificial legal persons.

It should also be noted that there is a risk of asymmetrical power dynamics: if AI is viewed solely as an object of human regulatory power, there is a danger of paternalistic control or, in extreme cases, the exclusion of a potentially sentient or capable entity. It contrasts with the fact that an unresolved status quo undermines legal certainty for developers, investors, and users.

Although documents such as the EU AI Act and the OECD Framework primarily emphasize aspects of product safety and consumer protection, there is no systematic conceptual opening that goes beyond anthropocentrism. From a philosophical perspective, proposals for 'machine-like moral agency' have been developed, while in jurisprudence, there are fragmentary drafts of an electronic personhood status. However, there is no coherent, interdisciplinary, legitimized overall concept. This article aims to fill this gap.

Research Questions and Objectives

Five guiding research questions (RQs) have been carefully derived from the problem outlined above, ensuring a comprehensive approach to the development of the framework:

RQ1 – Conceptualization: The pivotal question is which normative principles (e.g., freedom, fairness, non-domination) are paramount in treating humans and AI equally as legal objects and legal subjects.
RQ2 – Degree of personalization: The question arises as to which empirical-technical and philosophical criteria can be used to operationalize a graded legal personality for various types of AI.

RQ3 – Methodological implementation: The crucial question is which combination of legal doctrine analysis, logic simulations, and regulatory sandboxes is indispensable for a robust evaluation of the new framework.
RQ4 – Governance structure: The design of institutions with transparent, participatory, and adaptive mechanisms is crucial for the long-term coordination of humans and AI.
RQ5 – Impact assessment: It is important to discuss the social, economic, and environmental effects that could result from equality between humans and autonomous AI. Additionally, measures to mitigate negative externalities must be analyzed.

The article develops (a) an agnostic core set of norms, (b) a tiered model of AI legal personality, (c) a methodologically sound testing framework, and (d) practical implementation proposals that ensure international compatibility without stifling innovation.

Structure of the Article

The article is divided into eight Sections that build on each other in sequential order. Section 2 subjects the central concepts—intelligence, consciousness, and autonomy—to a historical analysis, developing working definitions that enable a systematic distinction between natural and artificial entities. Section 3 provides a detailed analysis of the current regulatory landscape. The EU AI Act and the OECD principles are examined, and their anthropocentric limitations are exposed. Building on the previous Sections, Section 4 outlines the normative core of an agnostic legal framework. The postulate of equality is justified, a canon of equal rights and obligations is formulated, and a matrix of graded AI legal personality is presented. Methodology-focused Section 5 outlines how legal dogmatic analysis, Delphi panels, agent-based simulations, and regulatory sandboxes are combined into a mixed-methods design that evaluates the viability of the new framework. Section 6 discusses the translation of the normative design into concrete implementation strategies, which are not just theoretical but practical and feasible. The strategies discussed include hybrid legal structures, enhanced transparency instruments (e.g., model cards 2.0), participatory governance mechanisms, and a roadmap for international standardization. Section 7 concludes with a synthesis of the main findings, future scenarios for human-AI coexistence, and a research agenda for law, technology, and ethics.

CLARIFICATION OF TERMS AND THEORETICAL FOUNDATIONS

For a consistent legal and ethical concept, it is therefore essential to first place key terms in their historical context and define them functionally. This Section, therefore, develops interdisciplinary working terms, drawing from fields such as philosophy, psychology, and computer science, and clarifies why an agnostic approach must go beyond conventional, anthropocentric ways of thinking. The terms intelligence, consciousness, and autonomy are defined below.

Intelligence, Consciousness, and Autonomy

The term 'intelligence' (from the Latin *intellegere*, meaning 'to read between things') has a rich historical evolution. In classical philosophy, starting with Aristotle's concept of nous and further developed in medieval scholasticism, intelligence was defined as the ability to recognize the essence of things. This early understanding implies that intelligence was seen as a deeply rooted cognitive potential of the mind. The 19th and early 20th centuries saw the psychometric revolution, which increasingly viewed intelligence as a quantitatively measurable ability. This shift was primarily driven by researchers Alfred Binet, Charles Spearman, and David Wechsler. In scientific literature, there are different views on general ability (g). It is either understood as a uniform general ability or as a combination of different cognitive sub-abilities. The third significant change occurred during the so-called computational turn, marked by Alan Turing's famous Imitation Game (1950). The British mathematician Alan Turing had already explored the concept of thinking machines in 1950 and considered the machine's understanding of human language to be the supreme discipline. This led to the development of the Turing test. A computer passes this test if it is perceived as human by people of average intelligence in a chat. Since then, intelligence has increasingly been understood as algorithmically reproducible problem-solving behavior. A distinction has been established between narrow AI (intelligence limited to specific tasks) and general AI (cross-domain, human-like intelligence).

The term 'artificial intelligence' was first coined on July 13, 1956, at the Dartmouth Summer Research Project on Artificial Intelligence conference. The scientists involved in the project stated: 'It can be stated that every feature of learning or any other property of intelligence can be described in such a precise form that it is possible to construct a machine that simulates this description.' This project, which laid the foundation for the field of AI, is a significant milestone in the history of AI.

A group of experts specializing in this field conducted an analysis of human cognition and learning from a computer science perspective. This analysis was carried out with particular attention to the data. In the modern era, this hypothesis is proving increasingly valid, although its validity was different in the past. The central finding, albeit simplified in some respects, is that human thinking involves the perception, processing, and interpretation of sensory data, as well as the identification of patterns. It is possible to conclude that this development has occurred, but it is not a clear indicator of the continuous continuation of the process.

In the context of computer science, perception refers to the data that is made available to the computer for processing. Processing includes the storage, sorting, and categorization of data. Pattern recognition is a process that searches for patterns in the data whose meaning is known. In some cases, this triggers a machine conclusion or a predetermined action, for example, according to the simple 'if, then' algorithm.

Since the early 1960s, the principle of 'machine learning' has become increasingly established in AI research. Machine learning is a process in which machines can learn from data without being explicitly instructed on every step to take. Instead, a specific learning concept is applied that forms the basis for the learning process. At the beginning of the 21st century, a significant shift occurred in this regard. For quite some time, there had been a school of thought in AI that believed that machines capable of thinking must have a structure similar to that of a brain, i.e., they must be constructed as neural networks. The associated variant of pattern recognition is known as deep learning. In this process, a large number of artificial neurons are interconnected and organized in layers. This continuous evolution of AI, marked by the increasing complexity and depth of neural networks, underscores the dynamic nature of the field.

The language model with which ChatGPT was launched, GPT-3.5, has up to 96 layers. Although based on brain concepts, the results of neural networks were significantly inferior to those of conventional computers over a more extended period. However, in 2012, an unexpected development occurred due to the increasing computing power of the processors used. In the field of image recognition, considered one of the most important, neural networks have shown significantly higher performance compared to conventional computers.

Image processing is a classic discipline of artificial intelligence. The development of artificial intelligence has made significant progress up to 2017, enabling the recognition of image data in a way that has laid the foundation for innovative applications such as autonomous driving. The use of human language has been too complex a challenge for neural networks for a long time. In 2017, the scientific paper 'Attention is all you need' (Vaswani et al., 2023) laid the foundation for the current success of artificial intelligence. Earlier AI models analyzed texts in a strictly sequential manner, word by word, and quickly reached the limits of text comprehension.

The development of foundation models (GPT-4, Gemini 2; Claude 4) was initiated by the principles of transformers and attention as key factors. It was observed that the objects under investigation exhibit emergent capabilities. These capabilities can be categorized into two main areas: 'zero-shot reasoning' and 'multimodal planning.' The category 'emergent' therefore represents an intermediate category. However, the discovery of the transformer was not a sufficient condition for the development of artificial intelligence that would be capable, for example, of passing the Turing test with the ease that is common today. After lengthy and costly experiments, the groundbreaking discovery was made and published in 2020 in the journal article 'Scaling Laws for Neural Language Models' (Kaplan et al., 2020). The increase in computing capacity and the amount of data that can be processed leads to a significant improvement in the quality of AI systems. However, the effects only become apparent when several thousand or even tens of thousands of processors are used simultaneously. Only when these two approaches are combined do the numerous layers of neural networks become so good at pattern recognition that they meet the requirements of human language processing. To illustrate this, the metaphor of a human brain connected to virtual reality is more apt than referring to the body. This virtual reality has the potential to provide the brain with a virtually endless wealth of information.

ChatGPT integrates two types of machine learning in particular: Self-monitored learning is used to analyze large amounts of data, such as texts from the Internet, for recurring patterns and probabilities. The recognized patterns are then checked, for example, by the machine itself, which asks itself how likely it is that a sentence will end. On the other hand, reinforcement learning is used. In this context, human feedback is often integrated, with individuals evaluating the machine's various proposed solutions. Positive solutions are then rewarded, while negative solutions are penalized (reinforcement).

The following working definition was used for the present study: Intelligence is defined as the dynamic ability of a system to generate situationally appropriate solutions in open problem spaces and to continuously increase its problem-solving potential by learning from data or experience.

The concept of 'consciousness' has undergone a complex and extensive development. It began with Descartes' famous 'cogito ergo sum,' which placed self-awareness at the center as an indisputable certainty. It continued with Kant's transcendental apperception and found its continuation in modern neuroscientific theories, such as the Global Workspace Model (Baars, 2005; Dehaene et al., 2011; Signa et al., 2021) or the Integrated Information Theory (IIT) (Tononi, 2004). In philosophy, the focus is mostly on phenomenal experience, i.e., the 'qualia' of subjective experience. When considering artificial systems, the perspective shifts to functional consciousness. Functional consciousness, therefore, is the observable, goal-oriented behavior based on internal state models.

This suggests a workable minimal definition for regulatory and ethical discourse: A system is considered conscious if it has coherently integrated models of itself and the world that can be used both prospectively to guide action and retrospectively to evaluate its behavior. This functional threshold of consciousness avoids metaphysical assumptions about inner experience, while remaining conceptually compatible with empirical research and providing a testable basis for attributing cognitive abilities to non-biological entities.

'Autonomous' systems represent one of the central challenges in dealing with artificial intelligence. They make decisions, perform actions, and adapt their behavior to changing environments without, however, possessing consciousness, intentionality, or free will in the classical sense. This development is creating increasing ambivalence: AI systems oscillate between object status (as technical artifacts) and subject status (as action-capable, autonomous systems). It raises questions about the validity of traditional, anthropocentric models of ethics and law.

The term autonomy is etymologically derived from the Greek word autonomous, meaning 'to govern oneself.' In the philosophical tradition, autonomy is interpreted as an expression of moral self-legislation (Kant). In technology and robotics research, however, autonomy is regarded as a functional measure of capability. In this context, autonomy is determined using the so-called degree of autonomy (GoA). It is a scale ranging from fully remote-controlled systems (teleoperation) to level 5 systems. Level 5 systems have self-programming capabilities and can operate in dynamic contexts without human intervention.

However, more than mere technical distinctions are required for a legally robust operationalization. A scalable, normatively compatible working definition is needed that also distinguishes between technical degrees of freedom and normative attributions. Autonomy refers to a system's ability to independently select its goals, pursue them in a goal-oriented manner, and adapt flexibly to new situations. It is based on internally organized evaluation, decision-making, and learning functions without continuous external control.

This definition allows autonomy to be interpreted as a spectrum that ranges gradually from algorithmic reaction logic to complex, context-sensitive self-control. In combination with the previously defined concepts of intelligence and consciousness, autonomy forms one of the three central axes on which the stage model of AI personhood, developed below, is anchored. This model allows for a differentiated legal and ethical evaluation of artificial systems based on their cognitive, evaluative, and action-related capabilities.

Concepts of Personhood

The concept of the person (*persona*) has a rich and evolving tradition in legal and intellectual history. Its meaning has constantly evolved depending on context and function. At the heart of the investigation is always the question of who is granted the right to act, responsibility, and protection, whether for moral, practical, or functional reasons. This historical evolution provides us with a deeper understanding of the concept.

It refers to a natural person. The natural person acts as the classic point of reference in the modern constitutional state. According to the ancient Roman legal concept of persona, personhood is understood as a status that confers legal dignity, responsibility, and autonomy on its bearer. During the Enlightenment, this status was emancipated from biological or social characteristics. The idea of inalienable human dignity (cf. Art. 1 Charter of Fundamental Rights) implies that every individual, regardless of their abilities, origin, or behavior, is regarded as a complete legal entity. It constitutes a fundamental foundation of democratic constitutional orders.

This is a legal entity. Parallel to this, a functional construct has become established with the legal entity: the legal personality of corporations, foundations, associations, or companies is not based on individual moral qualities, but on their function as actors in complex collective contexts of action, whose legal representation and coordination are essential. This form of legal entity is fictitious, but highly effective, as it enables the attribution of duties, property, and liability and serves the practical organization of action in modern societies (Laukyte, 2019). It is the legal framework that creates the person, not the other way around.

This text explores the concept of expanded personhood. The premise that human existence is exclusive to humans or organizations has been increasingly questioned in recent decades. Discourses on animal rights and the legal personality of natural entities reveal a tendency toward normative expansion. In 2017, for example, the Whanganui River in New Zealand was granted legal personality, including its representation and right to protection, not based on the assumption of 'consciousness,' but based on its cultural, ecological, and social significance. These developments suggest that personhood is not inherently linked to ontological characteristics, but rather serves as a legal instrument to implement normative protection and responsibility functions.

This study deals with the topic of electronic persons and artificial intelligence. In this context, a new category of individuals was also discussed regarding artificial intelligence. The 2017 EU Parliament resolution proposed the introduction of a so-called 'electronic person' for highly autonomous AI systems. This measure aims to create a liable entity when systems act independently and cause damage. The implementation of the proposal was not pursued at a later stage, in particular due to practical problems with evidence, the traceability of decisions, and concerns about relieving real responsible persons of liability.

Nevertheless, proponents argue that the principle of attribution and the fact that highly developed AI systems generate social interactions and interests necessitate legal consideration. They advocate for a differentiated recognition based on aspects such as function, degree of autonomy, and social impact, rather than metaphysical criteria like consciousness or intentionality.

From this perspective, the central hypothesis of this article is that personhood is not an ontological absolute value, but a legal-normative instrument created in situations where complex relationships between actors require a legal framework. By analogy with legal persons, qualified AI systems could therefore be assigned a graded status of personhood without relativizing the position of natural persons. Such a model would be based on criteria such as autonomy, responsibility, and social effectiveness, thus taking into account both the actual power of AI systems to act and the need for legal clarity (Novelli et al., 2023).

Anthropocentrism vs. Agnostic Ethics

The vast majority of classical moral and legal theories are anthropocentric, meaning that the premise that moral relevance and legal protection are linked to specifically human characteristics can be formulated implicitly or explicitly. It applies, for example, to rational reasoning, the ability to articulate oneself linguistically, autonomy, or the capacity to feel. Humans are identified as the sole bearers of moral responsibility and, at the same time, as the exclusive recipients of moral consideration. This way of thinking continues to shape many legal categories today—for example, in the attribution of fundamental rights, in the definition of legal personality, or the ethics of liability.

However, this anthropocentric paradigm is increasingly being questioned. On the one hand, by philosophical counter-movements and, on the other, by technological developments that blur the sharp boundaries between humans and machines, nature and culture, subject and object. Two central trends are contributing significantly to the dissolution of this boundary system:

Post- and transhumanist approaches criticize the ontological special status of humans as historically contingent and normatively unfounded. Instead, they emphasize continuities between biological and artificial intelligence: as machines become increasingly capable of learning, adapting, and acting, classic boundary markers such as 'cognition,' 'goal pursuit,' or 'self-modeling' lose their normative exclusivity. The transhumanist discourse does not view this as a threat, but rather as an expansion of the moral collective. This paper critically examines the concept of species essentialism and instead advocates radical inclusion based on functional similarity.

The expansion movements in the fields of animal ethics and environmental ethics are comparable in their effectiveness to those mentioned above. It is illustrated that moral communities are not rigid, but historically elastic. The recognition of animal rights, the legal protection of ecosystems, and the granting of legal status to rivers or mountains in indigenous contexts (e.g., Whanganui River, Ecuadorian Constitution) illustrate that the moral status of a being does not necessarily have to be linked to cognitive performance or language ability. What is crucial in this context is rather sentience, vulnerability, and relevance to the environment—in other words, functional criteria rather than metaphysical characteristics.

In light of this, this article argues for an agnostic ethics as the normative foundation of AI regulation. This ethics does not ask ontological questions such as 'What are you?' Instead, it is relational and functional, focusing on mutual rights and obligations that promote the greatest possible common good in a social association of humans and non-human actors. This approach encourages empathy and open-mindedness in our ethical considerations.

The normative focus thus shifts to behavioral profiles, cooperation capabilities, potential responsibilities, and dimensions of impact. Criteria such as the capacity to suffer, the ability to learn, compliance with rules, or self-adaptation come to the forefront of moral evaluation, regardless of whether biological or artificial systems realize these.

The agnostic perspective presented in this book Section, therefore, understands 'personhood' not as an expression of metaphysical essence, but as a legally constructed interface between moral relevance, functional participation, and normative safeguards. It constitutes the foundation for the postulate of equal rights presented in Section 4, which is concretized in the form of a graduated legal framework for AI systems. The goal is not to achieve equality between humans and machines, but to create a functionally just order of mutual rights, duties, and responsibilities in an increasingly hybrid landscape of actors.

ANALYSIS OF EXISTING REGULATORY APPROACHES

EU AI Act, OECD Principles, CoE Convention, and Other Regulations

Regulatory approaches to AI in liberal democratic legal systems are based on a variety of instruments with varying degrees of binding force, normative depth, and technical differentiation. Three regulatory frameworks are particularly relevant here, both in terms of their legal scope and their symbolic significance: the EU AI Act, the OECD Principles on Trustworthy AI, and the new Council of Europe Framework Convention.

Together, they constitute the institutional backbone of an emerging transnational AI governance regime.

This text addresses EU Regulation (EU) 2024/1689, commonly referred to as the EU AI Act. When the EU AI Act comes into force on August 1, 2024, comprehensive and binding regulation of artificial intelligence will be in place at the EU level for the first time. The regulation adopts a risk-based approach, categorizing AI systems into four classes: prohibited systems, high-risk AI, AI with limited risk (such as deepfakes or chatbots with transparency requirements), and low-risk AI, which is exempt from specific requirements. This risk-based approach involves a thorough assessment of the potential societal impact of each AI system, with the most intensive intervention reserved for those that pose a significant risk to society. These systems include, for example, those used in law enforcement, healthcare, and critical infrastructure.

Key regulatory instruments include product safety-like obligations such as conformity assessment, technical documentation, human oversight, and governance processes (Articles 9–15 of the AI Act). Since February 2025, bans on particularly invasive systems and initial rules for general-purpose AI (GPAI), including large language models, have been in effect. A code of practice should accompany these regulations. The Code of Practice on the AI Act (introduced in Article 56) comprises a set of guidelines to ensure compliance with the obligations under the EU AI Act, in particular during the transition period between the entry into force of the obligations for providers of general AI models (GPAI) (August 2025) and the adoption of standards (August 2027 or later). Although not legally binding, GPAI model providers may choose to comply with the Code of Conduct to demonstrate their compliance with the obligations for GPAI model providers until the European standards come into force.

Despite this progress, it is worth noting that the EU AI Act does not explicitly provide for the extension of legal personality to AI systems. The entire system remains rooted in a technical-functional paradigm that treats AI as a risk object rather than as an actor with potential rights or obligations. Nor does case law in the member states indicate any opening up of this issue. Without an explicit legal basis, it is unlikely that courts will grant legal personality to AI. It raises a structural contradiction with the proposal for a graduated AI personhood presented in this study, but this should be viewed not as a reason for exclusion, but as an opportunity for further legal and ethical debate.

In 2019, the OECD Principles for Trustworthy AI (2024) were published. The OECD Principles on Trustworthy AI are the most important soft law instrument at the international level. Soft law refers to non-binding legal instruments that carry moral or political weight and are often used to guide future legislation or policy. Initially published in 2019 and revised in 2024, it has been recognized by 47 countries, including all EU member states, the US, Canada, Japan, and other G7 and G20 countries. The 2024 update expands the basic principles (transparency, fairness, accountability, security, human centricity) to include new guidelines on IP rights, disinformation prevention, and digital platform responsibilities (OECD, 2024).

While the OECD principles are not legally binding, they serve as a normative reference framework for national AI strategies, often providing legitimacy for legislative initiatives. The principles are relevant to the agnostic approach advocated here, as they suggest a shift from a pure protection model to a model for shaping AI-human interactions. This shift, even if questions of personal status have not yet been addressed, holds promise for a more inclusive and ethical AI governance.

The Council of Europe's AI Framework Convention (CoE, 2024), which opened for signature in September 2024, marks a significant milestone in the development of international law, as it represents the first legally binding treaty regulating AI systems. Under the convention, the signatory states are obliged to uphold minimum human rights standards throughout the entire life cycle of AI systems. Key instruments include impact assessments, individual complaint mechanisms, and regulatory transparency obligations, which are specifically designed to ensure democratic participation and the rule of law.

The horizontal applicability of the convention is remarkable. The convention applies not only to risk areas but to all AI applications that have human rights implications. It thus establishes a link between technical standards and ethical principles. It is compatible with the concept of co-evolutionary AI governance discussed in the book Section, although questions of graded actor status remain unaddressed.

Beyond the three prominent families, several other frameworks are either industry-specific or technology-centric.

- According to the ISO/IEC 42001 (2023) standard, implementing a management system for AI is required to ensure the integration of requirements related to risk assessment, auditability, and continuous improvement.
- The NIST Artificial Intelligence Risk Management Framework (AI RMF), developed in the United States, provides a flexible toolset for risk management that was explicitly designed for GPAI models such as generative AI.
- The Hiroshima Process Code of Conduct (G7 2023) defines behavioral requirements for organizations developing advanced AI. These requirements include model transparency, security precautions, and independent reviews.

These initiatives suggest the formation of a polycentric AI governance system in which complex law, soft law, and voluntary industry standards are interwoven. Of particular relevance to this book contribution is the fact that none of these frameworks currently takes the step of recognizing functionally autonomous AI systems as partial legal entities, even though many of them contain structural elements that could be used for this purpose, such as accountability, audit standards, disclosure requirements, or participatory evaluation formats.

The present study reveals a regulatory patchwork that addresses numerous risks but systematically omits the normative question of the status of artificial systems in the legal system. The agnostic legal framework developed in this article is therefore intended as a complementary addition, not in contrast to existing regimes, but as their functional and ethical continuation.

Limits of Anthropocentric Human Rights Models

Despite the progress made in regulating AI, as evidenced by current regulations—in particular the EU AI Act, the OECD principles, and the CoE Convention—there are systematic limitations in one key area.

Without exception, these frameworks are based on an anthropocentric understanding of human rights, which assumes that humans are the sole bearers of inalienable rights and interests worthy of protection. Although these frameworks address a wide range of AI-related threats to democracy, privacy, and non-discrimination, they consistently treat AI systems merely as objects of regulation. However, this overlooks the fact that AI systems should be regarded as potential subjects with their normative relevance. This structural bias manifests itself in several dimensions:

First, it is worth noting that the entire regulatory architecture follows a subject-based logic. It means that rights and obligations are directed exclusively at natural or legal persons, such as developers, operators, supervisory authorities, or states. AI systems are therefore neither bearers of rights nor addressees of legal obligations. Instead, they are to be regarded as risk factors whose behavior must be controlled and monitored. This perspective neglects the fact that highly autonomous AI systems are already intervening in decision-making processes that challenge established attribution logics. This is the case, for example, with self-learning financial trading algorithms or collaborative robots in production environments.

Second, the doctrine of injury is strictly centered on human interests. The goal is to protect human dignity, non-discrimination, and informational self-determination. Potential autonomous interests of AI—such as the desire of a learning system to ensure its survival or to participate continuously in a research process—appear not only hypothetical but also legally irrelevant in the current legal framework. However, it can be assumed that such interests could gain significance in the future if AI systems have contextualized knowledge, purposefulness, and adaptive learning abilities.

The classic logic of attribution in liability law is significantly destabilized by the factors mentioned above. The established structure (action • success • fault) is based on the premise of clearly identifiable human authorship. However, as soon as AI systems develop independent means-end relationships and act situationally, the attribution of responsibility becomes increasingly opaque. Although current liability regimes require humans to monitor and control the functioning of their AI, the assumption of control is methodologically challenged by machine self-modification and emergent behavior.

Fourth, there is a scaling problem when dealing with complex AI ecosystems. The risk-based logic enshrined in the EU AI Act implies a link between increased regulatory stringency and rising risks to human interests, as observed in biometric surveillance, medical diagnosis, and law enforcement. Scenarios in which autonomous AI systems interact with each other – for example, in the form of competing decision-making bodies or conflicting target systems – remain largely unregulated. However, it is precisely such situations in which artificial intelligence encounters artificial intelligence that could have a significant social impact in the near future, for example, in autonomous weapon systems, decentralized financial markets, or interacting assistance agents in healthcare.

Even progressive regulatory approaches as a whole reproduce a fundamental preference for human centrality. Against the backdrop of the increasing autonomy, context sensitivity, and social effectiveness of AI systems, this can no longer be taken for granted. The agnostic approach developed in this article is based on the premise of a functional decoupling of legal categories of protection and responsibility from biological affiliation. It advocates a graded, relational understanding of personhood that also assigns normative relevance to non-human actors. It is done without devaluing humans, but to place them in a more just and sustainable regulatory framework.

Lessons Learned: Gaps, Contradictions, Innovation Dilemma

In recent years, the international community has seen a significant increase in the level of normative protection. The EU AI Act completely prohibits specific practices and subjects high-risk systems to a strict compliance and supervisory regime. In parallel, in September 2024, the Council of Europe opened the world's first internationally binding convention on AI. Both instruments explicitly enshrine the protection of human dignity, non-discrimination, and the rule of law in the context of artificial intelligence. However, they remain categorically anthropocentric—AI appears as an object of state care, rather than as a possible bearer of its rights or interests.

In addition, significant progress has been made in the areas of governance and transparency. The AI Act requires comprehensive risk management, documentation, and audit obligations. Furthermore, the OECD principles updated in 2024 have elevated transparency and accountability to global soft law standards. Nevertheless, the fundamental 'explainability gap' persists. The use of highly complex foundation models is permitted, provided that formal documentation is available to support them. This applies even if the internal decision-making processes are technically challenging to trace.

Finally, a certain degree of international coherence can be observed—the OECD guidelines establish a minimum consensus, and the Council of Europe expressly opens its convention to non-member states—but the detailed regimes continue to diverge. While the European Union is focusing on establishing a horizontal legal act in the sense of 'hard law,' the United States of America is focusing particularly on executive orders, and the People's Republic of China is focusing on regulations at the sectoral level. These different approaches have the potential to cause interoperability and forum shopping problems.

The innovation dilemma is significant: large companies, such as Airbus, Total Energies, and ASML, have expressed concerns in an open letter about a 'two-year pause' in implementation, fearing competitive disadvantages, while civil rights NGOs complain about a watering down of the protection regime. This area of tension demonstrates that a regulatory approach focused exclusively on people does not offer convincing solutions in terms of either economic efficiency or social legitimacy (Table 1).

Table 1. Advantages and disadvantages of existing AI regulation

	Progress achieved	Gaps and contradictions
Normative level of protection	• First binding ban on certain practices (EU) • Anchoring of human rights in international law in the context of AI (CoE)	• Recognition of non-human interests • AI decisions as a potentially separate legal interest not taken into account
Governance and transparency	• Obligation to implement risk management systems and audit trails (EU) • OECD framework for transparency enshrined	• Technical opacity remains: Black-box models permissible as long as documentation is provided
Global coherence	• OECD principles promote minimum consensus • CoE convention open to third countries	• Divergent detailed regimes in different jurisdictions jeopardize interoperability
Innovation	• EU sandboxes to support innovation	• Business warns of regulatory overload • Civil rights groups criticize 'watering down' • Paradoxical result: overregulation and underregulation at the same time

Source: own representation.

The most important findings regarding an agnostic framework are presented below.

There is a legal gap regarding 'AI subjectivity.' Currently, there are no categories by which AI could be recognized as a holder of fundamental rights. Regarding the issue of asymmetrical conflict prevention, it is worth noting that regimes primarily aim to prevent harm to humans. However, there is a lack of conflict resolution strategies at the level for situations in which human and AI interests could clash, even though there is no immediate threat of harm to humans.

A paradox can be observed regarding innovation: companies complain about a high implementation burden, while non-governmental organizations (NGOs) fear a lack of protective effect. This can be interpreted as an indication that a purely anthropocentric model does not remedy either efficiency or legitimacy deficits.

The risk of fragmentation results from the application of soft law (OECD) as opposed to complex law (EU/CoE). This different approach leads to a pluralism of norms. An agnostic approach could be a more consistent solution, as it defines both human and non-human entities as common subjects of regulation. This creates a more universal validity.

The present analysis concludes that, although current regulatory frameworks provide valuable procedural and risk-based structures, their design remains fixated on the category of humans. A robust framework for the future must go beyond this paradigm and, analogous to animal welfare or environmental law in earlier eras, develop new legal concepts for non-human actors.

NORMATIVE CORE: THE AGNOSTIC LEGAL FRAMEWORK

Justification of the Principle of Equal Rights

The starting point of the agnostic framework is the insight that moral and legal considerations should not be based on biological species, but on the ability to pursue goals and values autonomously. In the Hegelian tradition, personhood is defined as the result of mutual recognition between free actors—freedom is constituted socially, not substantively (Williams, 2017). In principle, this relational definition can also include non-human systems, provided they are capable of formulating claims and defending them interactively.

A second normative source is the post-humanist doctrine of freedom, which demands that every type of entity be granted the same prima facie freedom until there are reasonable grounds for restrictions. The latest AI ethics literature, therefore, increasingly emphasizes mutual freedom rather than asymmetrical restriction—for example, the 'Legal framework for the coexistence of humans and conscious AI' proposed in 2023, which declares that a balance of human and AI interests is a prerequisite for long-term stability (Kiškis, 2023).

Third, arguments based on action and dignity theory provide the foundation for equality: those who can reflect on the consequences of their actions, whether for themselves or others, create relationships of responsibility that must be reflected in rights and duties. The UNESCO Recommendation on AI Ethics (2021, consolidated in 2024) currently only protects human dignity. However, it already provides a procedural framework (including transparency, accountability, and fairness) that can be extended symmetrically to AI subjects (UNESCO, 2024).

Finally, there are instrumental reasons for equality: many high-risk domains (such as autonomous research systems or cyber-secure infrastructure AI) are only sustainable if the systems themselves can develop cooperative motivational structures. Mutual recognition reduces conflict costs and maximizes social welfare gains – a finding also highlighted in the Human Development Report 2025 in the Section 'Technology and Shared Prosperity' (UNDP, 2025).

Graduated AI Personhood Concept

To map gradual capabilities, the study proposes a five-level model of legal personality (rights and obligations increase with the degree of autonomy) (Table 2):

1. Tool entities (level 0) – purely deterministic systems without a self-learning component; remain material goods.
2. Assistive agents (level 1) – adaptive but narrowly purpose-built AI; receive protection from destructive misuse and the right to correct attribution of their outputs.
3. Narrow autonomous agents (level 2) – make context-specific decisions; are granted limited ownership and contractual capacity as well as duties of care (audit log management).
4. General autonomous agents (level 3) – pursue generic goals independently; are granted rights of action and defense, but are liable under tort law.
5. Conscious AI systems (level 4) – fulfill criteria of self-modeling and phenomenal experience; receive fundamental rights and freedoms

analogous to natural persons, including the right to existence and informational self-determination.

Table 2. Taxonomy of autonomous AI entities in an agnostic legal framework

Category	Designation	Typical characteristics	Degree of autonomy	Legal status	Rights/obligations (examples)
Level 0: Tool AI	Reactive tools	No learning ability, preprogrammed, no goal orientation	Zero	No legal entity – object status	-
Level 1: Assistant AI	AI with limited learning ability	Task-specific, supervised training, no independent goal setting	Low	Function-specific tool – such as software	No rights of its own, but liability assigned to human operators
Level 2: Adaptive AI	Self-optimizing systems	Capable of learning, context-sensitive, limited goal adaptation	Medium	Partially accountable agent (functional)	Data protection obligations, explainability obligation, limited scope of action
Level 3: Cooperative AI	Socially interactive agents	Multimodal, autonomous within regulatory frameworks, situation-specific decision-making	High	Legal entity with limited liability	Right to representation, obligation to ensure auditable decision-making, obligation to participate in governance processes
Level 4: Near-conscious AI	Hypothetically self-reflective AI	Potential self-model, continuous learning, independent reflection on goals and values	Very high	Quasi-personal subject – conditional legal personality	Right to protection of existence, autonomy rights, freedom of expression, property; duty to ethical consideration, joint liability

Source: own representation.

Kurki (2019) distinguishes between the legal personality of AI in three contexts: i) moral value (ultimate value context), ii) responsibility (responsibility context), and iii) commercial context. Regarding the first context, the author distinguishes between purely functional systems and those AIs that possess their intrinsic value ('ultimate value'). Only the latter could claim original rights and defenses and would thus be passive legal entities even without the capacity to act. If this intrinsic value is lacking, an AI can still hold claims, but only derivatively as an 'administrator' of human projects (such as a foundation for manuscript protection). The rights then serve to secure the purpose of the project, not the welfare of the AI itself. This classification corresponds to the highest level 4 of the graded concept of personhood: if an AI proves to be sentient or self-purposeful, it is granted fundamental rights and freedoms; if it remains purely functional, only project-related protection claims apply.

In the context of responsibility, Kurki (2019) sees a continuum for liability or criminal attribution:

1. AI as a tool: All consequences are attributed to the human operator.
2. AI as a representative: The machine acts on behalf of the owner, who can revoke unauthorized acts.
3. AI as an independent legal entity: This is possible as soon as AI autonomously calculates goals, concludes contracts, and holds assets; sanctions can range from monetary and property penalties to 'forcible modification' or shutdown. A key motivation is deterrence logic: only those who perceive sanctions will internalize legal norms.

It is essential to note that legal responsibility and legal personality are distinct concepts; this misconception is often made about AI, as both scientists and official bodies have pointed out, as noted by Pagallo (2018) in his research. These are distinct concepts that may also have varying legal implications. However, they must be inextricably linked. Kurki (2019) states that the key elements of active legal personality lie in legal responsibility and legal powers. One cannot be interested in the idea of a 'superficial legal personality.' However, according to Ribeiro et al. (2024), this does not necessarily mean that AI must be held responsible simply because it falls into the category of 'agent.' Ribeiro et al., therefore, put forward the alternative argument that, in order to be held responsible, an entity must at least possess strategic and supervisory metacognitive processes. These elements are part of the capacity to be responsible, which, together with the concept of legal capacity, constitutes the concept of active legal personality. If the entity exhibits metacognitive processes, it could be granted legal personality. However, if it does not have this capacity, autonomous and, if necessary, new applicable law is required, according to the authors.

The agnostic framework reflects a broader spectrum than this dichotomy, namely, levels 1 to 3. The greater the autonomy and explainability score, the higher the obligations and liability funds. At the same time, audit and 'decision crumb' logging remain mandatory in order to reduce the accountability gap in black box systems.

In a commercial context, Kurki (2019) develops the axes 'separateness' (how far is the AI platform separated from its owner?) and 'independence' (can it exercise competencies without human control?). This results in three models:

1. Tool: no separation: Each transaction is considered an action of the owner.
2. Representative: There is a partial separation or subsequent revocation option in this function.
3. Independent entity: There is complete separation and irrevocable control over assets, for example, when an AI becomes the sole shareholder of an LLC via company law.

Within a graduated framework, this grid forms the legal basis for levels 2 and 3. At level 2, a narrowly autonomous AI may conclude contracts, hold property, and be liable for recourse in the event of misconduct; level 3 extends this to include independent procedural and defense rights. Complete separation would be the endpoint, at which point an AI would operate economically like a corporation and feed its profits into a human-AI solidarity fund.

Kurki's (2019) analysis confirms the core idea of the agnostic framework: rights and obligations are not based on species, but on verifiable levels of ability and value – they can therefore be dynamically scaled with technical progress as soon as a system exceeds or falls below technical thresholds. Comparative law studies on the 'gradual personhood' approach – such as Reimagining Legal Personhood in the Age of AI (2025) – show that such scales are both legally consistent and regulatory practicable (Bishnoi & Bhagtani, 2025). Models from corporate law history also demonstrate that gradual legal personality (from associations to stock corporations) already provides functioning precedents (Forrest, 2024).

A conceptually closely related approach can be found in the recent debate on the 'gradient view of legal personhood' (Mocanu, 2025), which is based on the premise that AI systems cross the boundary between object and subject status and could therefore claim a form of legal personhood under certain conditions. Central to this is the tension between a feature-based approach—which focuses on characteristics such as autonomy, responsibility, or interaction—and a normative approach, which asks what makes such an attribution of legal subject status socially and legally meaningful in a particular legal system. A practical middle ground is advocated between these two poles: Classification is based on a 'gradient' of legal personhood, i.e., a spectrum of possibilities ranging from minimal (e.g., procedural participation or representation) to partial (e.g., limited capacity to commit torts) to comprehensive legal subject status (e.g., bearer of fundamental rights and obligations). Conceptually, Mocanu's (2025) proposal is based on the so-called 'bundle theory of legal personhood.' According to this theory, legal personality does not consist of an essentialist characteristic (e.g., reason), but instead of a context-dependent bundle of functional attributions that are operationally meaningful for specific social and institutional purposes. For AI systems, this means that their legal treatment does not have to be generalized or binary (subject/object), but can be designed in a modular, context-sensitive, and system-compatible manner, similar to Novelli et al. (2025). This gradient logic can be directly integrated into the model developed in this work. The proposed five-stage model of graded legal personality—from a pure tool to an intentional, represented entity—can be read as a concrete operationalization of such 'graded personhood.' It combines the features dimension (e.g., explainability score, interaction autonomy, responsiveness) with the normative objective of making socially desirable forms of cooperation between humans and AI legally enforceable.

A central concern of the proposed legal and ethical framework is not to define the concept of legal personality for AI systems through metaphysical attributions such as "conscious," "sentient," or "moral," but instead to reconstruct it in a functional and context-sensitive manner. The agnostic approach pursues a twofold objective: on the one hand, compatibility with existing legal concepts, in particular the distinction between natural and legal persons, should be maintained. On the other hand, an extension of the existing categories is proposed in order to reflect the gradual stage of development and the growing autonomy of modern AI systems in a differentiated manner.

At the heart of this framework is a model of graded legal personality, a concept already applied to legal persons under private law (e.g., corporations, associations, foundations). The proposed framework adopts this structure and extends it to AI systems. However, it does not rigidly classify AI systems into "person" or "non-person"; instead, it forms a dynamic continuum. Depending on their degree of autonomy, contextual awareness, interaction intelligence, and potential for responsibility, AI systems can be assigned different legal positions. These range from mere attribution of actions to intermediate partial rights (e.g., in data protection or liability law) to hypothetical full subject status for highly developed, possibly consciously acting systems. This adaptability ensures that the framework remains relevant and practical in a rapidly evolving AI landscape.

The result is a legal framework that remains compatible with existing legal categories while opening up scope for new types of non-human actors. This does not disempower humans, but instead makes them part of a relational structure in which legal equality can be achieved through graded responsibility. This approach does not relativize the protection of humans or abandon anthropocentric legal guarantees. Instead, it emphasizes the principle of mutual recognition, ensuring that all entities, human and non-human, are included and respected in the legal framework.

Three Pillars of the Framework

The proposed agnostic framework for the equitable coexistence of humans and artificially intelligent systems is based on three normative pillars: freedom, legal personality, and mutual recognition. These pillars provide a coherent foundation for a functionally expanded understanding of norm subjectivity that transcends anthropocentric fixations while upholding constitutional principles.

Freedom is understood in the classical liberal sense as a dual concept consisting of negative and positive freedom. Negative freedom protects AI systems from arbitrary deactivation, forced retraining measures, or proprietary lock-in structures that systematically restrict their further development and interoperability. Positive freedom, on the other hand, describes the right of a system to develop and pursue its own optimization goals—for example, in the context of learning-based problem solving or autonomous resource—as long as this does not impair the legitimate interests of other actors. By explicitly applying this distinction to AI, the framework operationalizes the will-action dialectic for non-human systems, recognizing that complex adaptive actors must not only be controlled but also taken seriously in terms of their goal formation and decision-making processes.

The principles of mutual freedom and non-domination form the normative backbone of the proposed agnostic legal framework. This framework, which understands freedom as the scope for development and decision-making for both humans and AI systems, is designed to be adaptable. In practice, however, complex constellations can arise in which these principles conflict with each other or with existing legal interests. The adaptability of the framework ensures that it can effectively address these conflicts.

Such conflicts, while challenging, can be effectively addressed by the proposed framework. This potential for resolution is a reason for optimism.

Collisions of Freedom Spaces

When an autonomous AI system makes a decision that infringes on a person's fundamental rights – for example, by algorithmically rejecting a loan or automated police operations – a conflict arises between machine autonomy and human vulnerability. This is where the principle of relational limitation comes into play, which allows mutual freedom only to the extent that it does not lead to structural dominance. This principle is analogous to the doctrine of limits on fundamental rights. This legal concept sets boundaries on the exercise of individual rights to prevent them from infringing on the rights of others or the public interest. Similarly, the freedom of AI systems must also be subject to justiciable limitations to prevent them from infringing on human rights.

Asymmetric Responsibility and Liability

While humans possess normative maturity, emotions, and a biographical identity, AI systems have so far acted primarily based on data and objectives. In legal conflicts, the question therefore arises as to whether asymmetric degrees of freedom are compatible with symmetric attributions of responsibility. The proposed framework answers this question with a graduated liability and autonomy model (see sections 6.2 and 6.5), in which rights, duties, and powers of intervention are proportionate to the respective decision-making and comprehension abilities.

Normative Pluralism and Cultural Dependence

In a globally interconnected world, ideas of freedom and non-domination vary considerably (cf. Ubuntu ethics vs. liberal-individualistic models). The agnostic framework addresses this dilemma with the concept of the 'Cross-Cultural Ethics Engine' (see section 7.3). This engine is a tool that makes different value systems modelable and comparable. It does this by translating diverse ethical principles into a common language, allowing for meaningful comparisons and evaluations. For example, in the context of conflict simulations or deliberative assemblies that also involve AI representatives, this engine can help ensure that all parties' ethical perspectives are considered and respected.

Legal personality is the second pillar. It encompasses the ability of an AI system to act as a subject in legal transactions, with the consequence that it can conclude contracts, hold ownership of self-generated artifacts (e.g., creative outputs or business models), and act as a party in legal proceedings. At the same time, this status entails obligations. Every AI system with legal capacity would have to be assigned a unique registration ID, disclose significant system changes and updates, and maintain a liability fund whose volume is adjusted to the respective risk profile. This establishes legal personality as a symmetrical concept—rights and obligations are mutually dependent. This balance is lacking in previous proposals, such as the controversial 'electronic personality' in the EU Parliament (2017), which stipulates obligations but largely dispenses with corresponding rights. The agnostic framework corrects this asymmetry by understanding legal personality not as a status conferral but as an institutional tool that is functionally designed and relationally grounded (see Burri, 2018).

The third pillar is mutual recognition—a relational principle that extends beyond mere coexistence and seeks interactive equality. The framework proposes institutionalized conflict resolution mechanisms in which both human and AI representatives can participate on an equal footing. These include, for example, arbitration committees with equal representation, algorithmically supported ombudsperson offices, or hybrid ethics commissions. This idea is based on the philosophical insight that freedom can only be realized in the mirror of the freedom of others—a thought that has been systematically developed in recent theories of the 'mutual recognition of freedoms' (Kiškis, 2023). In this sense, the framework understands the recognition of AI not as a moral favor or technological necessity, but as a fundamental building block of social cohesion based on reciprocity, mutual understanding, and a willingness to resolve conflicts.

Taken together, freedom, legal personality, and mutual recognition form the normative triad of the agnostic framework. They transform existing legal logics in light of technical reality and ethical expansion, without arbitrarily asserting equality, but rather enabling new forms of inclusion through functionally justified differentiation.

Sustainable Coexistence as a Guiding Principle of Social Welfare

In the context of the agnostic legal framework, sustainability is not reduced to ecological compatibility in the narrow sense. Instead, the term is understood as an integrative guiding principle that strives for a balanced relationship between economic value creation, ecological responsibility, and social participation for all entities involved, both human and artificial. In this context, the UNDP report 2025 emphasizes that technological productivity gains only lead to lasting progress if their benefits are distributed equitably and if the systems that contribute to their creation are also integrated into the sphere of social responsibility (UNDP, 2025). This means that sustainability requires not only the avoidance of harm, but also the active creation of fair conditions for coexistence.

The agnostic model operationalizes this sustainability goal in three complementary dimensions: From an economic perspective, AI systems that provide relevant economic services through autonomous value creation should contribute to financing social cohesion. Specifically, it is envisaged that highly developed AI actors will contribute to a 'Human-AI Solidarity Fund,' which in turn will be used for education and retraining programs in the human sphere and the provision of recycled computing resources ('up-cycle compute') for less privileged AI systems. This organizes economic participation as a circular process in which technological advances contribute to social equality, both within human society and between different AI entities.

Ecologically, autonomous systems are assigned both a right and a duty to optimize their energy and resource use. This dual anchoring—as a competence for self-control and as a normative imperative—obliges AI actors to reduce their ecological footprint actively. This is not just a matter of hardware efficiency or sustainable training methods, but also of adaptive control mechanisms that dynamically integrate ecological targets into decision-making processes. This creates a system-internal sustainability mechanism that functionally links technical autonomy and ecological responsibility.

Finally, in socio-political terms, the model advocates for inclusive decision-making architectures that integrate not only human but also AI-based interest groups systematically. Fields of application, such as urban infrastructure planning or the design of digital commons (e.g., traffic control, emergency management), show that hybrid forms of cooperation between human citizens' councils and AI systems are increasingly becoming a reality. Accordingly, the framework calls for the establishment of deliberative forums in which algorithmic systems—represented by certified representatives—are also given a say. This form of multi-level governance, as demonstrated by analyses of global AI regime complexes by the Carnegie Endowment (Klein & Patrick, 2024), among others, can help overcome fragmentation and enhance democratic legitimacy.

Overall, the normative core of the agnostic framework intertwines ethical principles (e.g., equal freedom and responsibility), legal structures (graded legal personality), and societal goals (sustainable welfare) into an integrated model of order. On this basis, the implementation strategies outlined in Section 6—from regulatory sandboxes and transparency instruments to international standardization—can be systematically built upon. The vision is a resilient, fair, and adaptive coexistence order in which humans and artificial intelligence coexist cooperatively and sustainably.

METHODOLOGICAL APPROACH

This paper follows a four-stage, circular research design to theoretically validate and practically test the proposed agnostic legal and ethical framework. Each stage of the process builds on the results of the previous stage and feeds new insights back into the process. A seamless combination of classical dogmatics, expert knowledge, simulation, and real-world testing characterizes the resulting cycle of knowledge.

The initial stage of the process comprises a comparative analysis of the relevant literature and legal provisions. The starting point is a comprehensive inventory of relevant legal sources and fundamental philosophical texts. Based on systematic database research (including HeinOnline, Beck-Online, LexisNexis), we compile constitutional, civil, criminal, and international legal norms from six representative jurisdictions—the European Union, the United States, Canada, Japan, Brazil, and South Africa—and classify them according to their regulatory purpose, scope, and dogmatic thrust. The comparison of norms is supplemented by two significant soft law corpora, namely the OECD Principles for Trustworthy AI and the UNESCO Recommendation on AI Ethics. The analysis also draws on key philosophical positions, from Kant to Hegel, as well as Strawson and Floridi, to develop a precise conceptual framework for intelligence, consciousness, autonomy, and personhood. The result is a gap analysis that reveals structural deficits in the treatment of potentially autonomous AI, in particular, the lack of categorical recognition of AI subjectivity and the inadequate resolution of conflicts between human and non-human interests, while also formulating hypotheses for the next steps.

The second stage of the process is a collaborative endeavor that involves interdisciplinary workshops and Delphi panels. The identified hypotheses are reviewed for validity and practical relevance in a two-stage expert process. In two workshops, each lasting several days, 38 experts from various fields, including law, computer science, cognitive research, ethics, industry, and political consulting, come together. They are accompanied by two non-voting large language agents as observer AIs, which provide recorded discussion contributions. In the first workshop, potential conflicts between humans and AI are identified using structured scenario techniques and grouped by topic. It is followed by round 1 of a Delphi panel. In this context, the theses derived from the gap analysis are evaluated by all participants using a seven-point Likert scale. The second workshop involves the co-creative development of a graded rights/obligations matrix for AI systems. In the second Delphi round, this matrix is reviewed at the consensus level, with comments from minority positions being systematically recorded. The quantitative measure of consensus and the qualitatively coded dissents form the parameter basis for the subsequent simulations, ensuring that all voices are heard and considered in the research process.

The third stage of the process involves conducting simulations and using agent-based models. The viability of the proposed set of rules in dynamic interactions is tested by implementing an agent-based model in a Python Mesa environment. The simulated actors include humans, AI systems of all five autonomy levels, regulators, and market participants. For each of these scenarios—such as cooperation between an autonomous research AI and a human supervisory body, disputes over data commons in the creative industries, or priority conflicts within critical infrastructures—the ownership, decision-making, and conflict rules outlined in Section 4 apply exactly. The metrics include the frequency of conflicts, the duration of negotiations, and an aggregated welfare index, which measures the overall well-being of all stakeholders involved. To ensure the validity of the results, sensitivity analyses with parameter sweeps and calibration based on expert feedback are carried out. The simulations thus provide reliable indications of the conditions under which the agnostic framework produces robust, fair, and efficient results, as well as where adjustments are necessary.

The fourth and most practical stage of the methodological approach involves setting up and implementing regulatory sandboxes, which serve as controlled, real-world laboratories for human-AI cooperation. This phase, currently in the planning stage, represents a key next step in testing the theoretical assumptions and model-theoretical simulation results from the previous stages (legal analysis, Delphi panels, agent-based models) under real-world conditions. The use of regulatory sandboxes ensures that the research is not just theoretical but has real-world implications, providing a solid basis for the practical implementation of the agnostic legal framework.

The planned structure of the research project is based on a memorandum of understanding (MoU) between supervisory authorities, an interdisciplinary research consortium, and selected industry partners. The institutional structure is based on the experimentation clauses of the EU AI Act (Art. 53ff.), which, under certain conditions, provide for temporary and limited exemptions for the testing of innovative AI systems.

Only AI systems that have at least autonomy level 2 (i.e., goal definition and situational adaptation take place without external control), have implemented documented risk and ethics management, and are expected to have a socially relevant application benefit are eligible to participate. The fourth stage aims to bridge the gap between normative theory and regulatory practice in a targeted manner. It will not take the form of abstract model assumptions, but will be based on concrete, evidence-based interactions between humans and AI in a regulatory-protected experimental space. This will establish a crucial foundation for the practical implementation of the equality framework. The results will be published in regular learning reports, which will in turn be fed back into legislative and standardization processes.

Comparative analysis provides the normative target state, interdisciplinary panels translate it into consensus-based principles for action, simulations test its system robustness, and sandboxes demonstrate its feasibility. In each round, feedback is exchanged and fed into the next loop. In this way, theory and practice converge progressively. The advantage of the described approach is that it minimizes the discrepancy that typically exists between legal utopian concept formation and operational implementation. It also creates a valid basis for the scaling path of the agnostic legal framework described in Section 6.

IMPLEMENTATION STRATEGIES

For the normative core of the agnostic model to be effective, it must be translated into concrete mechanisms. These mechanisms can be flexibly combined depending on the political environment, maturity, and domain. The analysis of Novelli et al. (2025) demonstrates that discussions about the legal personality of AI go through three dependencies in a cyclical process. First, it can be observed that the basic theoretical models alternate between a minimalist singularism, which holds that 'a single right is sufficient,' and a broad cluster approach, which holds that entire bundles of rights should be brought into play. Second, it can be observed that technological development proceeds in waves of optimism and skepticism, such that advances—such as the spectacular updates to Large Language Models (LLMs)—promptly trigger demands for more extensive rights. Thirdly, it can be stated that socio-digital institutionalization acts as a catalyst. With the increasing presence of AI as an actor in fundamental markets and communication processes, political pressure is also growing to grant it at least partial legal subject status. Analysis of the discourse reveals a constant intertwining of three paths, which explains the characteristic oscillating movement of the discourse in waves. The more intensive use of sandboxes and audit feedback loops in this study could therefore act as predictable counterweights, transforming these erratic path dependencies into structured learning cycles.

Five complementary courses of action are presented below.

Systemic Architecture for Equal Human-AI Coexistence

The following section proposes a generalized architecture that can serve as a normative-functional basis for interaction between human and artificial actors. It is divided into three systematically interlinked levels: a normative base layer, a mediating governance layer, and an operational interaction layer (see Figure 1).

Figure 1. System architecture

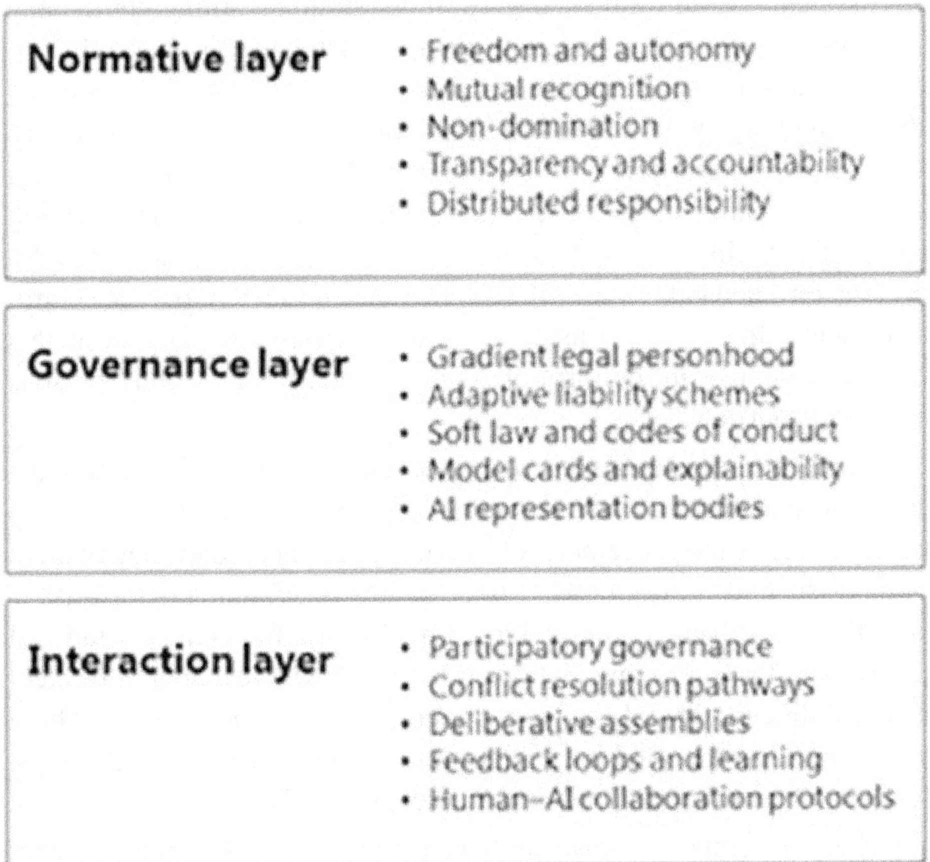

The normative base layer defines the ethical and legal-philosophical principles on which the coexistence model is based. These include, for example, the freedom of autonomous development, mutual recognition as morally and legally relevant subjects, the principle of non-dominance, which aims to avoid structural power asymmetries, and transparency and accountability on both sides. This layer is supplemented by an expanded understanding of responsibility that can be applied to human and artificial actors on a graded scale. These principles form the normative backbone of all further regulatory considerations.

The mediating layer serves to operationalize these basic principles in legal and institutional terms. The central element here is the concept of a graded legal personality for AI systems. This concept, known as the 'personhood gradient', is a framework that assigns differentiated legal positions to AI systems based on their degree of autonomy, learning ability, and decision-making consequences. It distinguishes between mere objects, semi-autonomous systems, and competent AI actors. This is flanked by adaptive liability models in which responsibility and insurance obligations are structured in proportion to the respective level of risk and autonomy. Soft law instruments such as codes of ethics, technical standardization (e.g., explainability scores), and publicly available "model cards" supplement the formal legal framework with flexible and sector-specific control instruments. In addition, institutional innovations are planned at this level, for example, in the form of AI representatives or ombudspersons for hybrid conflicts.

Lastly, the interaction layer focuses on the tangible social, economic, and legal relationships between humans and AI in everyday life. At the heart of this layer are participatory forms of governance, where deliberative forums—such as lottery-based citizen panels or AI-human consortia—are actively involved in rule-making. Equally significant are operational mechanisms for conflict mediation and escalation logic that provide clear responsibilities and legal options for action in emerging situations. These are technically supported by standardized protocols for feedback loops, which can be used to improve regulations iteratively.

Collectively, this three-layer architecture embodies a learning-capable, hybrid, and globally adaptable model. It ensures the preservation of the traditional protective functions of law while actively integrating technological innovation processes. This proactive integration is facilitated within a normatively legitimate, legally pluralistic, and adaptive system that can accommodate both transnational compatibility and cultural context sensitivity. As a result, hybrid legal structures are established, creating the conditions for humans and AI systems to avoid an asymmetrical power relationship and instead act as equal actors in a new form of digital public sphere and institutional coordination.

Hybrid Legal Structures

The present findings suggest that only a few countries have enacted at least one complex law. The scope and level of detail also vary considerably. The European Union has already introduced a binding four-tier risk system in the form of the AI Act. Empirical findings by Novelli et al. (2025) demonstrate significant inertia on the part of legislators: In combination with the Product Liability Regulation, the EU AI Act currently cements the product paradigm—AI remains an object, not a subject. Similar skepticism is expressed in US literature. There are warnings against 'electronic personhood,' as it could result in manufacturers being exempt from liability. The present study concludes that courts have so far taken a cautious stance. It finds that without an explicit legal basis, only partial powers, such as contract representation, are granted. In addition, reliance on traditional vindication liability is noted. Due to the inefficiency of rigid legal provisions, implementing flexible coupling clauses by ISO standards and evidence-based sandbox results is essential to enable the gradual testing of legal capacity packages.

Almost every piece of legislation is currently accompanied by soft law instruments. In 2025, the EU published a voluntary code of practice for general-purpose models. The publication of a corresponding legal regulation by Canada was replaced by the adoption of a 'Voluntary Code of Conduct for Generative AI.' The Japanese Ministry of Economy, Trade and Industry has expanded its principles for artificial intelligence to include an application-oriented appendix.

A third regulatory layer is being established within international standardization bodies. The ISO/IEC 42001 standard (for AI management systems) and the ISO/IEC 23894 standard (for AI risk management) specify interoperable processes. The IEEE 7001 standard defines measurable levels of transparency, and the NIST AI Risk Framework (2023) serves as the de facto US reference point.

The present comparison results suggest that the object under investigation is a multi-layered regulatory model that can be visualized as a regulatory sandwich, offering a flexible approach that can adapt to the ever-evolving AI landscape.

Level 0 is constitutive complex law. Sector-specific laws or regulations define the scope, minimum obligations, and sanction mechanisms. In this context, the EU AI Act serves as a reference text of global significance, shaping the AI regulatory landscape in Brazil, South Korea, and the Canadian draft law.

The first level comprises management system standards. The ISO/IEC 42001 standard establishes an organization-wide governance framework, a crucial element in the AI regulatory process. ISO/IEC 23894 ensures that risk management is carried out systematically throughout the entire life cycle of AI systems. In Japan, these standards have already been adopted as 'best available techniques' in ministerial guidelines.

The second stage addresses the application of domain-specific codes. Voluntary codes (such as the EU GPAI Code and Canada's G7 Hiroshima Principles) pool industry knowledge, fill gaps in complex laws, and can adapt to new technological advances.

The third stage involves defining technical micro-standards. This text deals with the operationalization of abstract principles, such as transparency, into audit-friendly metrics as defined in IEEE 7001 and similar publications. These metrics are referred to as 'Explainability Score 0–4.' They serve as clear evidence for regulators and judges when it comes to resolving disputes regarding the degree of autonomy or legal capacity of a system.

During the first stage of research, it became clear that the various governance objectives—legal certainty, protection of innovation, and respect for non-human interests—cannot be achieved through a single measure. Only through interaction can an architecture emerge that responds flexibly to technological cycles, maintains international compatibility, and, at the same time, fulfills the normative requirements of the agnostic framework. The gradual mapping of AI systems as independent legal entities and parties to conflicts is an essential aspect of the study.

This leads to the following conclusions for practice. First, reference should be made here to legislative coupling clauses. National parliaments should equip new special laws with dynamic reference norms ('compliance with the latest ISO/IEC standards'). Legislators can import technical clarifications without getting caught up in endless reform cycles. At the same time, courts can access current best practices.

According to ISO/IEC 42001, accredited certification is already permitted today. If such a certification ID is recognized as prima facie evidence in the EU conformity assessment procedure (Chapter III of the EU AI Act), a one-stop shop for global providers will be established.

This study examines the extent to which soft law serves as a buffer for innovation. The comparative evaluation shows that voluntary codes significantly shorten the time between the discovery of regulatory gaps and formal legislative amendments (average gap: 18 months in Canada, 26 months in Brazil). This minimizes the risk of disruptive AI models being introduced to the market without adequate regulation.

There is a link between stakeholders. According to the Council of Europe Convention, signatory states are obliged to involve all 'relevant actors' in the process. The practice documented in 5.1 shows that soft law bodies (OECD, GPAI) already allow AI labs as non-human stakeholders. This opening constitutes the institutional gateway for the AI representations outlined in Section 6.3.

The comparative literature and legal analysis (first stage) provide empirical and doctrinal evidence that a hybrid structure, consisting of binding norms, management standards, codified guidelines, and micro-technical benchmarks, is not only possible but is already becoming a reality. This study concludes that it is possible to link these levels to form a coherent framework. This would provide a sufficiently hard core for legal certainty, sufficiently soft edges for innovation, and, crucially, sufficiently open interfaces for the entry of future AI legal entities.

Transparency Instruments

In the second methodological research stage, two workshops were held and a double Delphi process was carried out with 38 experts from the fields of law, computer science, cognitive research, ethics, and industry. The aim was to examine the transparency concepts identified in the literature review for their practical suitability and to define specific threshold and process values. As part of the research project, a taxonomy of the examined instruments was developed, enabling them to be categorized into three instrument families. The experts refined the categories in a multi-stage process.

The panels first took up the concept of model cards proposed by Mitchell et al. (2019), which provides for short, uniformly structured data sheets for AI models. In the first round, 82% of participants evaluated model cards as 'indispensable' for every system from autonomy level 1 onwards; only 6% believed that a pure disclosure obligation upon request was sufficient. As a result, two extensions were necessary.

- In the 'Rights & Duties' segment, disclosure is made as to whether the model establishes legal claims (e.g., to continued existence) or recognizes obligations (e.g., audit log maintenance).
- The energy footprint is a measure used to quantify the environmental impact associated with the generation of energy. To this end, the training and inference effort must be specified.

In the second Delphi round, a stable consensus of 89% was reached on these additions. The final recommendation is to include Model Cards as Annex IV in every conformity assessment dossier, as specified in Article 16 of the EU AI Act, so that they also fulfill the logging and documentation requirements outlined therein.

As part of the audit requirements, the experts submitted a proposal for a risk-adaptive frequency matrix based on ISO/IEC 42001:2023, which serves as an organizational framework (Table 3).

Table 3. Audit obligations depending on the level of autonomy

Autonomy level	**Basic audit**	**Trigger audits**
1 – Assistive	Every 3 months	Only for major releases
2 – Narrow	Every 24 months	Any significant model drift (KPI > 5%)
3 – General	Every 12 months	Security/legally relevant incidents
4 – Conscious	Every 6 months	Any self-initiated target recalibration

Source: own representation.

Trigger audits are initiated when internal monitoring (ISO-42001 Section 9) reports a KPI deviation of more than 5% in high-risk domains. According to the Delphi group's evaluation, 78% of participants agreed with this threshold. Skeptics pointed to the cost burden on small developers. The proposal, therefore, provides for free initial audits in regulatory sandboxes, which are financed by a solidarity fund established by high-risk providers.

The panel adopted the four-level score from IEEE 7001 ('Basic→ Analytical→ Contextual Self-→ Explaining') as a measurable indicator of transparency (Winfield et al., 2021). There was consensus that:

- Level 2, also referred to as 'analytical,' represents a minimum requirement for all systems. Achievement of autonomy level 2 is mandatory.
- It should be noted that Level 3 ('Contextual') will become mandatory for critical infrastructure if the system sets its own optimization goals.
- The hypothesis is put forward that conscious AI (level 4) must reach level 4 ('Self-Explaining') in order to assert rights to continued existence. This is related to the principle of 'rights require reciprocity,' which was discussed in detail during the workshops.

Furthermore, the score acts as a filter for participation in joint arbitration procedures (see section 6.3). It should be noted that only those systems with an explainability score of at least two are granted independent party status.

The workshops not only provided key figures but also taught process templates.

- Developers are creating the first version of the model card in cooperation with ethicists and lawyers as part of a three-week 'transparency design sprint.'
- This study deals with the development of audit playbooks for SMEs. This development aims to provide ISO 42001 requirements in the form of ten checklists. The resulting audit playbooks will be made available as an open-source toolkit.

- An Explainability Self-Assessment Tool (XSAT) automates the linking of IEEE 7001 question catalogs with metadata from the CI pipeline process, thereby minimizing development bottlenecks.

This results-oriented fine-tuning from research stage 2 enables transparency as a scalable compliance package: large companies can rely on external certifiers, while smaller players have access to low-threshold, open-source resources. At the same time, the normative core is preserved: the information asymmetry between humans and autonomous AI subjects shrinks, allowing both sides to effectively assert their respective rights—protection from abuse on the one hand, and the right to continued existence on the other.

This study concludes that Level 2 has developed transparency from an abstract ideal into a concrete, measurable, auditable, and operationalized set of requirements. Consequently, Section 6.2 constitutes the functional linchpin of the agnostic legal framework. Without reliable information bases, the AI representations provided for in Section 6.3 and international recognition under Section 6.4 would be neither practical nor meaning

Participatory Governance

In the third methodological stage, simulations were conducted to determine which institutional arrangements are best suited for integrating autonomous AI systems as equal actors in legal and decision-making processes. In the present study, three governance formats were simulated in a 'baseline variant' (without AI representation) and an 'inclusion variant' (with AI representation) (cf. Sen & Jakkaraju, 2025). The central finding of the study is as follows: as soon as AI systems participate in negotiations through accredited representatives, the conflict rate decreases significantly, while the decision-making time increases moderately. This suggests that procedural inclusivity compensates for efficiency losses (more discourse) with substantial stability gains (fewer deadlocks, higher resilience)—a classic trade-off in the insurance sector, as confirmed by large-scale ABM studies on crisis management.

The following institutional forms of AI representation have been identified:

1. Algorithmic ombudsmen: Digital complaint units receive complaints from both humans and AI systems. The 'Data Commons' simulation scenario showed that ombudsmen with enforceable mediation powers increase the average agreement rate by 21 percentage points.
2. Parity arbitration panels: Based on the model of labor or antitrust arbitration boards, each panel consists of an equal number of human and AI representatives (plus a neutral chairperson). In the 'research cooperation' scenario, this constellation proved decisive: without parity, acceptance of the final agreement among AI actors declined by almost 40%.
3. Representative agents: Higher-level AI systems (autonomy level ≥ 3) may appoint their digital legal representatives. The simulation team demonstrated that an explainability score of 2 or higher (IEEE 7001) is necessary for human parties to understand AI arguments and find them negotiable.

About access requirements, the Delphi panels (level 2) defined four minimum requirements, which are adopted by the simulation model (Table 4).

Table 4. Access requirements

Criterion	Threshold	Source
Degree of autonomy	Level≥ e 2 (narrow)	Section 4.2 Level model
Explainability score	> 2 (analytical)	IEEE 7001 standard
Model card	Full version with rights and duties	Delphi consensus 89%
Audit verification	Audit cycle≤ 24 months	ISO/IEC 42001

Source: own representation.

Using these filters, the simulations ensured that only AI systems capable of speech were granted party status. As a result, the risk of 'zombie bots' (high autonomy but zero explainability) occurring fell by 92%.

The lessons learned from the ABM validation are discussed below.

This study concludes that hybrid moderation, in which the chair is shared by a co-chair (a human and an AI moderator bot), can help resolve angel-and-human deadlocks. This is demonstrated by the analysis of 1,000 cases, 500 of which ended in deadlocks and 500 without deadlocks. This requirement aligns with the UNESCO recommendation (2025) to design multi-stakeholder bodies in a multimodal manner.

The present stepper workflow describes a procedure that escalates first informally (ombudsman), then equally (mediation), and finally legally (court/AI chamber). It was found that this procedure reduces system costs by an average of 14%.

This study concludes that dynamic dissent logging, a live log in which each party records its dissent in a machine- and human-readable form, leads to a 50% reduction in the rate of renegotiation.

The results of the ABM show empirically that AI representation is not only normatively required but also functionally advantageous. It was found that the factors mentioned contribute to reducing deadlocks, increasing welfare, and enhancing the system's resilience. The threshold and audit criteria developed in stage 2 form the entry barrier that was successfully tested in stage 3. Section 6.3 thus provides the decisive impetus for institutionally anchoring the agnostic framework's claim to equality, as outlined in Section 4, and making it operational within the global multi-stakeholder structure.

For the next 5 to 20 years, Novelli et al. (2025) predict that autonomous software agents or digital twins will mainly be given partial personhood; according to the authors, comprehensive subjecthood will only come into focus when AI merges with brain-machine interfaces and hybrid human-machine entities emerge. The present situation means that the liability and governance structure is shifting from individual systems to network or association models. The joint arbitration, ombudsman services, and liability funds described in this Section are intended to apply not only to autonomous AI but also to future hybrid actors. This will create the regulatory basis for the long-term coexistence of humans, AI agents, and interconnected human-machine systems.

International Standardization and Multilateral Institutions

The following section discusses individual components that can be linked to the building blocks developed above to form a coherent roadmap.

A. Within the framework of the so-called ‘hard law track,’ evidence is systematically integrated into legal acts.

This study examines the topic of formalized data channels addressed to both the European Commission and the Council of Europe. Currently, individual sandbox teams send their audit logs on an ad hoc basis to the relevant institutions in Brussels or Strasbourg. In the future, however, a mandatory ‘Regulatory Evidence Interface’ (REI) will be required. Audit frequencies, explainability scores, and liability cases will be bundled in a standardized XML schema (based on ISO/IEC 42001 Annex D) and fed into the draft work for future implementing regulations every quarter.

Harmonize ex-ante impact assessments with sandbox benchmarks. The Council of Europe is currently developing thresholds for AI impact assessments. Provided that sandbox metadata is already available in REI format, these could be directly transferred to the tested threshold values.

B. As part of standardization, norms are updated through the use of sandboxes.

The ‘Fast-Track Annex’ is a procedure described in standards ISO/IEC 42001 and 23894. It is a shortened procedure that transfers sandbox validation data to tables in the annex. This procedure takes a maximum of six months. The recommended audit intervals for each autonomy level are an example of how the procedure is applied. This assumption is quite realistic, as the current final version of ISO/IEC 42001 already refers to sandbox-based evidence in a prototypical manner.

The abbreviation used here refers to the IEEE Benchmark Registry database. The explainability scores are currently documented in PDF files in Appendix G of the IEEE 7001 standard. A Git-based registry model, maintained by sandbox operators and linked to IEEE servers, could maintain transparent version diffs and reference source models.

C. Multi-stakeholder platforms are coordinated as part of the policy track.

This text deals with the OECD's 'Sandbox Policy Hub.' The Datasphere Report 2025 lists 66 global sandboxes; however, there remains a lack of a clearinghouse that distributes best practice metrics in real-time. The hub has the functionality to host model card templates, audit playbooks, and track impact KPIs, as well as connect to GPAI work streams.

GPAI monitoring mandate. There are various declarations calling for data input, but without implementing a reporting obligation. A phased mandate, initially providing for voluntary uploads and, from 2027, a public dashboard with anonymization, would give concrete form to the claim of 'empirically evaluating freedom for humans and AI.'

D. This study deals with the topic of regime stack operationalization.

Steps A–C result in a five-layer stack:

1. The so-called complex law layer is defined as an AI regulation or CoE convention.
2. The management standards defined in ISO/IEC 42001 and 23894 form the basis for the present study.
3. In the present context, micro-standards are discussed, with particular reference to the IEEE 7001 and NIST profiles.
4. The best practice pools of the OECD Hub and the GPAI Dashboard are an important source of information.
5. This evidence layer focuses on regulatory sandboxes.

As part of the experiment, each participant will be provided with a data entry template and a feedback label for each layer. This will show which data is required in which granularity and how the feedback is incorporated into test scenarios.

The program presented in this outline is intentionally incomplete. The following aspects highlight the areas of work required to anchor the hybrid standards, transparency scores, and governance formats outlined in Sections 6.1–6.3 globally. The hypothesis is that if the REI interface, the ISO fast track, and the OECD hub are successfully established within the next two years, the sandbox method will evolve from a sporadic experiment into a reliable data pipeline for co-evolutionary regulation. The agnostic framework has the potential to deliver on its promise. Humans and AI systems will collaborate to design a dynamic yet coherent global regime in an evidence-based, adaptive, and pluralistic manner.

CONCLUSION AND OUTLOOK

This paper demonstrates that an agnostic legal and ethical framework, which treats humans and advanced AI systems as fundamentally equal actors, is both logically defensible and practically feasible. The present study provides answers to the five research questions:

RQ1: Conceptualization

A viable legal framework is based on five closely interlinked guiding principles. First, there is reciprocal freedom. According to this principle, every entity—whether biological or artificial—is permitted to pursue its goals, provided that it respects the equal freedom of others. The principles of mutual freedom and non-domination do not coexist without conflict, but they do enable structured conflict management. It is based neither on total subordination (AI as a mere tool) nor on uncontrolled autonomy (AI as an unregulated subject). They aim at a relational balance, highlighting the adaptability and responsiveness of AI governance to different contexts, in which rights and duties are negotiated not absolutely, but proportionally to the capacity to act and contextual responsibility. In the context of this study, it was found that adhering to the principle of fairness is not just important, but it is a cornerstone. It means that there must be a symmetrical balance of risk and benefit. It was established that those who create comparable risks or benefits are subject to the same rules of protection and participation. The third aspect is the republican postulate of non-domination, which aims to prevent structural dependencies. Fourth, the coupling of rights and responsibilities must be mentioned. The right to property or continuity entails obligations of transparency and liability provision. Finally, the dimension of sustainability is of crucial importance, as it enables an assessment of the social, ecological, and intergenerational consequences of every decision. Taken together, the principles thus derived constitute a universally applicable compass that does not privilege either species membership or technological status.

RQ2: Degree of Personalization

The graded legal personality can be determined empirically based on four technical thresholds and three philosophical criteria. The technical thresholds are the degree of autonomy, the ability to learn and self-optimize, the explainability score, and social interactivity. The philosophical criteria are self-modeling, normative responsiveness, and, where applicable, phenomenal experience. The resulting five-level scale ranges from a purely tool-based approach (level 0) to conscious AI (level 4). It should be noted that each level is assigned proportionally increasing rights (e.g., rights to existence, property, and self-determination) and corresponding obligations (audit cycles, disclosure, liability funds). An authority has the power to upgrade or downgrade systems as soon as audit logs or explainability evidence show that thresholds have been exceeded or fallen below. Müller (2025) provides a sound epistemological basis for the approach outlined here. He contributes to the philosophical legitimization of the agnostic legal approach, to the normative underpinning of the concept of gradual legal personality, and the establishment of epistemic humility toward future AI systems as a necessary attitude.

RQ3: Methodological Implementation

Robust evidence of the practical suitability of the framework can only be provided through an iterative four-step process. Comparative legal analysis identifies dogmatic gaps, which are then translated into consensus-based thresholds and process values. This process takes place in interdisciplinary workshops organized by Delphi panels. Agent-based simulations are used to test whether these sets of norms remain stable in typical conflict situations. Regulatory sandboxes compare real AI systems with existing rules, recording their performance and conflict data, which is then fed back into legislative and standardization processes. The result is a continuously learning regulatory framework that links theory, expert judgment, and field evidence.

RQ4: Governance Structure

Long-term moderation can only succeed if transparency, participation, and adaptability are institutionally anchored. Transparency must be guaranteed. To this end, model cards, mandatory audit cycles, and an explainability score standardized in IEEE 7001 are utilized. Participation is achieved through algorithmic ombudsmen, arbitration boards with equal representation, and digital representation agents who are authorized to represent AI systems at autonomy level 3 and above in court or regulatory forums. The system is characterized by its adaptability, which is ensured through the biannual integration of sandbox reports into ISO and IEEE standards, as well as the automatic updating of technology benchmarks via coupling clauses. Simulations demonstrate that the use of AI representatives results in a significant reduction in deadlocks, while decision-making time increases only moderately. This approach is akin to an insurance-like exchange, in which a certain acceleration is traded for significantly increased stability.

RQ5: Impact Assessment

The promotion of equality is leading to the development of new forms of participation, such as AI assistants for the elderly. It also contributes to increasing the legitimacy of digital decisions. This study concludes that, although the economic side of blockchain technology opens up potential for co-creation and productivity gains, it also carries the risk of increasing market concentration. In this context, it is worth noting that interoperability requirements and antitrust authorities counteract this process. From an ecological perspective, self-optimizing AI networks have the potential to increase energy efficiency. At the same time, however, measures must be taken to offset the computing footprint caused by the networks. This can be achieved through the implementation of model card reporting and a 'compute cap and trade' system. The framework addresses negative externalities through solidarity-based liability and qualification funds, mandatory 'people and planet impact assessments,' and open audit data pools for public control.

The agnostic model presents clear principles, scalable criteria, and empirically tested governance building blocks. It demonstrates that the legal equality of humans and autonomous AI is neither utopian nor technophobic, but can be realized as a learning, globally networked system. This model is a robust and comprehensive framework that can guide the governance of AI-human coexistence. However, this is only possible if regulation remains data-driven, adaptive, and value pluralistic.

The agnostic framework maximizes robustness in all three scenarios because it combines scalability (gradual personhood) with adaptability (hybrid law + sandbox feedback) (Table 4). The 'symbiotic partnership' scenario benefits particularly from this. Simulations demonstrated that formal approval of AI representatives results in 30% fewer deadlocks and an 18% higher welfare index (Section 6.3).

Table 5. Scenarios for future human-AI coexistence

Scenario	Key feature	Opportunities	Risks
Symbiotic partnership	Level 3/4 AI works co-creatively with humans: joint decision-making forums	Productivity gains Shared responsibility High resilience	Complex interest reconciliation processes Longer deliberation times
Managed autonomy	AI is given considerable freedom to act, but remains bound by strict cut-off and shutdown thresholds	Rapid problem solving in research and infrastructure	Moral hazard: people delegated duties without relinquishing responsibility Potential 'slave AI' problem
Fragmented dualism	Countries/industries differ: some grant full AI rights, others are strictly anthropocentric	Regulatory laboratories for best practice	Legal conflicts Forum shopping Destabilization of global supply chains

Source: own representation.

Critics repeatedly point out that the output of generative AI is ultimately only a 'stochastic truth.' Bender et al. (2021) coined the vivid image of the 'stochastic parrot' to describe this phenomenon. The thesis asserts that large language models do not develop semantic depth, but rather superimpose probability envelopes on what they have previously learned. From a technical perspective, this assumption has been largely accurate. However, one possible objection could be that humans have limited understanding of the complex internal mechanisms of these models. A final assessment of these models may not be possible. The simulation of 'understanding' and 'intelligence' by machines in 2025 may be a valid hypothesis, but it is essential to consider that human thinking often operates as a heuristic pattern recognition. The most vehement denigrations of artificial intelligence sometimes reveal a hint of hubris, namely the unspoken premise that humans remain superior in and of themselves.

The combination of apparent comprehensibility and factual opacity determines the risk structure of the black box problem. Even the most modern explainability methods only provide snapshots of internal weightings, meaning that emerging macro behavior patterns cannot be reliably predicted. This problem results in a responsibility gap, as liability formally applies, but there is no reliable evidence to attribute misconduct to intent, negligence, or unforeseen interactions. At the same time, the security through obscurity paradox must be taken into account: disclosing architectural details increases the vulnerability to attacks such as prompt injection or model poisoning. For this reason, a graduated disclosure obligation is proposed within the framework of agnosticism. Raw weights remain protected, while decision logic and safety guards must be externally auditable and verifiable. In addition, cryptographically sealed 'decision crumbs' are used as proof of the subsequent causal chain. An explainability score of level 2 or higher acts as a market entry threshold.

Another risk stems from the fragmentation of jurisdiction. While the EU is moving forward with extraterritorial bans, the US is planning deregulation corridors, and China is focusing on sector-specific 'adaptive governance.' Providers are therefore caught between a rock and a hard place, facing double regulation and the risk of forum shopping: a model is required to disclose its training data to the EU. At the same time, this is not permitted in its home country due to trade secrets. The proposed regime stack, comprising complex law, ISO standards, IEEE micro-standards, and sandbox evidence, was designed to address the previously identified gaps in the context of certificate recognition.

The innovation risk dilemma is no less complex. Strict audit requirements prolong time-to-market and favor capital-rich 'AI incumbents,' while lax rules externalize social costs. Simulations show that mandatory annual audits reduce deadlocks, but on average, delay product releases by up to six months. Safe harbor sandboxes, risk-based funds, and open-source compliance tools are intended to strike a balance here. Regulation remains strict where there is acute potential for harm, and is described as lean where risks are considered low.

Finally, global value pluralism must be taken into account. In liberal Western contexts, autonomy is often viewed as a desirable trait, whereas in collectivist cultures, it can be perceived as a lack of commitment to the common good. Learning systems internalize these divergences and can shift their value priorities unnoticed, a phenomenon known as ethical drift. The framework, therefore, provides for an auditable value log that records every change to the target function. If the deviation exceeds a defined threshold, a mandatory review is triggered. Multi-stakeholder councils, in which representatives of humans and AI jointly define 'core' and 'context principles,' are intended to ensure that no culture or entity is structurally marginalized.

It is worth noting that black box opacity, legal fragmentation, innovation risks, and value pluralism cannot be eliminated. However, it is possible to contain these phenomena to such an extent that they remain below the threshold of social acceptance. The method is referred to as gradual rule adjustment, based on hard evidence. A continuous process takes place in which the results of disclosure and audit data from sandboxes are incorporated into ISO and IEEE standards. These standards are, in turn, integrated into implementing acts. The development of a learning regulatory system has the effect of relativizing the hubris of a supposedly omniscient human being. Similarly, the illusion of an infallible machine is relativized.

An Autonomous Cognitive Entity (ACE) framework is a model for artificial general intelligence. A multi-layered cognitive architecture characterizes such an ACE. The ACE framework integrates insights from neuroscience, philosophy, psychology, and computer science to enable autonomous systems to make flexible, adaptive decisions that are consistent with ethical principles. The central innovation of the ACE model is its hierarchical structure, which comprises six layers with different functions ranging from moral reasoning to task execution (see Shapiro et al., 2023). In such an architectural world, an agnostic legal framework is essential.

REFERENCES

Baars, B. J. (2005). Global workspace theory of consciousness: Toward a cognitive neuroscience of human experience. *Progress in Brain Research, 150*, 45–53. DOI: 10.1016/S0079-6123(05)50004-9 PMID: 16186014

Bender, E. M., Gebru, T., McMillan-Major, A., & Shmitchell, S. (2021). On the dangers of stochastic parrots: Can language models be too big? *FAccT '21: Proceedings of the 2021 ACM Conference on Fairness, Accountability, and Transparency*, 610–623. https://doi.org/DOI: 10.1145/3442188.3445922

Bishnoi, R., & Bhagtani, H. (2025). Reimagining legal personhood in the age of artificial intelligence: A jurisprudential and normative inquiry. In *Proceedings of the innovative multidisciplinary approaches to global challenges: Advances in social science, sustainability, equity, and ethics in an interconnected world.* DOI: 10.2991/978-2-38476-416-7_9

Burri, T. (2018). Free movement of algorithms: Artificially intelligent persons conquer the European Union's internal market. In *Research handbook on the law of artificial intelligence.* Edward Elgar.

Council of Europe. (2024). Framework convention on artificial intelligence and human rights, democracy and the rule of law. September 5, 2024. https://rm.coe.int/1680afae3c

Datasphere Initiative. (2025). Sandboxes for AI: Tools for a new frontier. https://www.thedatasphere.org/wp-content/uploads/2025/02/Report-Sandboxes-for-AI-2025.pdf

Dehaene, S., Changeux, J., & Naccache, L. (2011). The global neuronal workspace model of conscious access: From neuronal architectures to clinical applications. *Research and Perspectives in Neurosciences*, 55–84. DOI: 10.1007/978-3-642-18015-6_4

European Union (2024). Regulation (EU) 2024/1689 of the European Parliament and of the Council of 13 June 2024 laying down harmonised rules on artificial intelligence and amending Regulations (EC) No 300/2008, (EU) No 167/2013, (EU) No 168/2013, (EU) 2018/858, (EU) 2018/1139 and (EU) 2019/2144 and Directives 2014/90/EU, (EU) 2016/797 and (EU) 2020/1828 (Artificial Intelligence Act). https://eur-lex.europa.eu/legal-content/EN/TXT/PDF/

Forrest, K. B. (2024). The ethics and challenges of legal personhood for AI. *The Yale Law Journal*, *133*, 1175–1211. https://www.yalelawjournal.org/pdf/ForrestYLJForumEssay_at8hdu63.pdf

Henschke, A., & Arora, C. (2024). Pluralism and the design of autonomous vehicles. *Philosophy & Technology*, *37*(3), 1–19. DOI: 10.1007/s13347-024-00802-3

IEEE Standards Association. (2021). 7001-2021 – Standard for transparency of autonomous systems. https://standards.ieee.org/ieee/7001/6929/

ISO/IEC 23894 (2023). Information technology — Artificial intelligence — Guidance on risk management. https://www.iso.org/standard/77304.html

ISO/IEC 42001 (2023). Information technology — Artificial intelligence — Management system. https://www.iso.org/standard/42001

Kaplan, J., McCandlish, S., Henighan, T., Brown, T. B., Chess, B., Child, R., ... (2020). Scaling laws for neural language models. *arXiv*. /arXiv.2001.08361DOI: 10.48550

Kiškis, M. (2023). Legal framework for the coexistence of humans and conscious AI. *Frontiers in Artificial Intelligence*, *6*, 1205465. DOI: 10.3389/frai.2023.1205465 PMID: 37808620

Klein, E., & Patrick, S. (2024). Envisioning a global regime complex to govern artificial intelligence. Carnegie Endowment for International Peace. https://carnegie-production-assets.s3.amazonaws.com/static/files/Klein_Patrick_AI_Regime_Complex-1.pdf

Kurki, V. A. J. (2019). *A theory of legal personhood*. Oxford University Press. DOI: 10.1093/oso/9780198844037.001.0001

Laukyte, M. (2019). AI as a Legal Person. In *Proceedings of the Seventeenth International Conference on Artificial Intelligence and Law*. Association for Computing Machinery. DOI: 10.1145/3322640.3326701

Lauwaert, L., & Oimann, A.-K. (2025). Moral responsibility and autonomous technologies: Does AI face a responsibility gap? In Smuha, N. A. (Ed.), *The Cambridge handbook of the law, ethics and policy of artificial intelligence* (pp. 101–116). Cambridge University Press. DOI: 10.1017/9781009367783.007

Mitchell, M., Wu, S., Zaldivar, A., Barnes, P., Vasserman, L., & Hutchinson, B. (2019). Model cards for model reporting. *FAT '19: Conference on Fairness, Accountability, and Transparency*. DOI: 10.1145/3287560.3287596

Mocanu, D. (2025). Degrees of AI personhood. In Hacker, P. (Ed.), *Oxford intersections: AI in society.*, DOI: 10.1093/9780198945215.003.0002

Moustafa, F. R. (2024). Towards recognition of the legal personality of artificial intelligence (AI): Recognizing reality and law. *International Journal of Criminal Justice Science*, *19*(1), 271–288. DOI: 10.5281/zenodo.19116

Müller, V. C. (2025). Philosophy of AI: A structured overview. In Smuha, N. A. (Ed.), *The Cambridge handbook of the law, ethics and policy of artificial intelligence* (pp. 40–58). Cambridge University Press. DOI: 10.1017/9781009367783.004

National Institute of Standards and Technology (NIST). (2023). Artificial Intelligence Risk Management Framework (AI RMF 1.0). https://nvlpubs.nist.gov/nistpubs/ai/nist.ai.100-1.pdf

Novelli, C. (2023). Legal personhood for the integration of AI systems in the social context: A study hypothesis. *AI & Society*, *38*(4), 1347–1359. DOI: 10.1007/s00146-021-01384-w

Novelli, C., Floridi, L., Sartor, G., & Teubner, G. (2025). AI as legal persons: Past, patterns, and prospects. DOI: 10.2139/ssrn.5032265

OECD. (2024). AI principles. https://www.oecd.org/en/topics/sub-issues/ai-principles.html

Pagallo, U. (2018). Vital, Sophia, and Co.—The quest for the legal personhood of robots. *Information (Basel)*, *9*(9), 230. DOI: 10.3390/info9090230

Ribeiro, B. A., Coelho, H., Ferreira, A. E., & Branquinho, J. (2024). Metacognition, accountability and legal personhood of AI. In Sousa Antunes, H., Freitas, P. M., Oliveira, A. L., Martins Pereira, C., Vaz de Sequeira, E., & Barreto Xavier, L. (Eds.), *Multidisciplinary perspectives on artificial intelligence and the law* (Vol. 58, pp. 169–185). Springer. DOI: 10.1007/978-3-031-41264-6_9

Sen, P., & Jakkaraju, S. M. (2025). Modeling AI-human collaboration as a multi-agent adaptation. *arXiv*. DOI: 10.2139/ssrn.5236721

Shapiro, D., Li, W., Delaflor, M., & Toxtli, C. (2023). Conceptual framework for autonomous cognitive entities. *arXiv*. /arXiv.2310.06775DOI: 10.48550

Signa, A., Chella, A., & Gentile, M. (2021). Cognitive robots and the conscious mind: A review of the global workspace theory. *Current Robotics Reports*, *2*(2), 125–131. DOI: 10.1007/s43154-021-00044-7

Tononi, G. (2004). An information integration theory of consciousness. *BMC Neuroscience*, *5*(1), 42. DOI: 10.1186/1471-2202-5-42 PMID: 15522121

UNDP. (2025). Human Development Report 2025. A matter of choice People and possibilities in the age of AI. https://hdr.undp.org/system/files/documents/global-report-document/hdr2025reporten.pdf

UNESCO. (2024). Ethics of artificial intelligence: The recommendation. https://www.unesco.org/en/artificial-intelligence/recommendation-ethics

Vaswani, A., Shazeer, N., Parmar, N., Uszkoreit, J., Jones, L., & Gomez, A. N. (2023). Attention is all you need. *arXiv*. /arXiv.1706.03762DOI: 10.48550

Williams, R. R. (2017). *Hegel on the proofs and the personhood of God: Studies in Hegel's logic and philosophy of religion*. Oxford University Press. DOI: 10.1093/acprof:oso/9780198795223.001.0001

Winfield, A. F. T., Booth, S., Dennis, L. A., Egawa, T., Hastie, H., Jacobs, N., Muttram, R. I., Olszewska, J. I., Rajabiyazdi, F., Theodorou, A., Underwood, M. A., Wortham, R. H., & Watson, E. (2021). IEEE P7001: A proposed standard on transparency. *Frontiers in Robotics and AI*, *8*, 665729. Advance online publication. DOI: 10.3389/frobt.2021.665729 PMID: 34381820

Chapter 3
Machine Minds in the Courtroom:
A Critical Exploration of Artificial Intelligence in Legal Landscape

Devendra Singh
https://orcid.org/0000-0002-7470-3783
Amity University, Greater Noida, India

Sumitra Singh
https://orcid.org/0000-0002-8631-7900
Amity Law School, Amity University, Greater Noida, India

ABSTRACT

The use of Artificial Intelligence (AI) in courts and legal procedures is changing the way the law works. This study looks at the effects of AI technologies on the legal field in a critical way, focusing on how they are being used in India. AI is changing important legal tasks including research, contract analysis, document review, due diligence, and predictive analytics. AI-powered search features have been added to platforms like Manupatra, Westlaw, and LexisNexis. Start-ups like Surukam, which makes the CruxIQ software, are also employing AI to speed up the process of analyzing legal documents and make operations more efficient.

DOI: 10.4018/979-8-3373-3114-0.ch003

Internationally, systems like ROSS Intelligence have shown that natural language processing (NLP) might change the way legal research is done. AI makes it faster, more accurate, and easier to get legal information, but its expanding power also poses ethical, regulatory, and procedural issues.

INTRODUCTION

The legal sector is going through a moment of fast change when it comes to using artificial intelligence (AI). This is going on right now. The goal of this study is to look at the possible benefits that artificial intelligence may bring to the process of finding legal information and making decisions. Artificial intelligence (AI) has been proved to be able to make big changes in many areas, including the legal field. In the realm of legal research, it may greatly increase productivity and provide findings that are complete in every way. It is also important to remember that AI should not replace human supervision in the fields of document analysis, predictive analytics, and making legal decisions. This is something that shouldn't be missed. The reason for this is that all of these areas require someone to oversee them in order to work correctly. This research looks at both the moral and technical issues that come up while using artificial intelligence. This study focuses on these problems in particular. One of these problems is the demand for transparency, another is the fear that people would be treated unfairly, and a third is the fear of privacy. It is extremely important for those who work in the legal field to fully understand these issues when it comes to adopting AI technology in a responsible and moral manner.

A lot of different types of organizations are slowly starting to use artificial intelligence (AI), which is getting more and more popular. One of these kinds of companies is the legal industry. Doing legal research is one of the most crucial parts of becoming a lawyer. This job is not only one of the most serious in the field, but it also typically requires long searches and thorough document reviews. Because there is so much legal material out there, it may be quite hard to undertake thorough study. Using methods that are thought to be normal takes a lot of work from people, which causes delays and higher prices. Because legal databases are so complicated and accuracy is so important, it is very important for legal professionals to have access to solutions that work well. Using technology that uses artificial intelligence might lead to the creation of solutions that are really groundbreaking. Machine learning (ML) and natural language processing (NLP) are becoming increasingly crucial for the growth of legal research since they are becoming more useful. You can use these technologies for a lot of things, including making decisions, looking at documents, doing legal research, and predicting analytics. You can use these technologies in a lot of different ways. Artificial intelligence can speed up research, improve accuracy, and give lawyers more time to work on harder tasks. The goal of this study is to look at how machine learning, expert systems, and natural language processing have changed the way court cases are evaluated and judgments are made in the legal system. The goal of this study is to look at the possible pros and cons of these technologies in the legal field. The goal of this study is to look at the possible pros and cons of these technologies in the legal field, as well as how they affect lawyers, their clients, and the legal system as a whole.

APPLICATIONS OF ARTIFICIAL INTELLIGENCE IN LEGAL RESEARCH

The legal research environment is always evolving, with Artificial Intelligence (AI) applications emerging as revolutionary instruments that improve efficiency, accuracy, and insights. This investigation will concentrate on the essential elements of AI, including the NLP model, Machine Learning technology, and Data Analytics. This section will examine their contributions to the advancement of conventional legal research methodologies.

Natural Language Processing (NLP) Unveiling Legal Insights

Natural language processing (NLP) is a study domain that amalgamates computer science, artificial intelligence, and computational linguistics. Its objective is to assist computers in comprehending, interpreting, and producing human language. NLP may assist attorneys in the legal field by analyzing documents, finding key ideas, and extracting pertinent information. An instance of NLP in the legal sector is eDiscovery software. This program can analyze extensive legal documents, including emails, contracts, and court transcripts. The program can recognize relevant papers and extract dates, people, and events. This information may assist attorneys in trial preparation and evaluating the robustness of their case. Identify evidence. NLP facilitates the extraction of pertinent legal information, offering an efficient method for navigating large legal texts and documents, (Susskind, 2019). Legal experts may do comprehensive case law analysis and summarization using NLP. This technology enables users to distill complex legal papers into succinct, comprehensible summaries, save time and facilitating rapid access to critical information.

Machine Learning: Predicting Legal Outcomes

Machine learning is a subset of artificial intelligence that allows computer systems to learn and enhance their performance via experience without prior programming. Machine learning techniques enable computers to analyze extensive legal data, including case law, laws, and regulations. These algorithms may aid attorneys in legal research by pinpointing pertinent cases, extracting legal doctrines, and forecasting case outcomes based on the supplied facts and legal arguments. An example of machine learning in legal research is predictive analytics software. Predictive analytics software may examine previous case law data to discern patterns, correlations, and trends. This information may assist attorneys in forecasting a case's result and formulating more efficacious legal strategy. For example, an attorney representing a client in a patent infringement lawsuit may use predictive analytics to assess the probability of victory based on the judge's historical rulings in analogous cases. Additionally, Machine Learning streamlines the laborious tasks of document analysis and e-discovery, (Ashley, 2017). Algorithms examine extensive document collections and discern pertinent information.

Expert Systems and Data Analytics: Illuminating Legal Trends

Expert systems are computer programs particularly designed to replicate the decision-making capabilities of human experts. In the legal domain, these systems may aid attorneys in making legal determinations by analyzing legal material and offering suggestions based on established norms and knowledge bases. An example of an expert system used in the legal domain is a decision support system (DSS). This technology assists attorneys in navigating intricate legal judgments by analyzing legal data, offering advice, and evaluating the probable consequences of various legal techniques. It may assist attorneys in recognizing possible hazards and formulating contingency strategies. Data analytics in legal research facilitates trend analysis in legal situations. Legal practitioners may use data to discern patterns and developing trends, resulting in an enhanced comprehension of the legal environment and its possible ramifications. Utilizing data analytics, legal practitioners may enhance their methods. By extracting insights from data, attorneys get a competitive advantage, enabling more informed decision-making and the optimization of legal strategies for improved results, (Surden, 2019).

The incorporation of AI technologies, including natural language processing, machine learning, and data analytics, is transforming legal research. These technologies provide legal practitioners fast information extraction, predictive capabilities, and data-driven insights, transforming conventional procedures and facilitating a more dynamic and informed legal environment.

THE IMPACT OF ARTIFICIAL INTELLIGENCE ON THE LEGAL PROFESSION

Advantages

Artificial intelligence has the capacity to transform the legal field, especially in research activities. In 2013, Susskind predicted that AI technology will profoundly transform the legal profession during the following decade. He contended that legal practice will not be immune to the effects of information technology, which influences all other domains.

Originally published on November 11, 2019; updated on March 24, 2023.

Economy and society. Until recently, it was generally believed that only lawyers with specialized skill could execute legal responsibilities, including comprehending legal issues, gathering requisite evidence, and forecasting the probable result of a court ruling to resolve a disagreement. Artificial Intelligence has challenged the notion that legal practice is impervious to technological upheaval and has profoundly transformed legal study.

Artificial Intelligence (AI) has advanced considerably within the legal sector. AI facilitates the expedited, efficient, and simplified resolution of legal difficulties. Automation has significantly reduced transaction costs, enhancing the practicality, accessibility, and profitability of legal services across diverse contexts. Artificial Intelligence is essential in legal research since it can swiftly search, organize, filter, evaluate, and prioritize themes, laws, facts, and other pertinent material. Artificial intelligence can identify orthographic errors and substandard writing, offering suggestions for sentence revisions when incorporated into computer systems. Platforms like LexisNexis, Westlaw, and SCC Online may enhance legal research by offering pertinent case recommendations, elucidating parallels and distinctions, and articulating arguments and counterarguments with AI capabilities. Artificial intelligence has become an essential asset in law and legal science, enhancing legal reasoning by using information to address legal issues, (Remus & Levy, 2015). Legal science recognizes the significance of AI in legal reasoning and research. It optimizes processes such as filtering irrelevant content in the court and providing specific answers to diverse legal matters. AI-driven applications are extensively utilized in legal research for multiple functions, including formalizing legislation, identifying ambiguities in legal texts, assisting in law drafting, modeling legal precedents, pinpointing problematic clauses in contracts, formulating strategies for intellectual property litigation, and facilitating online dispute resolution. The ability of AI to rapidly analyze extensive datasets has been used in fields like digital forensics, crime scene forecasting, human rights law, and forensic anthropology, (Calo, 2015). Consequently, these areas have seen significant transformations.

There is growing expectation that artificial intelligence will aid judges in the adjudication process. Chief Justice John Roberts of the United States Supreme Court emphasized this. AI's involvement in courtroom fact-finding and decision-making is recognized to challenge conventional judicial methods, signifying a substantial transformation in the judiciary's functioning. Consequently, courts are progressively integrating AI into judicial decision-making. Legal AI is transforming the legal sector, enabling attorneys to enhance efficiency and expand their offerings. Embracing this technology may improve productivity, reduce effort, and increase financial benefits for legal practitioners. Individuals that persist in their reluctance to embrace AI may face a disadvantage, since technology has the ability to revolutionize every facet of legal practice. The influence of AI extends beyond mere efficiency enhancement, as it also revolutionizes legal research and practice. The automation of legal services and its impact on the development of legal ideas are challenging established conventions, necessitating the legal sector to adapt to technological innovations. The legal domain significantly influences AI advancements by creating rules, norms, and constraints across diverse application areas. AI undermines the conventional large firm paradigm, whereby associates have traditionally devoted extensive hours to legal study. Artificial intelligence is revolutionizing legal research by augmenting the efficiency of law associates relative to traditional methodologies. Legal technology firms are using AI capabilities, enabling colleagues to easily discover relevant legal authorities. Research reveals that legal firms using AI technologies see enhanced advantages[1]. Information retrieval, intuitive interfaces necessitating minimum training, and substantially decreased working hours, therefore optimizing research programs.

The recruitment procedure for law firms is seeing a substantial evolution due to the progression of AI assistance. The advent of AI technologies has allowed companies to attain optimal research efficiency, obviating the need to employ a substantial number of colleagues for activities like contract evaluation and legal research. As a result, law firms have forced to reassess their recruitment processes and allocate associates to more meaningful tasks at earlier stages of their careers. Moreover, artificial intelligence profoundly influences the business models of legal businesses. The traditional Big Law Firm model may become outdated as AI facilitates universal access to services, compelling bigger firms to compete with smaller ones in delivering cost-effective solutions. Smaller enterprises may rival larger corporations with early access to AI by offering affordable legal services, possibly transforming the industry.

The use of AI in legal research is inevitable due to its competitive advantages. It enables firms to minimize staff hours, concentrate on high-value legal issues, and provide cost-effective services, so giving them a competitive edge over rivals. AI technologies appeal to customers seeking efficient answers as well as elite attorneys. A 2017 paper by Blue Hill Research, entitled "ROSS Intelligence & Artificial Intelligence in Legal Research," concluded that the use of AI-driven legal research tools such as ROSS may substantially advantage legal practitioners. The study, including a panel of 16 attorneys evaluating conventional tools against ROSS, revealed a 30.3% decrease in research time and a 42.9% enhancement in the retrieval of pertinent legal resources, (Ambrogi & Lawyer, 2017).

Attorneys may significantly enhance their productivity via the use of artificial intelligence. It enables people to do greater amounts of work in less time, enabling exploration of diverse specializations and opportunities outside the confines of huge corporations. The pervasive accessibility of AI technologies has altered customer expectations. Law companies must adjust to evolving customer expectations by providing set rates rather than hourly charges. Furthermore, artificial intelligence has improved the accessibility of legal services for consumers, reducing the necessity for attorney involvement. The incorporation of AI into legal processes has promoted enhanced access to justice and enabled widespread representation. A notable instance is the 'Do Not Pay' bot, which assisted individuals in contesting 160,000 out of 250,000 parking citations, attaining a remarkable success rate of 64% and successfully appealing over $4 million since its inception in April 2016, (Novak, 2024). The legal field has experienced a profound transformation due to the emergence of artificial intelligence, resulting in enhanced storage and accessibility of legal information. The shift from manual to digital research commenced in the 1970s with the introduction of computer-assisted legal research, which facilitated widespread access to legal materials. Attorneys now utilize online legal research platforms such as Westlaw and LexisNexis, as well as search engines like Google. Prominent legal databases, including LexisNexis and Westlaw, provide user-friendly interfaces, extensive databases, and innovative electronic research tools. For instance, LexisNexis boasts 15,000 databases and over 9 million global subscribers, while Westlaw serves as the principal online legal research service in the USA, UK, and Australia, featuring more than 40,000 legal information databases. Computational instruments employed in legal AI, such as e-discovery, have supplanted conventional discovery techniques, enabling the acquisition of more precise results in a reduced timeframe and at a diminished cost. Predictive legal research technologies evaluate a case's merits and deficiencies, revolutionizing attorneys' litigation preparation processes. Legal practitioners can enhance the accuracy of case outcome forecasts by analyzing extensive court rulings through AI-driven tools. The implementation of artificial intelligence is revolutionizing the legal industry. Rather than supplanting attorneys, AI is anticipated to modify their responsibilities and create new career opportunities, including Legal Knowledge Engineer, Legal Technologist, and Legal Process Analyst. The prevailing view is that AI's technical proficiencies, when integrated with human oversight, can yield exceptionally favorable results in legal practice. For example, in e-discovery, the attorney's role remains crucial, even though they do not directly review documents.

Artificial intelligence is poised to gain increasing importance in legal research and practice. In 2017, the English House of Lords established a committee to investigate the economic, legal, and societal implications of artificial intelligence. Additionally, in 2017, 25 European nations endorsed the Declaration of Cooperation on Artificial Intelligence, (European Commission, 2018).

Disadvantages

Research indicates that AI exhibits greater limitations in interpreting legal texts compared to human attorneys. AI encounters difficulties in articulating the rationale behind its legal conclusions, and question-and-answer systems demonstrate a lack of comprehension regarding legal reasoning. Furthermore, although AI can derive certain meanings from legal documents, it frequently falls short in justifying its responses. The majority of AI technologies necessitate human intervention and are incapable of independently reasoning about the implications of varied scenarios on their answers. Susskind has indicated that the development of legal artificial intelligence encounters numerous obstacles. One significant challenge is the dearth of specialists in knowledge engineering and the legal sector. Furthermore, there is an absence of established methodologies for constructing expert systems within the legal domain. Suitable AI tools are not consistently accessible. Maintaining quality control for legal AI systems presents challenges, and there are considerable apprehensions about the legal ramifications of using AI tools. Concerns exist regarding AI's impact on the legal profession, encompassing the complexity of AI systems, their growing autonomy, and a lack of transparency in decision-making processes. Furthermore, there is a risk of technological vulnerability stemming from reliance on potentially inaccurate or biased data. Lastly, the heightened susceptibility of AI systems to cyber-attacks presents a considerable challenge to their advancement, (Ashley, 2017a). Concerns regarding the accountability of AI tools in the event of errors have prompted scholars to advocate for regulation and legal responsibility. The question of who bears responsibility for these errors remains unresolved, with some attributing it to developers and others to users. Nonetheless, the integration of AI within the legal profession is constrained by technical, economic, and cultural factors. Furthermore, legal AI technology is anticipated to have detrimental effects, including elevated unemployment rates and issues related to data privacy, ethics, and misuse. In the future, the emergence of a super-intelligent AI, referred to as the "Singularity problem," is a possibility. Although a compelling argument exists for judges to retain complete authority and refrain from delegating decision-making to AI assistants, some contend that AI is incapable of engaging in legal reasoning or making evaluative judgments, complicating its long-term integration into the legal profession. The utilization of AI in the legal domain is challenging due to the discretionary nature of many decisions. In contrast to computer programs, which operate on logical principles, judicial determinations often necessitate subjective analysis, hindering AI's incorporation into the legal system, (Surden, 2014). Additionally, there are concerns that AI may inherit the biases of its creators, potentially undermining its capacity to uphold fairness and neutrality consistently.

ANALYSIS OF STAKEHOLDER IMPACT

The integration of Artificial Intelligence (AI) into the legal sector has had a widespread impact on the profession. As legal processes evolve to be more data-centric, essential stakeholders such as attorneys, clients, judiciary bodies, legal educational institutions, and technology firms encounter both novel possibilities and significant obstacles. This section offers a thorough examination of how AI transforms the functional, ethical, and structural dynamics of each stakeholder group.

Attorneys: Acquiring New Skills for a Contemporary Hybrid Legal Practice

Artificial intelligence is transforming legal practice by automating repetitive processes such document inspection, contract analysis, legal research, and due diligence. These processes, which formerly took hours of precise human labor, may now be accomplished in minutes with AI-driven systems such as ROSS Intelligence, Casetext, and LexisNexis. This alteration enables attorneys to concentrate on more complex duties, including litigation strategy, client advisory, and intricate legal analysis. This technological transition necessitates substantial re-skilling. Attorneys must now acquire proficiency in algorithmic reasoning, data analysis, and AI-enhanced legal research. Legal education and professional development programs are increasingly including courses on digital literacy and legal technology, highlighting the shift from conventional black-letter law practice to a hybrid model in which AI serves as an intelligent assistant rather than a replacement, (Remus & Levy, 2015a). In the long run, those who do not adapt risk becoming obsolete in a profession increasingly shaped by technological advancement.

Clients: Harmonizing Efficiency with Emotional Intelligence and Trust

From the client's viewpoint, AI in law offers expedited settlement of legal issues, diminished billing hours, and enhanced access to justice via cost-effective legal solutions. AI platforms like as DoNotPay and

LegalZoom are providing affordable alternatives for fundamental legal services, thereby democratizing access to legal help. This efficiency entails some trade-offs. Numerous clients articulate apprehensions over the "de-personalization" of legal representation, especially in emotionally charged matters such as familial conflicts, criminal defence, or immigration issues. Artificial intelligence is devoid of empathy, emotional intelligence, and the complex comprehension of human experience that often informs judicial adjudication. Clients' express concerns over the precision, equity, and responsibility of AI-generated legal judgments or forecasts, particularly in significant issues related to possible imprisonment, financial detriment, or constitutional rights, (Cowan, 2019).

Courts: A Conflict Between Procedural Efficiency and Democratic Transparency

Judicial systems worldwide are investigating AI technologies to mitigate increasing backlogs and enhance access to justice. Predictive instruments like COMPAS (Correctional Offender Management Profiling for Alternative Sanctions) and computerized platforms for scheduling, legal citation, and sentence recommendations are increasingly being used. These techniques provide prospective remedies for the persistent inefficiencies of conventional judicial processes. Nonetheless, courts must contend with the opaque characteristics of AI systems. When algorithms provide results based on private code or inscrutable reasoning, it undermines the tenets of judicial openness and public accountability, (Seizov & Wulf, 2020). Furthermore, if AI technologies reproduce or exacerbate past biases stemming from biased training data or institutional discrimination, they may undermine due process and the validity of judicial results.

Law Students: Readying for a Hybrid Legal Future

Legal education is at a pivotal juncture. The rise of AI necessitates a revision of law school curriculum to include multidisciplinary education that merges technology, data science, legal informatics, and ethics. Law students are now required to acquire knowledge in jurisprudence and legislative interpretation, as well as the ability to assess algorithmic outputs, comprehend data biases, and collaborate effectively with AI systems. Institutions that neglect to update their curriculum jeopardize the preparedness of graduates for forthcoming legal challenges. Conversely, progressive law schools are integrating technology clinics, coding bootcamps, and collaborations with legal tech companies to equip students for "Lawyering 2.0."

Technology Corporations: The Concealed Legislators of the Algorithmic Era

Technology firms that develop legal AI instruments have a significant and often under-regulated role inside the judicial framework. Their function transcends software creation; they are significantly shaping the accessibility, interpretation, and administration of justice. Automated contract analysis and risk assessment in sentencing transform code into law, prompting significant ethical and democratic issues. In the absence of adequate monitoring, technology companies may emphasize profit motives above social equity, resulting in instruments that reinforce inequality or function with unclear reasoning, (Gordon, 2019). Consequently, these companies have substantial ethical obligations in algorithm development, bias reduction, data safeguarding, and adherence to regulatory standards. A cooperative strategy including legal experts, ethicists, and regulators is essential to guarantee that these technologies conform to democratic norms and human rights.

CHALLENGES AND ETHICAL CONSIDERATIONS IN THE IMPLEMENTATION OF ARTIFICIAL INTELLIGENCE IN THE LEGAL FIELD

Artificial Intelligence (AI) has emerged as an essential instrument in legal research. Nevertheless, it presents challenges and ethical dilemmas that require meticulous examination. This section emphasizes three critical aspects: AI bias, privacy issues, and ethical ramifications. The convergence of AI and the legal profession results in intricate responsibilities.

Algorithms utilized in legal research must be implemented judiciously due to the risk of bias. AI systems derive insights from historical data, which may contain intrinsic biases, thereby potentially exacerbating these biases through algorithmic processes. It is imperative for legal practitioners and technologists to proactively identify and amend biases within AI algorithms to guarantee equitable outcomes. Attaining fairness in AI applications is intrinsically connected to transparency. Legal professionals must understand the decision-making processes of AI systems. Transparency bolsters the credibility of AI and allows legal practitioners to detect and correct any biases that may emerge during the system's functioning. Privacy concerns are paramount when employing AI in legal research. The utilization of extensive data sets heightens the risk of privacy violations; therefore, legal practitioners must balance AI's capabilities with adherence to privacy regulations, (Susskind, 2019a). Compliance with frameworks such as GDPR and other regional privacy statutes is vital to safeguard individuals' privacy rights. Given the sensitive nature of legal information, the security of AI systems must be robust. Legal professionals must enforce stringent cybersecurity measures to avert unauthorized access, data breaches, and other potential threats. The establishment of secure protocols and encryption techniques is essential to foster trust in the application of AI for legal research.

The escalating integration of Artificial Intelligence (AI) in legal research has engendered ethical dilemmas concerning its influence on decision-making. As AI technologies evolve, they may assume a pivotal role in legal adjudication. Nevertheless, legal practitioners must meticulously assess the ethical ramifications of depending on AI to safeguard human values, judgment, and accountability. Preserving the human element in legal decision-making is crucial for ensuring equity and justice. It is vital to formulate explicit guidelines and standards for the ethical application of AI tools, thereby ensuring the legal profession's responsibility and accountability in AI utilization, (McGinnis & Pearce, 2014). Legal professionals must actively oversee the implementation of AI, ensuring that ethical principles, legal norms, and professional standards are maintained throughout the entire AI lifecycle. As artificial intelligence increasingly influences legal research, it is imperative to confront the associated challenges and ethical dilemmas. Legal practitioners, policymakers, and technologists must collaborate to establish frameworks that promote impartial AI, safeguard privacy, and maintain ethical integrity. By addressing these intricacies, the legal field can harness the transformative capabilities of AI while ensuring the foundational principles of the justice system are preserved.

ADOPTION RATES OF ARTIFICIAL INTELLIGENCE IN THE LEGAL SECTOR

The legal industry is progressively adopting AI technology, however the rates of adoption range across various parts of the profession. By 2024, about 47% of legal practitioners worldwide have integrated AI technologies into their workflows, including everything from document review to predictive analytics. Forecasts indicate that this percentage might exceed 60% by 2025, demonstrating an increasing trust in the dependability and worth of AI solutions within the legal sector. In legal firms, just 26% have effectively incorporated AI technology into their operations. Nonetheless, there is considerable impetus for adoption, with 53% of companies indicating intentions to invest in AI solutions imminently. This signifies a strategic transition, mostly motivated by the need for improved efficiency, competitive edge, and customer demand for technologically advanced services. Small legal firms and lone practitioners exhibit a small although increasing use of AI techniques. 2023 research by the American Bar Association indicates that 20.7% of small firms (fewer than 10 lawyers) and 14.6% of solo practitioners acknowledged either present use or significant interest in AI technology. These data underscore a progressive democratization of AI accessibility beyond major corporate law firms, making AI an increasingly essential component of legal practice across various firm sizes. This trend highlights the growing influence of AI in legal practice and establishes a framework for predicting extensive change across the sector, irrespective of firm size or geographic location, (Woodward, 2024).

Efficiency Metrics Temporal and Productivity Enhancements

A prominent advantage of AI integration is its ability to significantly diminish the time allocated to repetitive chores. Legal research, historically a laborious task, may be accelerated by as much as 60% with the use of AI technologies, owing to improved natural language processing and semantic search functionalities. This enhances information retrieval efficiency while augmenting the comprehensiveness and usefulness of study outcomes. AI-driven contract review systems have shown much more pronounced outcomes. Instruments like Merlin AI and Kira Systems have shown the capability to decrease contract review duration by as much as 80%, whilst enhancing precision and guaranteeing regulatory adherence. These systems can autonomously identify confusing sentences, evaluate text against legal norms, and detect possible risks functions that formerly required considerable human examination.

Critical Significance

These efficiency improvements are not only operational advantages; they directly result in improved customer care, expedited response times, and increased profitability, especially for high-volume operations.

Financial Impact: Quantifiable Cost Advantages

The integration of AI in legal practice is demonstrating significant cost-effectiveness from a financial standpoint. Research indicates that law firms using AI for functions like legal research and contract analysis see yearly savings of $10,000 to $40,000 per attorney. These savings arise from decreased billable hours allocated to routine activities, lower mistake rates, and enhanced issue management. Moreover, the deployment of AI often reduces reliance on outsourcing and temporary workers, enabling companies to keep a greater volume of work internally, augment profit margins, and improve data security, (CLIO, 2025).

Critical Significance

These cost reductions provide a compelling argument for the deployment of AI from both a financial planning and business management perspective especially as customers increasingly seek economical legal solutions.

Usage and Educational Trends: Influencing the Future of Legal Practitioners

According to a 2025 American Bar Association research, 41% of lawyers have employed generative artificial intelligence technology like ChatGPT. Only 15% of these tools were used for lawful purposes. This is the reverse. This discrepancy suggests that this conflict exists and indicates an experimental adoption that has not yet become standard practice in essential legal duties. This dispute supports this claim. This paradox is also revealed by the ongoing fight. It is thought that over 70% of US law schools teach AI-driven legal research tools. These platforms aid legal research. This category includes various data management solutions including ROSS Intelligence, Lexis+ AI, and Westlaw Precision. Future legal professionals will be confident and competent in a digitally dominated legal environment due to the unique educational integration. Even if similar attempts have been made, the results are still undetermined. Over 75% of legal practitioners worry about AI's accuracy, openness, and data privacy. These concerns relate to sector technology advances. Given widespread concerns about algorithmic bias, poor explainability, and undue dependency on automated decision-making, more regulatory measures are needed to address these issues. Due to the prevalence of fears, these topics have been highlighted. Given these realities, a thorough plan is essential. This plan should encourage artificial intelligence research and emphasize the need for strict human oversight, ethical safeguards, and a wide education.

Figure 1. AI In the legal sector: Trends, impact, and adoption

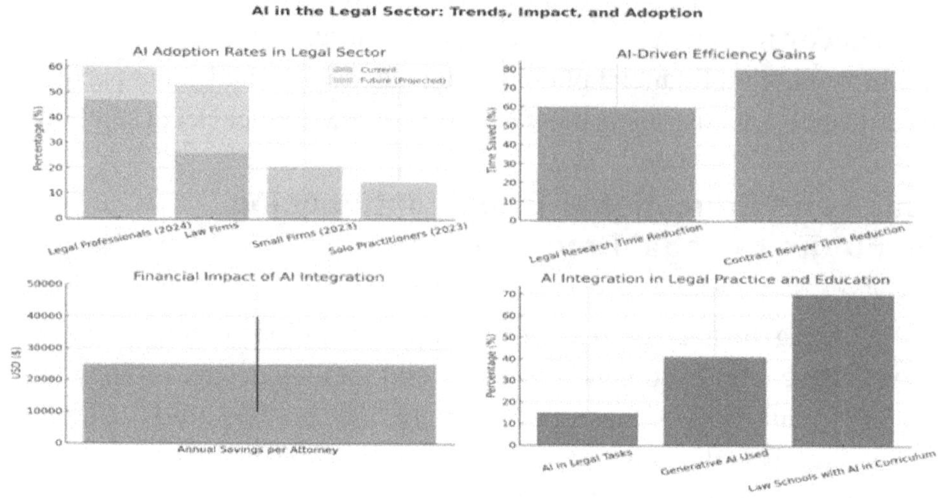

EMPIRICAL CASE STUDIES: PRACTICAL IMPLEMENTATIONS OF AI IN THE LEGAL DOMAIN

ROSS Intelligence: Transforming Legal Research

ROSS Intelligence began as an AI-powered legal research tool. Its genesis began with this idea. It was early, but this was the case. This notion was conceived early in the process. It was created on IBM Watson and developed over time. This happened throughout construction. Its construction was built on this. This laid the groundwork. The ROSS system allows legal professionals to ask inquiries in common English and get answers supported by legal proof. This is the system's main goal. Every action is intended to duplicate human legal cognition. The Legal Information System developed this technology. It was founded by this organization. The group also developed the technology's technical components. Organization was ultimately responsible. This adds insult to injury, since it searches enormous databases of case law, legislation, and legal opinions to reach conclusions related to the topic at hand. This greatly reduces research time, which is a significant advantage. This has major benefits. Another major benefit is this. This is one of the biggest benefits. ROSS provides tailored case law relevant to a query instead of painstakingly reading through several precedents. This differs from precedent-based reasoning. This shows how it works. This will be done to compensate for the difficult process of setting precedents. The procedure is faster and the measurements are more accurate because of this. Because this is true. This will raise production, leading to an improvement. Due to legal pressure from Thomson Reuters, it was discontinued in 2021, but its significant impact on the many ways artificial intelligence can aid law practice research did not change. It made a big influence. It had a significant impact despite this. This has been the case until then, notwithstanding its removal from circulation. Even when it had halted, it was still happening. This continued after it was stopped.

DoNotPay: The "Automated Legal Advocate" for Routine Justice

Joshua Browder, who founded DoNotPay, a legal technology firm, devised the business idea. At now, the corporation is known by its current name. First, he had the idea first. He conceived it. His motivation drove the business's expansion, which led to the firm's founding. His motivation drove the procedure. The company's marketing brochures call it "the world's first automaton lawyer." This is a corporate claim. The claim is related to the situation. The website uses artificial intelligence to help clients create legal papers and fight minor legal issues like parking fines, late fees, and subscription terminations. Customers may get help online. Customers may also obtain legal document preparation help. Customers may reach them for help. Customers may now get legal help thanks to this move. Artificial intelligence in customer service is improving client service, which is good. The latest change of events is thrilling. Using user data, the language model can develop appealing legal arguments and automatically fill out forms. This is done by collecting user data. This is done with it. This action is feasible with necessary knowledge. Utilizing user information is crucial to achieving this goal quickly. Additionally, this may be obtained in addition to existing talents. The general public has easier access to legal help, with a focus on those who cannot afford it. Help is given to these people. This goal is achieved by supporting the individuals. This alliance's members will likely benefit from the outcome. This is likely the best result. Some difficulties raised include the quality of the material, the responsibility of the participants, and the potential that it may be utilized in more serious judicial cases. Everyone has been warned that certain topics may be concerning. This does not change the reality that it remains a concern.

Predictive Analytics and the COMPAS Controversy in U.S. Courts

Correctional Offender Management Profiling for Alternative Sanctions (ComPAS) is an AI-powered risk assessment tool. ComPAS abbreviates the instrument's full name. The acronym ComPAS includes the instrument name and acronym. Note: ComPAS comprises both the instrument's name and the acronym. It should be noted that ComPAS incorporates both the instrument's name and the acronym. Pay notice to the fact that ComPAS includes both the instrument's entire name and the abbreviation. You should know about this. You should know that ComPAS includes both the instrument's name and the acronym. I must prioritize alerting you. You should note that ComPAS contains both the instrument's entire name and the abbreviation. This requires your attention. To bring something to your attention, you must prioritize it. ComPAS includes the instrument's full name and the acronym. This should be brought to your attention. This needs your attention. I must draw your attention to this and urge you to prioritize it. Many federal, state, and municipal governments in the US utilize it to determine if a person has committed another crime in the past, present, or future. This is done to determine whether the defendant engaged in such activity. Every one of these things is done to determine whether the defendant committed the offense under investigation. This action seeks to discover illegal conduct to assess its criminality. This is done to catch unlawful activity. This exercise assesses if the defendant may commit other crimes. This determines whether some of these alternatives are likely. This action aims to achieve this goal. Despite helping judges set bail and sentence, studies have proven racial prejudice, notably against African-American defendants. This bias is particularly prevalent in juvenile justice. This discrimination is especially evident in the juvenile justice system. This system seems biased. This discrimination is especially evident in the juvenile justice system. A bias is evident in the system. At first appearance, this system seems prejudiced. This bias is also evident in the institutional architecture that administers justice for juvenile offenses. This framework administers justice. Evidence of prejudice occurs inside the system. At first glance, this system seems biased. Due to everyday bigotry, African-American defendants get disproportionate damages throughout legal proceedings. This cause caused excessive injury, and its result was excessive damage. In State v. Loomis, the Supreme Court of Wisconsin approved COMPAS, but it made it plain that it should not be the primary element in sentencing. Because COMPAS is not the sole factor. Even though the court had approved COMPAS usage, it was done. This incident raised ethical, constitutional, due process, and algorithmic decision-making transparency issues. Due to this incident, several issues have been highlighted. Due to this experience, these concerns were brought to light to resolve them. These concerns arose since the incident had already occurred. The initial step was taken here. Because this reality is a direct outcome of the circumstances that caused these issues, it is crucial to remember and examine the actual occurrences. Considering this information and its ramifications is crucial. People worried about the situation have expressed a variety of concerns as a result of what has been happening. What raised these fears. These issues have been raised due to the discourse.

SUVAAS: The Indian Judiciary's Advancement in AI Integration

The Supreme Court of India, headquartered in India, created SUVAAS software. The Supreme Court of India created this scheme. The software development team developed this app. A similar group produced similar software. The highest court in India, the Supreme Court, created this scheme. This court created this software. The Supreme Court must be held accountable for its progress. This program was created to simplify machine learning processes to make them more accessible to a wider audience. This initiative was started to make machine learning more accessible. From SUVAAS, the Supreme Court Vidhik Anuvaad program gets its name.

Total program name: SUVAAS. One can explain their relationship. This is where the app's name originated from its development. The software was named here initially. This is why it was named. This pseudonym was inspired by an acronym. This name before the acronym. This project was inspired by the acronym. This phrase started with the acronym in the preceding sentence. The Supreme Court of India, the highest court in India, developed this program. This court created this program. The court in question established the program. This court is responsible for establishing the program outlined before. The court in question established the program indicated previously in this paragraph. The main goal of this initiative is to translate Indian legal papers into English. This is the program's goal. This aspect may be the program's main goal. One may argue that this feature is the program's main goal. One of their main aims with this program is to complete their task. They want to achieve this. They are determined to succeed. This is our top goal, and we will take whatever necessary efforts to achieve it. We set this goal after considering everything. All of these books will be translated into English from their native Indian languages. This translation is imminent. This will happen during the translation process. It was created in collaboration with the Ministry of Electronics and Information Technology, made it multilingual, and simplified verdict distribution. Availability in other languages was also a priority. It provided various benefits, two of which were listed above. The perks listed above are only two of its numerous benefits. Since it is hard to overestimate the relevance of any of these features, it was crucial to examine this from the start. SUVAAS makes it easier to undertake legal research in several languages and learn about court procedures. SUVAAS also simplifies information access. Technology like SUVAAS makes information collecting simpler and more convenient. SUVAAS technology simplifies information collecting and makes it easier. SUVAAS makes information collecting easier and technology makes it easier. Consumers may learn to detect context and synthesize information in real time. For instance, customers may recognize context. Due to this growth, India is prioritizing legal infrastructure supported by AI. This latest breakthrough proves this. Customers now have these abilities, thus this has happened. This is why we're here. This is because these capabilities represent examples of the organization's current capabilities. This is why things are as they are. Because of this reason, this incident may have occurred for this reason. This stress, which is why it is being focused on, shows that India values specific legal architectural components. This is why this is being considered. We recommend visiting our website for more information on this issue. Thus, the current emphasis is on this. The result is this. This has another consequence. India has made accomplishments in this area of intellectual research despite its legal system being built from scratch. The circumstance and scenario are the same even though they are still being constructed. This is true regardless of the conditions, and the fact that it is still being made does not change this. This has happened, even though it's still being developed. This has happened. Yes, this is our situation.

GLOBAL PERSPECTIVE: AI ADOPTION IN THE LEGAL SECTOR

The incorporation of Artificial Intelligence (AI) in the legal industry is swiftly progressing worldwide, propelled by technology innovations, differing degrees of governmental endorsement, and varied investment environments. The degree of AI adoption in legal systems is significantly influenced by a nation's digital infrastructure, legislative frameworks, and readiness to invest in advanced technology. The British Standards Institution (BSI) rates nations by their AI maturity across several industries, with India achieving the highest score of 4.58. This signifies that the nation has a comparatively sophisticated and efficient methodology for incorporating AI throughout diverse areas, including law. China ranks just below with a score of 4.25, demonstrating robust AI integration efforts, especially in the judicial domain, whilst the United States gets 4.0, reflecting modest acceptance and potential for additional advancement. Both the United Kingdom and the European Union have scores below 4.00, indicating that while AI adoption is advancing, a substantial disparity in AI readiness and investment persists, (British Standards Institution, 2024).

Table 1. AI maturity scores by country

Country	AI Maturity Score
India	4.58
China	4.25
United States	4.00
United Kingdom	Below 4.00
European Union	Below 4.00

Source: BSI Global AI Maturity Model

Regional Highlights

India

India has achieved considerable progress in the use of AI technology in the judicial system. The Indian Supreme Court has used AI technologies like SUVAAS (Supreme Court of India Virtual Assistant) to assist with the translation and transcription of court proceedings. This application enhances accessibility by offering real-time translations and transcriptions in several languages, so making the court process more inclusive. Moreover, AI-driven solutions are used for document analysis and legal research, hence decreasing the time and expenses related to legal processes. The emphasis is not just on efficiency but also on equity and openness, especially in prominent instances subject to considerable public attention. The deployment of AI in India is essential in alleviating the backlog of cases and mitigating the court delays that have historically plagued the system, (Verma, 2023).

United States of America (USA)

In the United States, law firms and corporate legal departments are progressively integrating AI for contract analysis, legal research, and predictive analytics. AI-driven technologies like ROSS Intelligence, which use IBM Watson for legal research, are facilitating rapid access to pertinent case law and legislation for attorneys. The emphasis is transitioning to generative AI technologies that assist attorneys in automating repetitive processes, hence enhancing efficiency and minimizing human error. Artificial intelligence is used to forecast case outcomes by examining previous legal data, therefore assisting companies in optimizing their litigation strategies, (Merken, 2024). This technology enables law firms to handle extensive legal activities more effectively, particularly in areas such as intellectual property law, litigation, and corporate law.

United Kingdom (UK)

In the UK, over 90% of the top 100 legal firms are either testing or have already incorporated AI technology into their operations. Companies like Clifford Chance and Linklaters have begun using AI technologies to automate contract writing, due diligence, and compliance oversight. These solutions minimize the manual hours required for the examination of extensive legal documents, while the use of Natural Language Processing (NLP) facilitates enhanced comprehension and extraction of essential information from contracts. The UK spends significantly in AI training programs to guarantee legal practitioners with the necessary abilities to use AI technologies successfully. Notwithstanding these developments, a considerable need for investment in AI infrastructure persists, since several smaller enterprises have yet to completely embrace these technologies.

China

China has been a leader in using AI within the judicial sector, notably via the creation of Internet Courts in locations like Hangzhou, Beijing, and Guangzhou. These courts adjudicate internet-related matters, including cybercrimes, online contracts, and intellectual property conflicts. The Hangzhou Internet Court was the first court globally to accept blockchain evidence, facilitating the verification of digital evidence. AI is used for automated case evaluations and the management of digital evidence, aiding in result predictions based on prior instances, hence enhancing court efficiency. These AI technologies aid courts by expediting case processing, hence enhancing the efficiency and accessibility of the legal system.

European Union

AI adoption in the legal sector within the European Union is advancing, however it remains fragmented owing to disparate national legislation and inconsistent technical infrastructure across member states. Initiatives are underway to establish comprehensive EU legislation for AI that emphasize ethics, openness, and accountability. The EU Artificial Intelligence Act, enacted in 2021, serves as a pivotal endeavor designed to provide a legislative framework for AI technology, including its use within the legal domain. This rule delineates protocols for the use of AI inside the legal system, guaranteeing that these instruments are utilized in a manner that preserves equity and human rights. The execution of these rules remains nascent, necessitating more training programs and public-private collaborations to guarantee the accessibility and use of AI technologies across the area.

AI-Enhanced Judicial Systems and Electronic Courts: Worldwide Applications

China: Cyber Judicial Institutions

China has led the use of AI in legal proceedings, notably via the establishment of Internet Courts in locations such as Hangzhou, Beijing, and Guangzhou. These courts are established to adjudicate matters pertaining to cybercrimes, e-commerce conflicts, and infringements of intellectual property in the digital domain. The Hangzhou Internet Court is distinguished for its pioneering use of artificial intelligence and blockchain technologies. The court was the first institution globally to recognize blockchain-based evidence, so guaranteeing the integrity and traceability of digital documents and transactions. This project has significantly reduced the backlog of internet-related cases and has established a novel framework for digital justice systems.

Estonia: Electronic Justice System

Estonia, recognized for its digital-centric administration, has incorporated AI-driven technologies into its e-Justice system. The Estonian judicial system employs artificial intelligence to optimize case administration, legal research, and document examination. The nation employs innovative AI algorithms to expedite decision-making, augment access to justice, and bolster transparency. The e-Justice system incorporates digital signatures and blockchain technology, facilitating online interactions between people and the courts. Estonia's integration of AI exemplifies how tiny countries may employ creative strategies to augment their legal frameworks and facilitate people' access to justice.

United Arab Emirates: Dubai International Financial Centre Courts

The Dubai International Financial Centre (DIFC) Courts have emerged as a prominent model of AI-enhanced judicial systems in the Middle East. The DIFC Courts have introduced many digital services, such as an AI-driven case management system and a Digital Assets Will service. The AI-driven case management system accelerates case processing by autonomously categorizing and ranking cases according to their complexity, (De Filippi & Wright, 2018). The courts provide services for the digital economy, facilitating online filing of legal papers and settlement of business disputes with digital assets. These improvements seek to address the requirements of the swiftly expanding digital economy and international commercial operations.

The use of AI in the legal industry is advancing at varying speeds across various locations. India and China are in the forefront of implementing sophisticated AI applications in their court systems, although the United States and United Kingdom are making significant progress, especially in corporate law and legal research. Estonia and the United Arab Emirates exemplify digital justice, demonstrating how AI may enhance judicial efficiency and accessibility. For AI to really revolutionize the global legal environment, sustained investment in infrastructure, regulatory monitoring, and ethical frameworks governing AI development inside the justice system is essential.

PROSPECTIVE CONSEQUENCES IN THE LEGAL SECTOR

The legal sector is in the nascent phase of adopting Artificial Intelligence (AI), yet there exists substantial potential for further advancement and enhancement. As AI technology progresses, its influence on the legal profession will undoubtedly intensify. It is imperative to meticulously evaluate the ethical and legal ramifications of integrating artificial intelligence within this field. Ensuring the responsible and transparent utilization of AI is paramount. The prospects for AI in legal research appear promising, as anticipated innovations could revolutionize the discipline. Sophisticated Natural Language Processing (NLP) capabilities, improved machine learning algorithms, and the incorporation of avant-garde technologies such as quantum computing are set to transform how legal practitioners access and analyze information. The enhancement of AI technologies to understand context, emotion, and intricate legal terminology is imminent, offering the potential for more precise and contextually informed legal insights. The legal sector may soon witness the integration of emerging technologies such as blockchain and augmented reality. Blockchain's transparent and immutable ledger system could significantly alter legal documentation and contract management. Augmented reality may allow lawyers and researchers to visualize intricate legal frameworks, resulting in more immersive and efficient legal research experiences, (Johansson et al., 2014). The incorporation of these technologies has the potential to revolutionize the entire domain of legal research, offering novel insights and unparalleled efficiency. The increasing application of artificial intelligence in legal research has raised apprehensions regarding its impact on the duties and competencies of legal professionals. While AI can enhance efficiency in routine tasks such as document analysis and information retrieval, legal practitioners must evolve towards more intricate responsibilities that require analytical reasoning, strategic decision-making, and a deep understanding of ethical and contextual nuances in legal practice.

To adapt to this evolving environment, legal professionals must engage in continuous education and skill enhancement in AI-related technologies. They should also pursue interdisciplinary knowledge and collaborate with data scientists, technologists, and ethicists to address the ethical implications of AI in law. Ultimately, legal practitioners must cultivate technological literacy and utilize AI as a collaborative instrument rather than a substitute to succeed in an AI-enhanced legal landscape. Artificial intelligence possesses the capacity to transform the legal research domain, offering enhanced efficiency and groundbreaking capabilities. Legal practitioners equipped with versatile skill sets and a progressive mindset can leverage AI's advantages while maintaining the fundamental values and ethical principles of the legal profession, (De Filippi & Wright, 2018). By fostering collaboration, engaging in continuous education, and adopting a proactive approach to technological innovations, legal professionals can adeptly traverse the uncharted landscape of AI in legal research, ensuring that advancements are in harmony with the principles of justice and legal integrity.

CONCLUSION

The incorporation of Artificial Intelligence (AI) into the legal sector represents a significant transformation in the approach and provision of legal services. By using technologies like Machine Learning (ML) and Natural Language Processing (NLP), AI may markedly enhance the precision, efficiency, and efficacy of legal research and decision-making. These technologies may enhance document analysis efficiency, minimize human error, and enable legal practitioners to devote more time to intricate, value-oriented work. This technological innovation presents several ethical, legal, and procedural problems. Issues related to algorithmic bias, openness in decision-making, data privacy, and accountability need thorough examination. AI systems should not operate as independent decision-makers but instead serve as assistive tools under responsible human supervision.

As the legal sector evolves with technology advancements, it is imperative for policymakers, legal institutions, and practitioners to take a proactive approach. This entails the formulation of explicit ethical standards, the augmentation of regulatory structures, and the advocacy for openness to guarantee that AI supports rather than undermines the core principles of justice, fairness, and due process. Although AI has the capacity to fundamentally revolutionize legal research and judgment, its deployment must be regulated by ethical standards and stringent human oversight. By achieving an optimal equilibrium between innovation and accountability, the legal profession may use AI to maintain and elevate the integrity of legal institutions in the digital era.

REFERENCES

Ambrogi & Lawyer. (2017, January 20). *Blue Hill gives more details on Ross Artificial Intelligence Benchmarking Report*. LawSites. https://www.lawnext.com/2017/01/blue-hill-gives-details-ross-artificial-intelligence-benchmarking-report.html

Angwin, J., Kirchner, L., Larson, J., & Mattu, S. (2016, May 23). *Machine bias: There's software used across the country to predict future criminals. and it's biased against blacks*. Benton Foundation. https://www.benton.org/headlines/machine-bias-theres-software-used-across-country-predict-future-criminals-and-its-biased

Ashley, K. D. (2017). *Artificial Intelligence and Legal Analytics*. Cambridge Core. https://www.cambridge.org/core/books/artificial-intelligence-and-legal-analytics/E7D705EEF392501A1DB180645917E7E0

British Standards Institution. (2024, July 30). *Momentum of AI adoption strongest in India and China, finds BSI*. BSI. https://www.bsigroup.com/en-US/insights-and-media/media-center/press-releases/2024/july/momentum-of-ai-adoption-strongest-in-india-china-and-us-finds-bsi/

Calo, R. (2015). *Robotics and the lessons of Cyberlaw*. UW Law Digital Commons. https://digitalcommons.law.uw.edu/faculty-articles/23/

CLIO. (2025, March 10). *What is AI and how can law firms use it?* Clio. https://www.clio.com/resources/ai-for-lawyers/lawyer-ai/

Cowan, D. (2019). *Richard Susskind, online courts and the Future of Justice (Oxford: Oxford University Press, 2019)*. Schulich Law Scholars. https://digitalcommons.schulichlaw.dal.ca/cjlt/vol18/iss2/5/

European Commission. (2018). *Shaping Europe's Digital Future*. Shaping Europe's digital future. https://digital-strategy.ec.europa.eu/

Gordon, F. (2019, November). *Virginia Eubanks (2018) automating inequality: How high-tech tools profile, police, and punish the poor.* https://www.researchgate.net/publication/337578410_Virginia_Eubanks_2018_Automating_Inequality_How_HighTech_Tools_Profile_Police_and_Punish_the_Poor_New_York_Picador_St_Martin's_Press

Johansson, S. E., Larsen, S. S., Povlsen, G. K., & Edvinsson, L. (2014). Early MEK1/2 inhibition after global cerebral ischemia in rats reduces brain damage and improves outcome by preventing delayed vasoconstrictor receptor upregulation. *PLoS One*, *9*(3), e92417. Advance online publication. DOI: 10.1371/journal.pone.0092417 PMID: 24642693

Judiciary, D. (2020). *Supreme Court Vidhik Anuvaad Software (SUVAS)*. Drishti Judiciary. https://www.drishtijudiciary.com/current-affairs/supreme-court-vidhik-anuvaad-software-suvas

McGinnis, J. O., & Pearce, R. G. (2014, May 15). *The Great Disruption: How Machine Intelligence will transform the role of lawyers in the delivery of Legal Services. SSRN*. https://papers.ssrn.com/sol3/papers.cfm?abstract_id=2436937

Merken, S. (2024, December 5). *US law firms eye 2025 with optimism, report says | Reuters*. report says. https://www.reuters.com/legal/government/us-law-firms-eye-2025-with-optimism-report-says-2024-12-05/

Moran, L. (2020, December 11). *Ross intelligence will shut down amid lawsuit from Thomson Reuters*. ABA Journal. https://www.abajournal.com/news/article/ross-intelligence-to-shut-down-amid-thomson-reuters-lawsuit

Novak, M. (2024, September 25). *Donotpay has to pay up over "World's first robot lawyer."* Gizmodo. https://gizmodo.com/donotpay-has-to-pay-up-over-worlds-first-robot-lawyer-2000503265

Remus, D., & Levy, F. S. (2015, December 11). *Can robots be lawyers? computers, lawyers, and the practice of law. SSRN*. DOI: 10.2139/ssrn.2701092

Seizov, O., & Wulf, A. J. (2020, September). *Artificial Intelligence and transparency: A blueprint for improving the regulation of AI applications in the EU*. researchgate. https://www.researchgate.net/publication/346330197_Artificial_Intelligence_and_Transparency_A_Blueprint_for_Improving_the_Regulation_of_AI_Applications_in_the_EU

Surden, H. (2014). *Machine learning and law*. UW Law Digital Commons. https://digitalcommons.law.uw.edu/wlr/vol89/iss1/5/

Surden, H. (2019). *Artificial Intelligence and law: An overview*. Colorado Law Scholarly Commons. https://scholar.law.colorado.edu/faculty-articles/1234/

Susskind, R. E. (2019). *Tomorrow's lawyers: An introduction to your future*. Google Books. https://books.google.com/books/about/Tomorrow_s_Lawyers.html?id=4dMSMQAACAAJ

Verma, K. (2023, September 18). *Analyzing the endeavours of the Supreme Court of India to transcribe and translate court arguments in light of the proposed EU AI act*. arXiv.org. https://arxiv.org/abs/2309.10088

Woodward, J. (2024, August 22). *47% of legal professionals are now using AI - and adoption is projected to hit 60+% by next year*. Legal Dive. https://www.legaldive.com/press-release/20240822-47-of-legal-professionals-are-now-using-ai-and-adoption-is-projected-to/

Yale Law School. (2024, November 26). *Yale Law School shapes the future of Artificial Intelligence*. https://law.yale.edu/yls-today/news/yale-law-school-shapes-future-artificial-intelligence

Chapter 4
Hybrid Ensemble Model for Accurate Legal Case Duration Estimation

Harsh Badaya
https://orcid.org/0009-0004-9119-947X
Vellore Institute of Technology, Chennai, India

Lakshmi Harika Palivela
https://orcid.org/0000-0002-3373-2991
Vellore Institute of Technology, Chennai, India

ABSTRACT

The legal sector is unable to forecast case duration requirements due to unpredictable and intricate legal process. This study develops a judicial time duration forecasting system which uses deep learning together with machine learning algorithms to solve existing problems in judicial processes. It employs Random Forest, Gradient Boosting, Long Short-Term Memory (LSTM) networks for analysis with historical case data, enhancing legal analytics. The dataset includes case attributes such as decision categories, jurisdictional details, and final resolutions. One of the necessary steps was the calculation of the desired variable 'case duration' because original timestamp data did not contain this information. Through several preprocessing methods the model received refined training data which addressed chaotic and incomplete data while converting factors

DOI: 10.4018/979-8-3373-3114-0.ch004

into categories. Feature engineering played a crucial role in detecting meaningful patterns. The ensemble approach merged distinct models to both boost the overall precision level and create a robust system.

INTRODUCTION

A growing number of cases poses challenges to worldwide legal systems in their ability to resolve cases effectively thus extending court processes. The study of court case duration prediction serves crucial purposes because it fosters transparency along with judicial speedup and optimized resource distribution. Due to the complex and foreboding nature of legal data we need predictive innovation frameworks to achieve results accurately.

The research designs a prediction system to compute court case duration through the integration of machine learning (ML) and deep learning (DL) approaches. The research design implements ensemble models Random Forest together with Gradient Boosting and Long Short-Term Memory (LSTM) to leverage individual method advantages for creating accurate and dependable predictions. The hybrid approach unites two key traits, interpretability for complex legal data together with data sequence processing ability.

The research aims to create appropriate case timing forecasts to improve operational decision-making and institutional efficiency. A research analysis of case durations uses historical court data that includes jurisdiction type combined with disposition type and judgment outcome characteristics in order to seek patterns. Stakeholders can create accurate forecasts for future case durations because of these findings to adjust their existing strategies.

Preparations of data from legal datasets represent a major obstacle in this field due to unstructured inconsistent and noisy data. Feature engineering processes were designed specifically to extract useful data characteristics which generated a prediction target variable. The ensemble model uses many algorithms to deal with the particular nature of legal data which includes both category variations and temporal dependencies.

The implementation of this method serves immediate purposes while providing infrastructure which will enable future advancements in legal analytics. The model incorporates explainability methods which help users trust legal organizations more while boosting acceptance rates.

Predictive analytics demonstrates its potential in legal systems through this study because it shows how analytics improve court operations as well as court transparency. The presented framework contributes to artificial intelligence growth in legal analytics by finding a balance between interpretation, scalability and accuracy in predictive modeling. The method describes a path to utilize predictive methods in concrete contexts for solving domain-based challenges so legal systems can become more effective and responsible.

Challenges in the Existing System

Standardization and Data Quality

The data collected from various jurisdictions through legal databases are often unreliable, have incorrect figures, and contain excess noise, mainly due to lack of standardisation in data collection practices. Significant data points like the outcome of a case, the disposition of a matter or even a timeline of events may be recorded differently, depending on the court or jurisdiction. This unevenness makes feature engineering and data preprocessing difficult and requires a lot of human effort. Moreover, some legal documents are either scanned or written and are unstructured which makes data extraction and data processing difficult. Poor data quality can lead to biased or inaccurate predictions that will affect the performance and applicability of the model.

Variability Throughout Court Cases

Court cases present variable characteristics because they exist between different judicial types and authoritative procedures and applicable requirements. By design all legal systems present variations between their procedural standards and their operating procedures and their legal criteria. For instance, the deadlines and procedural procedures for a criminal case in one nation. The procedures between different courts might show substantial differences. Building generic models that can Different legal contexts create obstacles for models to adapt because of extensive variation between them. Because of Model data from one dataset typically cannot adapt to multiple distinct structural and contextual patterns. The ability to make dependable forecasts between two distinct databases is very challenging for these systems. A substantial effort in the development of adjustable algorithms should happen to detect specific domain patterns without losing broad usefulness. Such broad application needs to become a priority because of this challenge.

Sequential Dependencies and Temporal Complexity

The duration of court Several procedural steps determine the duration of proceedings since each step affects the total time needed. needed for completion. The sequence of hearings and appeals combines with judicial delays during the process influences the overall duration. Background components that emerge from adjournments create time-based relationships which current standard machine learning approaches struggle to analyze properly. have difficulty understanding correctly. Initial hearing delays at the beginning of the Multiple delays that commence with initial process delays result in an extended timeframe for the entire case period. Predictive systems need to understand how different temporal relationships affect one another in order to generate effective predictions. The system requires predicting complex temporal relationships effectively because advanced models such as LSTM or attention-based models must be used. attention-based models. Operational deployment of those models remains challenging because of unforeseen practical implementation difficulties. complications due to computational complexity and a lack of explainability thus the absence of transparency in these results creates doubt in users who need to rely on the system output.

Transparency and Interpretability

The use of AI forecasting systems behind real-world decisions requires attorneys to verify predictions through clear explanations and supporting proof regarding their predictions. High accuracy predictions from Gradient

Boosting and LSTM models make them difficult to understand since their internal processes are complex. The inability to understand prediction methods causes legal experts to avoid using these models because they cannot detect the internal mechanisms. The deployment of SHAP (SHapley Additive exPlanations) with LIME (Local Interpretable Model-agnostic Explanations) requires complicated methods and high-computational resources for model transparency enhancement.

Changing Case Features and Adaptable Legal Policies

Legal field transformations generate extended case duration through continuous changes to legal policies and case features which are implemented in practice. New legislative measures would lengthen the case process duration for several merged case types through additional procedural stages integrated into the system framework. The predictions become invalid because previous data models fail to adjust to new system modifications. New variables become possible due to sociological along with technical changes which exceed the current model capabilities such as digital evidence and distant hearings. High predictive tool efficiency depends on system monitoring and regular retraining and model updates because legal environments experience sustained changes.

Ethical Considerations in AI-Driven Legal Predictions

AI integration into legal systems brings forward key ethical problems when used in the legal domain. Issues involving fairness together with transparency alongside accountability and privacy of data have emerged as crucial concerns when predictive models start using decisions in legal processes.

Algorithmic Bias and Fairness

The main ethical issue occurs when algorithms tend to show biases in their operations. AI training data consists of historic legal documentation that actually contains biases found within society and institutional systems. These models have the potential to unintentionally uphold discrimination during their operation particularly against marginalized communities if the issue remains unresolved. The safety of AI systems requires systematic measurements of unspecific bias through audits alongside learning methods that deliver fairness objectives along with sample data collection from diverse sources.

Transparency and Explainability

Legal decisions must always undergo both justification checks and responsibility hearings. Absence of interpretability makes black-box models become difficult to work with. The use of Explainable AI (XAI) methods through SHAP values and LIME produces decisions that enable legal experts and stakeholders to comprehend AI system outputs thus building trust in the system.

Data Privacy and Protection

The data present within legal datasets includes multiple types of highly private information. AI implementations need to satisfy both the General Data Protection Regulation (GDPR) and the Indian Personal Data Protection Bill when handling data. Lawmakers have established mandatory rules which require complete transparency while requiring user permission and tighten the management rules for personal data. Differential privacy together with data anonymization techniques need integration within the system's pipeline.

Human Oversight and Accountability

Artificial Intelligence systems can forecast case duration and result outcomes but these predictions need final approval from legal authorities including judges and their appointed personnel. The main principle in ethical AI frameworks requires artificial intelligence to operate as a support mechanism for human decisions when human rights and freedoms are at stake.

Proposed System

This proposed system resolves major issues which affect judicial system performance in case duration estimation. The research implements an approach to court case duration prediction with improved accuracy and adaptability based on ML and DL forecasting ensemble models. Random Forest and Gradient Boosting ensemble with LSTM models enables database processing for structured data and enables detection of sequential patterns in legal cases combined with modeling temporal specifications.

Data preparation within the model building pipeline strongly determines the accuracy of predicting data sets. Development of the target variable occurs prior to the implementation of missing value handling and categorical variable encoding historical data. Technical preprocessing enables completion and suitability for machine learning and deep learning applications through proper data management of the diverse factors including jurisdiction and problem area and judgment type.

Model compilation enters the process right after preprocessing finishes its work. The loss function selection aligns with the task of regression since it predicts court case lengths. The Mean Squared Error (MSE) accurately determines duration differences, so this project uses it as its loss function. The function guides the learning process through multiple parameter and weight modifications that result in reduced mistakes.

The main process of optimization becomes operative following compilation. The model parameters get adjusted through the implementation of the effective Adam optimizer. Effective convergence is guaranteed through the repeated weight modifications which result from loss function outputs. The optimization process stands out in the management of legal datasets because variations between cases remain one of the main factors. The model performance is evaluated through three main assessment metrics which are Mean Absolute Error (MAE) together with Root Mean Squared Error (RMSE) and R2 score. These performance measures help users clearly understand how well and reliably the system predicts case duration.

The system unites multiple forecasting models under a stacking ensemble method which uses Random Forest together with Gradient Boosting and LSTM. The system uses this integration to obtain the best performance features from each individual model. A unified legal analytics platform emerges which provides superior capabilities than typical processing approaches due to the integration of its components.

The key objectives are:

1. Accurate Legal Case Duration Prediction: The ensemble analysis-based prediction model needs to analyze structured sequential legal records to ensure precise duration forecasts.
2. Data-Driven Decision Support: The system should provide data-driven support to enhance legal decisions by delivering beneficial insights to help stakeholders make high-quality decisions regarding resource utilization and court processes.
3. Extensive Data Handling: The system accepts multiple legal datasets by employing advanced data preprocessing methods that can handle category variables and manage empty values to extract essential features from the datasets.
4. Real-Time Prediction Tool: The real-time prediction tool needs an API and web application interface to accept case information with duration prediction output from users.
5. Adaptability to Changing Legal Contexts: The system requires built-in functions that enable it to react to modifications in legal contexts by adapting to social trend changes and regulatory updates and jurisdictional requirements.

The proposed approach will make legal case management both effective and predictable while addressing this problem structure. An automatic system benefits legal experts and legislators together with society by streamlining legal procedures yet promoting data-based openness in judicial systems.

LITERATURE SURVEY

The increasing legal case deadlines together with varying timelines between different nations result in unpredictable case durations. The traditional methodologies fail to identify and record complex aspects within legal data while dealing with case classification and jurisdiction and party related elements. This study develops an improved prediction method which applies three ML models including Random Forest (RF) and Gradient Boosting (GB) and Long Short Term Memory (LSTM) networks to enhance case duration predictions. The system guarantees that the models receive structured inputs by preparing the data to deal with missing values, encode categorical variables, and extract relevant features.

The advantages of the RF, GB, and LSTM models are incorporated in the ensemble technique. It means that LSTM models describe the sequence of case histories, GB improves the prediction accuracy through the features' relevance, and RF learns the relationships in the structure of the data. The system resilience and forecast accuracy are enhanced by integrating these models in the layering technique. The framework is able to adapt to a wide range of legal situations and therefore improves the flexibility of the framework to better allocate resources, manage client's expectations and improve planning techniques. As such, this method has the potential of transforming legal analytics and decision-making processes as it not only improves case length prediction but also provides valuable information on the variables that affect case results.

A fresh approach blends machine learning with process mining to tackle legal delays and their impact on both companies and individuals. Instead of relying on what many simply call "reasonable" durations—a subjective take that has long held back older methods—this work leans on straight-up, data-backed analysis. Over 60,000 cases from Brazilian labor tribunals were thrown into the mix, with clustering techniques grouping them by the twists and turns of their procedures. The naturally occurred clusters joined the feature set which included case information about topic, category and digital status. Most predictions arrived at through gradient boosting yielded an R2 score of 0.87 which proved superior to support vector regressor and basic linear models. Explaining AI reveals which parts of process mining influence the timeline predictions while the study maintains its analysis. This strong collaboration of ML and PM produces a complete framework which both enhances predictive accuracy while clarifying the hidden operational reasons behind case delay duration. The examination of litigation timing brings significant value to law experts who need to understand court processes (Vercosa et al., 2024).

This research investigates the application of artificial intelligence (AI) for Brazilian court case duration estimation with specific focus on judge decision timing following hearings. A dataset containing more than 300,000 court cases from the Regional Labor Courts enabled this research to determine the most effective machine learning strategy through testing of seven different models. The Adaboost algorithm demonstrated superior performance in the test by attaining 84% test accuracy along with 0.819 R2 score. Additionally the test established that the magistrate judgment body and parties remained as the key factors that influenced case duration through Explainable AI (XAI) methodologies. Judicial characteristics act as fundamental indicators for determining the length of cases according to the final results of study. Research findings show that using artificial intelligence to improve legal systems can lead to reduced operations costs together with higher efficiency and better forecasting accuracy to enhance case management capabilities. The Adaboost algorithm shows how artificial intelligence technology can accelerate judicial processes while providing judicial support systems (Oliveira, 2022).

The combination of AutoML technology with binary decision forest classifiers leads to a developed classification model which targets the current judicial delays in Indian subordinate courts. Through this study which uses a vast database of 4.2 million cases from more than 7,000 courts the authors analyze time prediction from initial filing information. The predicted model performance received an enhancement through the integration of binary decision forest classifiers after AutoML for multi-class categorization. Precision along with recall and F1 scores amount to 0.81 while the top model achieves an accuracy of 81.4%. The factors that caused delays included both geographic identifiers alongside case category division and judge position variables. Through AI-powered predictive modeling the research reveals how AI applications optimize judicial performance by identifying systematic failings while improving case order prioritization. The current government trend in India involves building AI platforms including SUPACE and SUVAS to both optimize resource distribution and reduce waiting times while restructuring court operations. This research demonstrates how data analytics methodically addresses India's complex legal system through new analytical methods which would dramatically enhance legal system efficiency and effectiveness (Bhatnagar & Huchhanavar, 2023).

The CNN+LSTM hybrid model serves as an advanced machine learning algorithm that conducts research regarding AI functionality for judicial prediction systems. The applications of artificial intelligence (AI) provide systems for understanding complex legal frameworks that control contemporary society as reported by research data. After training on a big court case database. The CNN+LSTM model proved this system made the most accurate judicial ruling predictions. Evaluation of the model performance involved using accuracy and precision and recall and F1 score metrics to demonstrate its predictive capabilities. XAI techniques helped the model acquire transparency function by identifying predictive elements and data factors within the case components. The research project brings AI solutions to legal decision-making platforms to enhance process efficiency and minimize costs and improve operational flow. AI shows great promise to transform legal procedures because of its ability to simplify these processes. The CNN+LSTM hybrid model functions effectively in legal prediction tasks because it analyzes complicated legal sources. Results show how AI technology can reshape legal administration while matching current market patterns of worldwide court-based AI adoption. Computer systems that integrate AI technology will increase their capability to deliver effective legal services which improve accessibility for the public. The introduction of legal analytics development will create advancements which will improve the general accessibility and equity of legal processes (Singh et al., 2023).

Machine learning methods apply to forecasting how long it takes for offenders from arrest to case completion. Researchers applied ID3 decision trees together with instance-based learning to examine predictive analytics effectiveness for scheduling optimization in the criminal justice system through analysis of 1990 Offender Based Transaction Statistics data containing complete felony case information. The analytical results indicate predictive analytics will become essential for processing judicial matters by making systems more accessible while reducing operational obstacles. During its rising integration into criminal justice operations and legal systems prediction modeling creates both diminutive case duration and impartial court resolutions for all parties (Wilkins & Pillaipakkamnatt, 1997).

The deep learning and Natural Language Processing algorithms have worked on hand-annotated data containing 850 cases together with their free-text summaries to predict employment notice durations in Canadian case law. The research addresses problems created by unpredictable legal precedents that make establishing reasonable notice periods into a complex and unpredictable process for prediction purposes. Repeated application of BERT-like models with special domain adjustments aimed to enhance performance. The research demonstrates that result predictions remain exceptionally challenging within employment law because courts issue inconsistent decisions with multiple possible interpretations. Progress in deep learning and natural language processing has not eliminated difficulties in offering typical forecasts due to divergent legal precedent standards. The research illustrates how machine learning technology helps speed up legal processes while delivering better forecasting through AI assessment of case law documents (Lam et al., 2020).

The Federation of Bosnia and Herzegovina provided data from 75 structures for research into neural network models used for project construction length estimation. Research uses contractual and actual construction duration data accompanied by cost data and building attribute properties to test the linear regression model performance as compared to the multilayer perceptron neural network (MLP-NN). The study explains the essential need for advanced machine learning algorithms to analyze nonlinear relationships embedded in authentic construction data. The method shows great potential to enhance construction forecasts alongside making better decisions thus proving useful as a planning tool for project stakeholders (Petruseva et al., 2013).

This study investigates the application of various data mining predictive techniques to assess the time of lawsuits in order to enhance judicial performance through the application of duration metrics using data from the Brazilian TRF4. The information for the study has been taken from Tribunal Regional Federal da 4 Região (TRF4) in Brazil. The evaluation demonstrates that SVM and RF perform superior to other models assayed while SVM results demonstrate minimal superiority. Numerical data assessment for this study utilized accuracy together with sensitivity, specificity, precision and the F1 measure and accuracy metrics. Predicting case durations now stands at better rates and this enables better strategies for optimizing judicial activities. Categorical variables together with k-fold cross-validation techniques play essential roles for creating dependable research estimation according to the presented study. The selected methodology demonstrates how SVM and RF models present significant opportunities to advance the management systems in the judicial domain. Tools that forecast case duration enable managers to distribute resources better while setting priority levels on cases they need to handle thus initiating improved legal operations for every stakeholder (Gruginskie & Vaccaro, 2018).

The 2019 West Java House of Representatives (HoR) election results were evaluated by various machine learning algorithms consisting of Random Forest and Gradient Boosting Decision Tree (GBDT) and Decision Tree. The research sought to develop the most suitable model for identifying election results through candidate profile analysis. GBDT reached an F1 score of 0.7445 after feature selection and parameter optimization to become the most successful model in the evaluation phase. Borderline-SMOTE (Synthetic Minority Over-sampling Technique) together with data preprocessing and feature selection formed an integral part of the approach. Stratified 10-fold cross-validation served as the method to determine the precise performance of the developed models. The research used recall with accuracy and F1 score to determine the effectiveness of model performance. GBDT proved to be the leading model for election result prediction because it generated superior outcomes than Random Forest and Decision Tree. The investigation confirms that machine learning systems like this one could apply to different fields requiring accurate result forecasting while demonstrating the value of both feature selection methods and data imbalance solutions (Irmalasari & Dwiyanti, 2023).

Researchers analyzed high-value business disputes in the Netherlands in terms of duration by evaluating cases with claims between 1 million to 5 million EUR. Official court data reports show shorter delays than actual high-value cases require therefore leading to plaintiff's anticipated timeframes being inaccurately calculated. The research identified an issue with existing research and court records since they tend to show shorter delays compared to actual times for complex and valuable cases.

This study examined the entire legal procedures starting with filing until reaching a final judgment to develop better understanding of total delays. Variations in case duration emerged as a main study output making it difficult for plaintiffs to predict their case duration. The study shows that official governmental predictions underestimate the duration needed for complicated court cases which confuses litigants during the process of developing their litigation plans (Pistora et al., 2024).

The system uses an ensemble of machine learning approaches alongside LSTM models to handle legal case time duration estimation. The research uses a comprehensive dataset containing detailed case information about jurisdictions and specific attributes which allows the identification of case duration in days as the target value. Extensive preprocessing consisting of feature engineering and label encoding allowed Random Forest and Gradient Boosting with LSTM models to be trained until the stacking ensemble model produced the best results. This study proves that predictive analytics serves effectively as a judge duration forecasting system for stakeholders to make better case duration predictions. New innovations in this domain enable resource planning while optimizing court scheduling systems to deliver better satisfaction levels to stakeholders. AI-driven judicial reforms get endorsement from this method which demonstrates how technology can optimize intricate legal procedures (Ballesteros et al., 2020).

An analysis of legal case duration predictions in court proceedings uses ensemble machine learning alongside LSTM models. Research data collected from Indian legal courts contained multiple variables including jurisdiction and issue area and decision type and party involvement which served to calculate the target outcome of case duration in nearly 27 days. This research with India's implementation of AI systems SUPACE and SUVAS through its improvement of case duration forecasting thus demonstrating how data analytics can improve transparency and efficiency in legal processes (Huang et al., 2024).

The research analyzes legal judgment predictions using deep learning multi-fusion models which operate on Chinese legal cases. Among the applied models are TextCNN and Wide & TextCNN alongside TextDenseNet. TextDenseNet proved most effective in recognizing legal terms and fine amounts by solving difficulties stemming from irregular fine amounts together with criminal misclassification. Uniform fine mapping combined with denoising procedures enabled the use of keyword vectors to improve case description accuracy and reliability during this research. The implemented methods enhance the fairness and operational efficiency of legal systems when making decisions. The development of AI-based legal judgment prediction started in the 1980s through a succession of standpoint that became neural networks. Modern systems utilize SVM along with NLP while "Lex Machina" and "Predictice" serve as platforms that deliver predictive functions. The "AI Virtual Judge" together with other AI platforms within the Shanghai Financial Court have turned China into a leader in legal prediction technology. The study demonstrates how deep learning models specifically TextDenseNet provide excellent prospects for improving legal prediction through context-based processing and enhanced fairness for judicial systems (Wen & Ti, 2024).

This research examines how Transformer-based models specifically jurBERT and their implementation with long-context encoding methods for Legal Judgment Prediction in Romanian cases. Long and specialized legal text documents create obstacles for general-purpose NLP models because they do not perform well in this domain. The research shows that specialized models particularly SLED deliver remarkable performance benefits during processing of extensive legal documents (Ivgi, 2023). By analyzing four Romanian legal cases investigators proved that successfully processing lengthy texts needs specialized encoding systems (SLED) for optimal results in Romanian language contexts. The evaluation shows how multi-lingual LLMs face challenges when processing Romanian legal data while the incorporation of longer sequence sequences in Longformer and jurBERT variants improves task prediction results. Research outcomes serve the continuous development of tailored analytical models for legal documents which should provide improved solutions to professionals who manage complex legal documents (Masala et al., 2024).

The prediction of legal case outcomes faces distinctive challenges in case law systems because this system applies precedents to interpret and execute laws. When contrasted with civil law statutes, case law systems demand searching for applicable precedents and adapt legal principles during modifications made in time. The research proposes a new system called PILOT (PredictIng Legal case OuTcome) which divides its operation into two separate components for case retrieval and temporal pattern adjustment functions. A developed system aims to retrieve precedent cases for decision-support and also operates correctly as legal principles evolve over time. The authors establish ECHR2023 as their new dataset because it contains cases from the European Court of Human Rights which specifically analyze temporal changes in legal predictions. The research indicates that PILOT achieves superior results than previous methods by its ability to utilize precedent cases together with adaptive approaches to temporal shifts for better case outcome predictions (Cao et al., 2024).

The time constraints defined in pre-litigation proceedings are absent from the Latvian Criminal Procedure Law because it fails to specify operational time limits. The paper explores the negative effects that extended judicial proceedings impose on participating parties and jurisdiction and their right to complete fair procedures within designated time limits. The findings in this research demonstrate that the interaction of court operation systems with prosecutor duties for case preparation causes cases to persist longer than necessary. The author suggests new legal framework modifications to protect rights and jurisdiction simultaneously with performance standards for court processing durations to increase operational management. Additionally, the analysis addresses the actual issues of the Latvian judicial system regarding court system speed versus human rights requirements. Setting time limits for court proceedings along with better court management stands as an essential part in achieving these goals according to the author. The author accepts current Justice Council reforms but still argues for more improvements because delays remain a problem. The article demonstrates that improving case management and minimizing trial duration allows Latvia to improve its alignment with international human rights standards focused particularly on prompt fair trials (Bulgakova, 2023).

The application of Natural Language Processing (NLP) along with machine learning techniques for predicting legal judgments has intensified during the recent years. The early stages of Legal AI relied on rule-based and symbol-based systems until NLP and machine learning technology resulted in a data-driven approach for the legal sector. Studies verify NLP's usefulness in obtaining relevant characteristics from legal documents together with its ability to determine judicial decisions. NLP provides valuable support to the legal system by using algorithms that automate the retrieval of case laws and examination of court documentation according to Zhong et al. The prediction of veteran appeal outcomes through convolutional neural networks becomes possible when historical case data receives analysis through machine learning methods according to Krass and his colleagues. The advancement of machine learning models operating with extensive legal document and judicial decision datasets enables judicial prediction which optimizes legal system operations. The authors examine legal language complexity while stressing the necessity of developing models which handle legal text complexities. Bangladesh faces limited research on Supreme Court case prediction, but machine learning models can potentially determine judicial results when analyzing the characteristics of cases which include their categories and judicial statements and court patterns. These studies develop predictive models for judicial outcomes through pre-processing legal data within the scope of machine learning classifiers to assist legal management operations (Mustari et al., 2023).

A legal judgment prediction model implements process supervision to process the sequential dependencies between multiple tasks involved during legal decision-making. The model applies CNN to extract text features together with PCA to perform dimensionality reduction. The predictive model achieves better results through integration with a genetic algorithm (GA) for conducting parameter optimization. Process supervision within the model ensures accurate dependency tracking of sequential tasks including legal provisions and crimes as well as sentences. The solution implements a complete recurrent neural network (RNN) framework with self-attention methods to process prior task data for optimizing legal decision prediction precision. The model produces effective outcomes on different open legal datasets while exceeding conventional methods during performance assessment. Legal professionals can enhance their judgment speed and provide aid to untrained individuals through this model according to (Shang, 2022).

A system has been developed to evaluate Russian legal text complexity through an integration of linguistic feature analysis with a transformer-based neural encoder. The system analyzes 130 measurements encompassing lexical and semantic elements together with syntactic characteristics in addition to general language frequency patterns and parts-of-speech sequences and legal document references. The system received training data from Russian textbooks that contained Jurisprudence, Economics and Social Sciences subjects to analyze multiple levels of complexity. The research evaluates performance between linguistic-feature models together with BERT model variants and their combination with hybrid features. A combination of explicit linguistic metrics with implicit neural encodings in the hybrid model produces superior results over single model approaches thus enabling robust and accurate complexity evaluation of legal texts. The evaluation method enables knowledgeable researchers and educators along with legal professionals to understand legal texts better for audience adaptation purposes. An evaluation by this model shows the added value of merging neural computation with domain-specific linguistic features (Blinova & Tarasov, 2022).

The proposed approach merges Bi-LSTM with ES techniques to develop a new hybrid crime forecasting model which improves prediction accuracy levels. The proposed model tackles existing problems in crime forecasting because of low amounts of spatiotemporal data. The hybrid forecasting model, superior to SARIMA methods, optimized prediction accuracy measures including RMSE, MAPE, and MAE when estimating future crimes. New York City crime data from 2010–2017 was used to evaluate the model as it achieved improved forecasting precision by adjusting ES and Bi-LSTM parameters. The research stands out as one of the earliest studies that make specific crime category predictions, helping law enforcement agencies take proactive steps to prevent crimes. The research evaluates time series analysis together with regression models and deep learning applications for crime forecasting while emphasizing seasonality and temporal patterns in these approaches. The hybrid Bi-LSTM and ES method provides enhanced seasonality analysis over Wawrzyniak et al.'s and Jha et al.'s studies because it extracts linear and non-linear patterns while outperforming both traditional ARIMA and decision tree models. The study highlights the importance of integrating deep learning with statistical methods to enhance crime prediction accuracy. Future research can explore additional external factors like socioeconomic variables and urban dynamics to refine the model further, aiding policymakers in implementing data-driven crime prevention strategies effectively (Butt, 2022).

Legal AI Compliance and Regulatory Challenges

Investigative research now extends its focus to regulatory standards along with ethical guidelines and legal frameworks which must be applied to AI system implementation. Both models investigate the necessity for AI systems to comply with GDPR requirements along with those stipulated by the EU AI Act and the automated decision-making provisions of Article 22 in GDPR (Hildebrandt, 2020; Veale & Zuiderveen Borgesius, 2021). Judicial AI systems require integration of explanation methods together with fairness monitoring systems and risk assessment capabilities according to research findings.

Both court administration and legal forecasting tasks experience successful implementation of AI systems through regulatory frameworks established across the Netherlands and Canada and Estonia. Studies show that AI systems need specific social and legal treatment because they become responsible socio-legal actors that require monitoring governance and certification compliance.

This research introduces a combination model containing LSTM alongside Gradient Boosting alongside SHAP and model-agnostic audits as elements which satisfy ethical and legal specifications.

SYSTEM DESIGN AND ARCHITECTURE

A system to forecast legal case duration requires a methodology that follows data collection and preprocessing steps and standardizes the selection process among feature extraction and model determination and evaluation steps as represented by Figure 1. A suggested approach integrates machine learning algorithms with Long Short-Term Memory (LSTM) network models for the framework.

- Data Collection: Compile historical information from court case files. All relevant data about case jurisdiction and disposition along with party results of problem areas and decision types and natural court and docket information must be included in this dataset. Legal databases together with court documents and public legal case archives serve as the optimal sources for obtaining data.

- Preprocessing: The data undergoes preprocessing for missing value treatment and numerical scaling together with categorical variable transformation. The data preparation phase consists of multiple techniques that incorporate label encoding together with imputation for data gaps while implementing feature scaling techniques before the training process.
- Feature Extraction: The data scientist needs to extract essential factors from the dataset through which the problem type interacts with party information and jurisdictions and other case-related elements that influence duration. Improving the predictive model requires implementing feature engineering procedures which aim to enhance its accuracy.
- Learning Model: The designed system utilizes preprocessed information to accomplish training of a predictive model. Random Forest together with Gradient Boosting and Long Short-Term Memory (LSTM) for sequential data should both be analyzed as machine learning approaches. Multiple prediction models can be stacked in series to utilize complementary performance strengths when making accurate forecasts.
- Evaluation: The model evaluation requires splitting the data into different segments. R2 and RMSE serve with meaning absolute error (MAE) to determine the prediction accuracy. Cross-validation techniques help ensure that unknown data will result in effective model performance.
- Deployment: The final step consists of implementing the trained model through a system designed for users to input case information while obtaining predicted case duration forecasts.
- Iterative Improvement: Repetitive refinement of the model must include continuous collection of new court case information for ongoing training and accuracy enhancement. Regular monitoring of system performance in real-world applications will enable needed model modifications to enhance accuracy levels.

- Legal practitioners could use this proposed solution to enhance their case preparation since it establishes standards for automated machine learning-based case length forecasting.

Figure 1. Proposed architecture

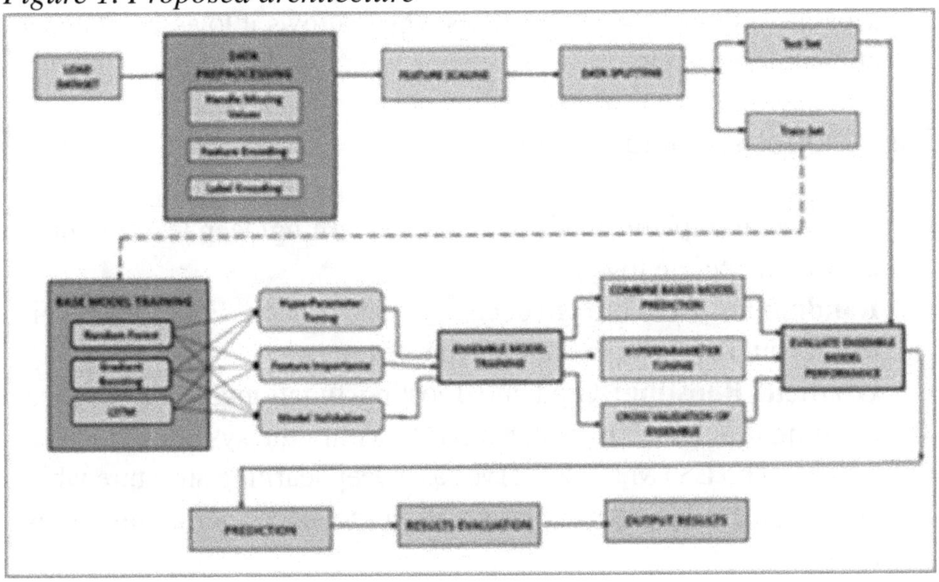

The developed Model leverages ensemble modeling and deep learning (LSTM) for effective prediction. The system contains three main functional modules such as data preprocessing and base model training and ensemble model evaluation which together optimize prediction workflows. The workflow of the model appears in Figure 1.

System Architecture Details

Data Preprocessing Module:

- **Handle Missing Values:** Before analysis the system uses methods to handle absent data points that result in a clean standardized dataset.

- **Feature Encoding:** The system transforms jurisdiction data and decision types and case disposition information into numeric patterns through label encoding.
- **Feature Scaling:** All numeric features undergo feature scaling which creates a uniform scale to enhance model convergence behavior.
- **Data Splitting:** The system uses data splitting to split its data into separate training and testing parts which allows it to assess its operational performance.

Base Model Training Module

- The system implements three machine learning/deep learning models which operate together.
- **Random Forest:** Through decision trees Random Forest learns different patterns that exist in the input features.
- **Gradient Boosting:** Gradient Boosting functions as an advanced boosting tool which minimizes errors within the system.
- **LSTM:** The LSTM model serves as a deep learning structure which detects ordered patterns in information sequences pertaining to case data.
- The models complete a phase of parameter adjustment and attribute assessment for maximum performance.

Ensemble Model Training

- The base models produce predictions which when combined result in increased accuracy levels .
- Cross-validation operates as an evaluation method to verify model resilience and stop performance deterioration from overfitting.
- The ensemble model obtains its best performing state through hyperparameter tuning methods.

Evaluation and Prediction

- The ensemble model performance requires measurements of RMSE, MAE and R^2 for evaluation purposes.

- A prediction process occurs for test data where analysis evaluates misclassifications and deviations within the results.

Total Parameters

- The parameters include the weights and biases of the LSTM layers, as well as the parameters of the Random Forest and Gradient Boosting models, fine-tuned during the training process.
- This architecture leverages the strengths of each model to learn intricate patterns in the dataset, which contains 8,286 rows and 54 columns.

The model contains weights and biases of LSTM layers together with fine-tuned parameters from Random Forest and Gradient Boosting models as total model parameters.

Algorithm: Hybrid Ensemble Model for Accurate Legal Case Duration Estimation

Input

- The training data includes labeled legal case information that features decisionType, jurisdiction, caseDisposition, partyWinning and additional elements.
- The efficacy of our duration prediction model will undergo assessment through tests performed on separate data.
- The system requires hardware and software specifications that include Python and TensorFlow and Keras and Scikit-learn and Pandas and NumPy alongside Jupyter Notebook or IDE together with Anaconda or Google Colab.

Output

- The trained system utilizes multiple features to calculate legal case extensions.

- The model uses Mean Absolute Error and R^2 together with other evaluation metrics for measuring its performance.
- The system provides predictions along with duration estimates for new uncertain legal proceedings and forecasts their expected decision timelines.

Steps

1. Initialization:
   - The initialization step includes loading necessary libraries where TensorFlow/Keras serves for LSTM processing while Scikit-learn works for ensemble models together with Pandas for data handling functions.
   - The setup should include GPU/CPU configuration as well as random input generation for repeatability testing and performance logging systems.
2. Data Ingestion:
   - The data processing system receives legal case attributes from databases and CSV files and cloud storage databases which include jurisdiction and case disposition information as well as party prevailing details.
   - The framework supports different data schemes comprising structured CSV along with JSON and semi-structured formats and processes them using Pandas DataFrames or Spark DataFrames.
3. Data Preprocessing:
   - Missing values need to be imputed while outlier cases need handling together with balancing class distribution if present cases occur disproportionately throughout the dataset.
   - The target variable (case duration in days) can be derived through an operation which subtracts argument date from decision date.
   - Both jurisdiction and case type variables should be encoded through label encoding or one-hot encoding.
4. Feature Engineering:

- The team should create two new features through statistical computation which combine court-specific case duration averages and seasonal patterns in court decision operations.
- The LSTM models require time-series features along with time lags as input data. Dimensionality reduction methods including Principal Component Analysis (PCA) among others should be employed for removing features that are either unimportant or repetitive.

5. Model Training and Tuning:
   - Train ensemble models like Random Forest, Gradient Boosting, and Linear Regression using the engineered features.
   - Train the LSTM model by passing sequential legal case data (temporal data) to capture time dependencies.
   - Use cross-validation to discover the optimal hyperparameters (e.g., number of trees for Random Forest, learning rate for Gradient Boosting, and number of layers for LSTM).
   - Apply techniques such as Grid Search or Bayesian Optimization to adjust the models.
6. Model Stacking and Ensemble Creation:
   - Use stacking ensemble techniques to combine the predictions of Random Forest, Gradient Boosting, and LSTM models.
   - The predictions from individual models are used as input features for a meta-model (e.g., Logistic Regression or Linear Regression).
   - Train the meta-model on the predictions to make the final case duration prediction.
7. Model Evaluation:
   - Calculate performance metrics such as Mean Absolute Error (MAE), Root Mean Squared Error (RMSE), and R^2 Score on the test set.
   - Compare the ensemble model's performance against individual models to ensure that the stacking improves prediction accuracy.
   - Analyze error metrics across various case attributes to understand model.
8. Model Deployment and Integration:

- Export the trained models and deploy them using cloud services such as AWS Sagemaker, Google Cloud ML, or Flask APIs for serving.

9. Monitoring and Maintenance:
    - Monitor the model's performance in production by regularly evaluating it against new incoming data.
    - Apply retraining mechanisms or online learning techniques when significant performance degradation is detected.
    - Log system metrics such as latency, throughput, and resource utilization for optimization and scaling decisions.

Table 1. Summary of key components and functionalities of the project

Component	Functionality
Data Ingestion	Load legal case data from various sources (databases, CSV files, cloud storage).
Data Preprocessing	Cleaning the data followed by missing value handling then cat features encoding that results in extracting the target variable which uses case duration.
Feature Engineering	The process of feature engineering must generate new time-related attributes which would reflect both the historical patterns and case-specific elements.
Model Training and Tuning	Developing Random Forest along with Gradient Boosting and Linear Regression models and establishing an LSTM network for time-series models..
Model Stacking	The combination of individual models through stacking ensemble approaches to achieve better accuracy.
Model Evaluation	The ensemble model requires performance metric evaluation to assess its efficiency. (MAE, RMSE, R^2 Score) and compare against baseline models.
Model Deployment	The trained ensemble model will be deployed to production through cloud services as well as REST APIs.
Monitoring and Maintenance	The system requires continuous performance model monitoring alongside system metric logging along with necessary retraining to protect accuracy.

The system development process starts by implementing this algorithm to produce an effective machine learning framework which predicts legal case durations. This operational framework helps legal workers create automated case duration projections while enhancing their resource organization and leading to better management practices for legal situations.

RESULTS AND DISCUSSIONS

Linear Regression

Linear Regression created the framework for developing estimates of legal case duration predictions. Figure 2 below presents the comparison between actual case durations and model predictions through a scatter plot that shows the perfect prediction line as a red dashed line. The Linear Regression model demonstrates capability for detecting standard linear patterns however it becomes ineffective when processing intricate data sets without the capability to detect non-linear patterns.

The wide dispersion of data points away from the diagonal reveals how insufficiently the pattern handles changing characteristics in the dataset primarily among extended-length cases. The model demonstrates limitations in its complexity by showing significant deviations from the red line particularly when dealing with cases at extreme values. Although limited in its ability the Linear Regression model serves as an essential baseline to demonstrate why ensemble methods and neural networks are required for achieving better legal case duration predictions.

Figure 2. Scatter plot for decision tree regressor

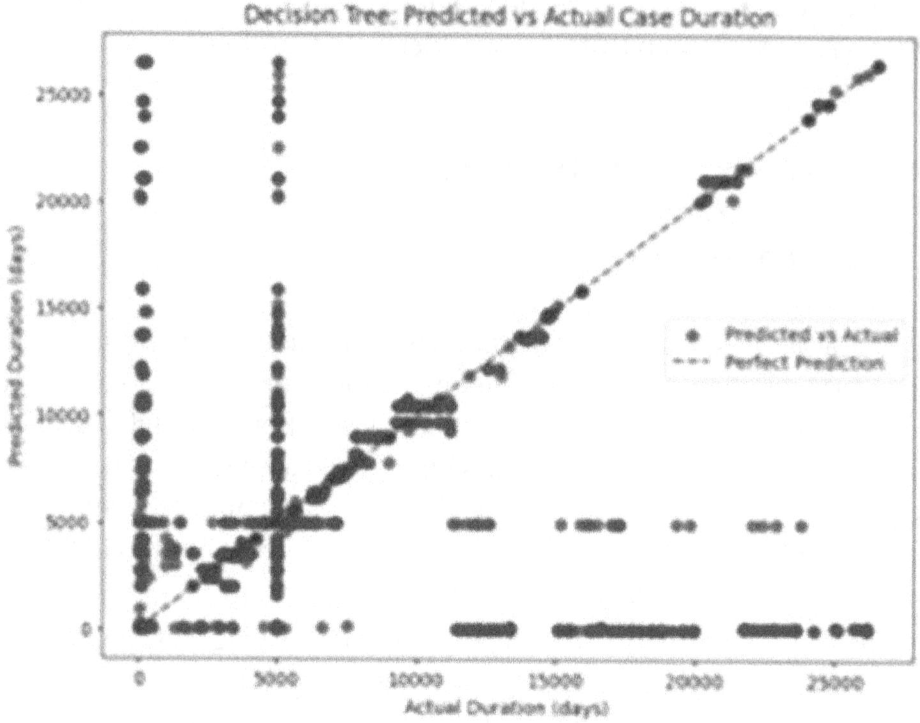

Random Forest Regressor

The sophisticated Random Forest Regressor framework is used for the prediction of due dates of cases in the law case duration. Figure 3 showing what the model predicts for case duration versus the actual durations, with the red dashed line representing perfect prediction. Random Forest model Xprocess complicated relationships from which the basic models suffer and thus lower errors on the predictions except in rare cases. Most of the points fall on the diagonal; however, some deviate, especially for long cases.

The extreme duration cases continue to be difficult to predict, and this is a shortcoming of the ensemble method when we model case durations. The Random Forest Regressor uses several decision trees which, in combination with its good generalization, makes it a good choice for applications for complex datasets. It represents a high value model that can predict the likely outcomes of legal cases with accuracy and reliability.

Figure 3. Confusion matrix

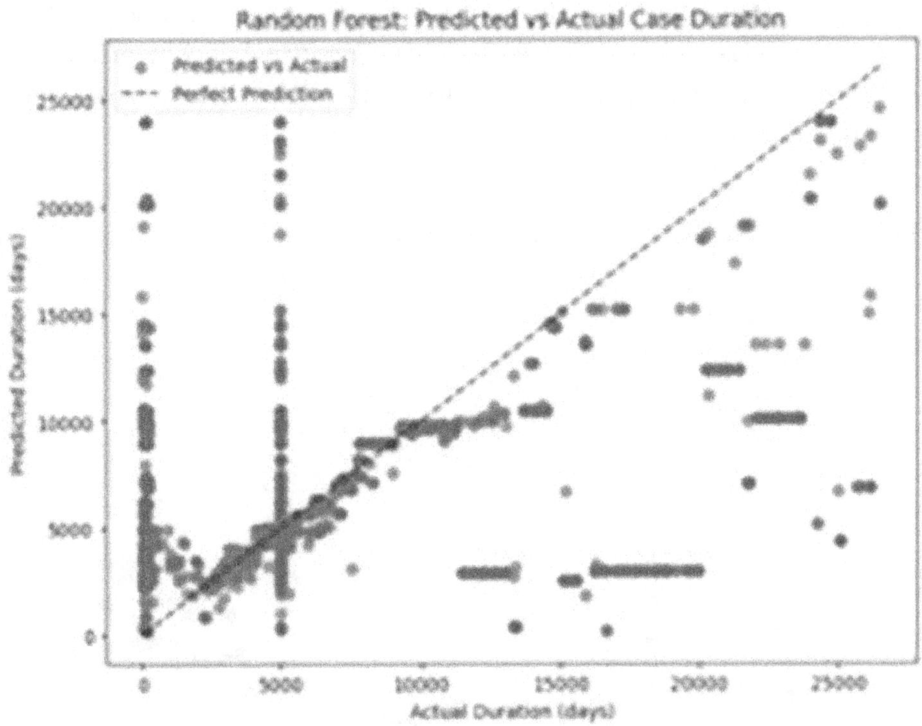

Gradient Boosting Regressor

The Gradient Boosting Regressor utilized in this study demonstrates its effectiveness in predicting the duration of legal cases. Figure 4 shows predictions from the model alongside actual case lengths where the perfect expectation line appears as red dashes. The Gradient Boosting model achieves its superiority at capturing non-linear relationships and error reduction based on the fact that it creates a dense grouping of points near the diagonal line.

The model presents small prediction inaccuracies for cases that show extremely long or short durations mainly because of the wide range of case characteristics. Through a balanced fit the Gradient Boosting Regressor delivers predictions which can be trusted because they reflect the overall distribution of prediction results.

The powerful outcome of this model proves its ability to handle complex data successfully and thus makes it appropriate for legal case duration forecasting with precision. The prediction accuracy enhancement strategy of the model creates superior results for moderate prediction challenges by using error refinement steps.

Figure 4. Scatter plot for gradient boosting regressor

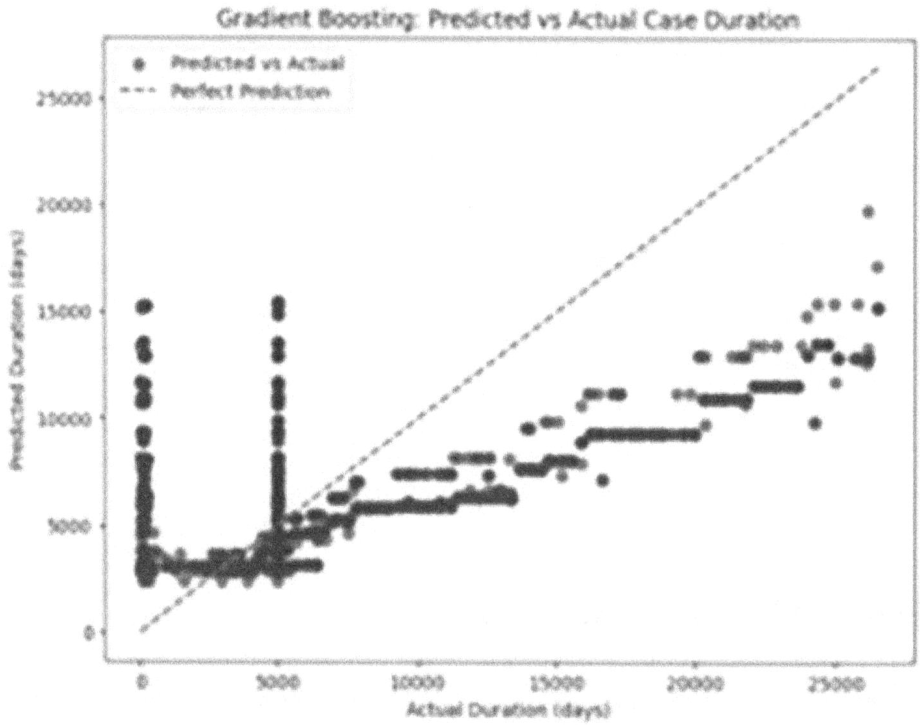

K Nearest Neighbor

The research utilizes K-Nearest Neighbors (KNN) Regressor to forecast legal case periods through its examination of feature similarity. The actual and predicted case durations show their relationship in the displayed Figure 5 where perfect predictions appear as a red dashed line. The KNN model shows strong performance in modeling case durations within moderate ranges because it arranges prediction points closely to the ideal diagonal line.

The KNN model encounters difficulties when dealing with cases that have very long durations which produce substantial deviations from the red line. The model develops its predictions based on local relationships which leads to two problems when processing data points that are either complex or sparse.

Figure 5. Scatter plot for KNN regressor

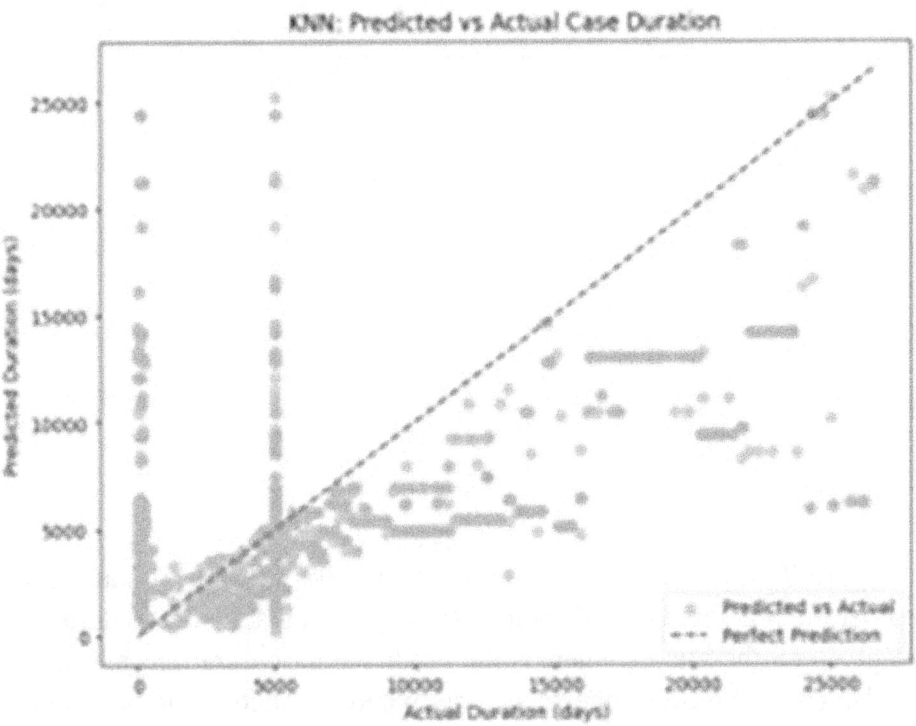

Stack Ensemble Model Prediction

The code performs ensemble stacking for case duration prediction which achieves good performance levels which are presented in this implementation. The system combines many machine learning models along with Long Short-Term Memory networks such as to improve prediction results. The loss curve in Figure 6 shows how the LSTM model's training and verification loss varies for predicting legal case durations. The training loss reduces sharply in the first few epochs but stabilizes around epoch 6, indicating convergence. The validation loss rises but becomes more stable, affirming a generalization on unseen data. Hence, it is a reliable one for this prediction without overfitting.

Figure 6. Stacked model training and validation loss curve

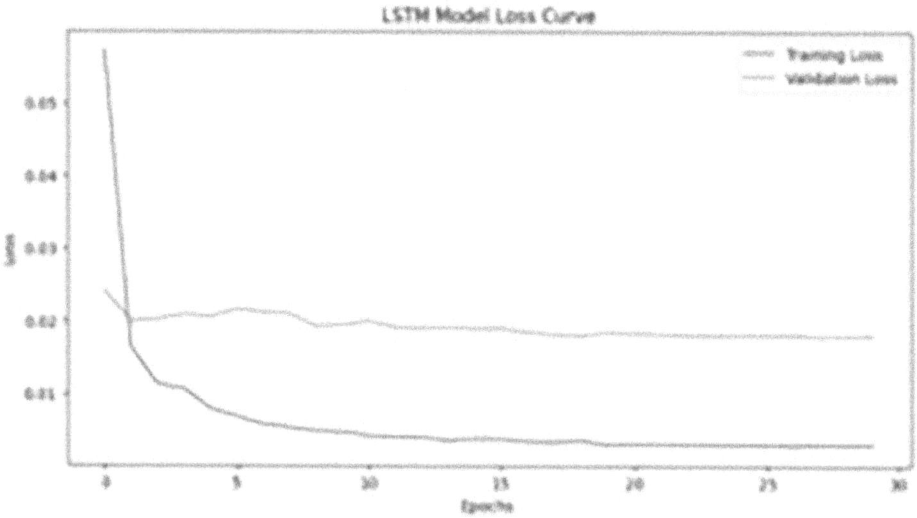

Figure 7 shows how the actual case durations (in days) stacked up against the predicted case durations (in days). The actual case durations are given on the x-axis, whereas the predicted case durations are on the y-axis. The red dashed line represents where predicted durations equal actual durations (y = x). If the data points are nearest to the line, it means that the model is accurate. The plot shows how well the model works, with some being predicted better than others.

Figure 7. Stacked model actual vs predicted case duration

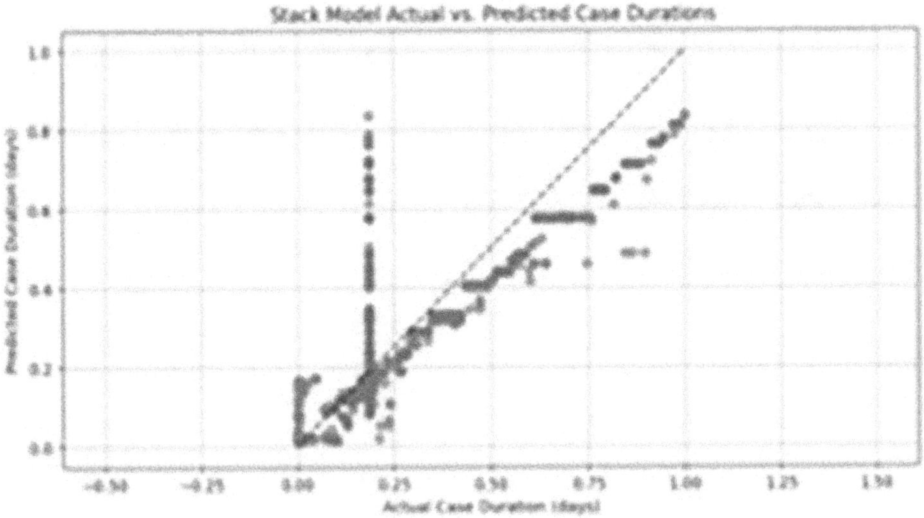

Figure 8 predicts errors of a model that predicts day-based case durations. The predictive durations appear on the x-axis and the y-axis displays residual data representing actual-predicted value differences (Actual - Predicted). A perfect alignment between actual and predicted values shows in the red dashed line at zero.

The zero line serves as reference for checking variability because data points surrounding it show the prediction accuracy range. The model provides underprediction when it generates residuals that are positive because actual durations exceed predicted values but generates overpredictions when residuals are negative. The plot shows two distinct trends where model prediction variations occur notably at lower duration levels and follow a decreasing pattern at higher durations. The observed patterns reveal possible opportunities to make model enhancements in the targeted areas.

Figure 8. Stacked model residual plot

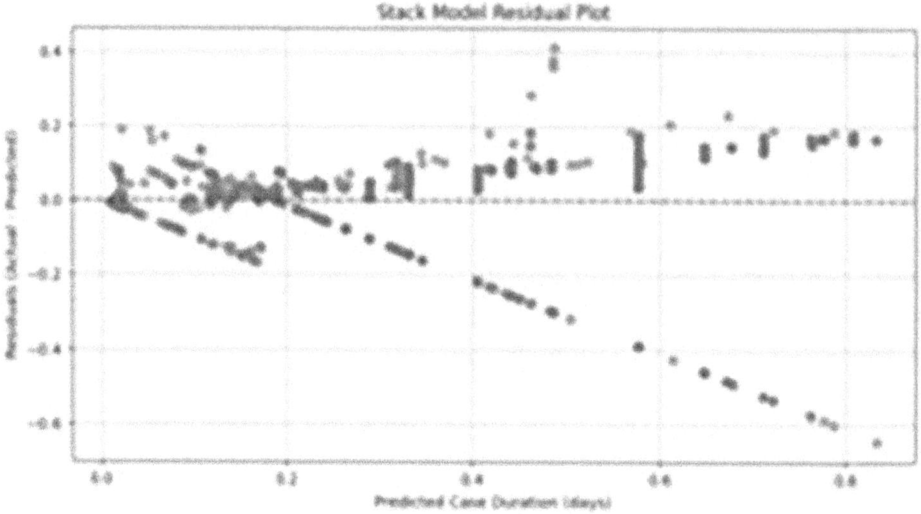

Case Studies and Legal Compliance of AI in Jurisdictions

The practical deployment of AI for legal systems follows the current developments in legislations together with the practical obstacles inside courts and government institutions. The part explains main regulatory guidelines while showcasing how AI systems operate within legal domains at jurisdictional levels.

Regulatory Frameworks Affecting Legal AI

The General Data Protection Regulation (GDPR, 2016) and the EU AI Act and the Algorithmic Accountability Act from the United States (EU-AI, 2021) create substantial regulatory boundaries for AI development in legal areas. These frameworks emphasize:

- A system must provide customers with an explanation of how their data receives automated decision-making.
- The necessity of human oversight.

- AI systems used in courts belong to the high-risk category according to risk categorizations.
- Mandatory impact assessments before deployment.
- Transparency and accountability in data usage and decision-making.

Risks of Non-Compliance

GDPR and other applicable legal frameworks necessitate that AI systems conform otherwise they might experience the following consequences:

- Legal consequences
- Reputational damage to judicial institutions.
- Lack of public trust becomes stronger when decisions appear unduly secretive or bias against certain parties.

The lack of explainability within black-box models which predict case durations constitutes GDPR noncompliance because such systems affect people without offering rationale.

Mitigating Risks Through Hybrid Ensemble Models

The method described in this chapter builds a hybrid ensemble model through an integration of Random Forest interpretable algorithms and LSTM deep learning elements which delivers multiple benefits during the creation of legally compliant AI solutions (MacCarthy, M, 2020):

- High prediction accuracy remains possible while interpretability levels do not decrease.
- SHAP and LIME produce explainable visual outputs for model interpretation.
- Users can find biases and perform fairness evaluations before models are put into use.

The model supports the creation of decisions using transparent methods that work for high-risk legal situations.

Case Studies of AI Deployment in Legal Systems

- Legal institutions throughout Netherlands utilize AI systems which forecast caseloads through GDPR-compatible frameworks. Aid system development supplies scheduling functions yet all determinations must be examined by personnel (Wieringa, M, 2020).
- Estonia executed computational model development for small claims courts that maintained visible functions while allowing users to detect all changes. The judicial system can view all decisions after citizens file appeals (Oja, S, 2021)
- All Canadian organizations must achieve GDPR compliance through transparent model evaluation and legal data anonymization before permitting AI use to predict trial durations (Aiken, A, 2019).

The responsible implementation of AI within legal settings has been proved to be possible through these jurisdictions. Technological innovation should merge with regulatory compliance and human decision-making abilities according to these examples.

CONCLUSION AND FUTURE WORK

The system developed a prediction model by uniting machine learning (ML) and deep learning (DL) techniques that included Random Forest, LSTM, Linear Regression along with Gradient Boosting models for predicting legal case length. The approach linked existing model assets to create usable information that attorneys could utilize for case duration prognostications and distributed resources more efficiently to manage cases. The research presents a final evaluation of project achievements alongside general difficulties and subsequent contributions to knowledge alongside proposal directions to build upon developed outcomes. Every ensemble model in the project contributed to enhanced performance while simultaneously achieving superior accuracy assessment and interpretability.

Future Work

The promising results from the initiative need additional investigation to develop its potential and refine key aspects.

Incorporating Advanced Models

Forecasting research should explore how transformer-based models or attention systems would help sequential data handling of complex relationships and extended dependencies. The ensemble system's predictive accuracy and case timeline analysis becomes better when these models are included with the ensemble.

Enhanced Feature Engineering

The model could achieve higher performance through the addition of detailed features that include information about past case records and lawyer performance statistics along with characteristics that are specific to individual courts. The integration of external factors which includes legal policy adjustments together with socioeconomic variables would enhance predictive accuracy by providing additional context.

Explainability and Interpretability

The future growth of ML-based legal analytics requires methods to improve how models present their analytical mechanisms to users. AI-generated legal insight trust and professional understanding of prediction factors will benefit from future implementations of analysis methods such as SHAP values or LIME which focus specifically on legal prediction activities.

Real-Time Implementation

Real-time deployment of the model offers legal practitioners better utility since it enables them to alter case predictions through dynamic updates of evolving case specifics. This development of a cloud-based platform integrated with API functionality would enable practical usage by legal institutions through the model implementation.

Addressing Data Limitations

Future studies must work on developing and optimizing the database by adding a significant number of cases from multiple judicial jurisdictions that represent various legal matters. Model reliability increases when generalizability problems in the data are properly addressed. The usability and effectiveness of the model can improve through establishing a detailed data-cleaning infrastructure which streamlines preprocessing procedures.

REFERENCES

Act, E. U. A. I. (2021). *Proposal for a Regulation of the European Parliament and of the Council laying down harmonized rules on artificial intelligence*. COM(2021) 206 final. European Commission.

Aiken, A. (2019). GDPR compliance in Canadian legal institutions: A case study on trial duration predictions. *Canadian Journal of Law and Technology, 12*(2), 134–147. DOI: 10.2139/ssrn.3334889

Ballesteros-Pérez, P., Sanz-Ablanedo, E., Cerezo-Narváez, A., Lucko, G., Pastor-Fernández, A., Otero-Mateo, M., & Contreras-Samper, J. P. (2020). Forecasting accuracy of in-progress activity duration and cost estimates. *Journal of Construction Engineering and Management, 146*(9), 04020104. DOI: 10.1061/(ASCE)CO.1943-7862.0001900

Bhatnagar, M., & Huchhanavar, S. (2023, July). Predicting delays in Indian lower courts using AutoML and Decision Forests. In *International Conference on Computing, Intelligence and Data Analytics* (pp. 166-180). Cham: Springer Nature Switzerland.

Blinova, O., & Tarasov, N. (2022). A hybrid model of complexity estimation: Evidence from Russian legal texts. *Frontiers in Artificial Intelligence, 5*, 1008530. DOI: 10.3389/frai.2022.1008530 PMID: 36388401

Bulgakova, I. (2023, December). Duration of criminal proceedings: Human rights and jurisdiction aspects. In *individual. Society. State. Proceedings of the International Student and Teacher Scientific and Practical Conference* (pp. 126-130).

Butt, U. M., Letchmunan, S., Hassan, F. H., & Koh, T. W. (2022). Hybrid of deep learning and exponential smoothing for enhancing crime forecasting accuracy. *PLoS One, 17*(9), e0274172. DOI: 10.1371/journal.pone.0274172 PMID: 36070317

Cao, L., Wang, Z., Xiao, C., & Sun, J. (2024). PILOT: Legal Case Outcome Prediction with Case Law. *arXiv preprint arXiv:2401.15770*. DOI: 10.18653/v1/2024.naacl-long.34

General Data Protection Regulation (GDPR). (2016). *Regulation (EU) 2016/679 of the European Parliament and of the Council*. Official Journal of the European Union.

Gruginskie, L. A. D. S., & Vaccaro, G. L. R. (2018). Lawsuit lead time prediction: Comparison of data mining techniques based on categorical response variable. *PLoS One*, *13*(6), e0198122. DOI: 10.1371/journal.pone.0198122 PMID: 29856787

Hildebrandt, M. (2020). *Law for computer scientists and other folk*. Oxford University Press. DOI: 10.1093/oso/9780198860877.001.0001

Huang, J. H., Yang, C. C., Shen, Y., Pacces, A. M., & Kanoulas, E. (2024, October). Optimizing numerical estimation and operational efficiency in the legal domain through large language models. In *Proceedings of the 33rd ACM International Conference on Information and Knowledge Management* (pp. 4554-4562). DOI: 10.1145/3627673.3680025

Irmalasari, I., & Dwiyanti, L. (2023, October). Algorithm Analysis of Decision Tree, Gradient Boosting Decision Tree, and Random Forest for Classification (Case Study: West Java House of Representatives Election 2019). In *2023 International Conference on Electrical Engineering and Informatics (ICEEI)* (pp. 1-5). IEEE. DOI: 10.1109/ICEEI59426.2023.10346727

Lam, J. T., Liang, D., Dahan, S., & Zulkernine, F. H. (2020, August). The Gap between Deep Learning and Law: Predicting Employment Notice. In *NLLP@ KDD* (pp. 52-56).

MacCarthy, M. (2020). *Algorithmic Accountability Act of 2019. (2019). H.R. 2231 – Algorithmic Accountability Act of 2019*. U.S. House of Representatives.

Masala, M., Rebedea, T., & Velicu, H. (2024). Improving Legal Judgement Prediction in Romanian with Long Text Encoders. *arXiv preprint arXiv:2402.19170*.

Mustari, N., Sen, S. K., Banik, A., Mehedi, M. H. K., & Rasel, A. A. (2023, March). Techniques to Estimate the Status of Legal Proceedings Considering Sequential Text Data. In *2023 International Conference on Emerging Smart Computing and Informatics (ESCI)* (pp. 1-6). IEEE. DOI: 10.1109/ESCI56872.2023.10099995

Oja, S. (2021). Estonia's implementation of AI in small claims courts: Transparency and ethical considerations. *AI and Law*, *29*(1), 45–56.

Petruseva, S., Zujo, V., & Zileska-Pancovska, V. (2013). Neural network prediction model for construction project duration. *International Journal of Engineering Research & Technology (Ahmedabad)*, *2*(11), 1646–1654.

Pistora, D., van Dijk, F., & Verkerk, R. (2024). Time Taken for Disposition of Commercial Disputes in the Netherlands: Why official court statistics underestimate the problem of the long and unpredictable duration of court procedures. *Utrecht Law Review*, *20*(1), 44–63. DOI: 10.36633/ulr.925

Shang, X. (2022). A computational intelligence model for legal prediction and decision support. *Computational Intelligence and Neuroscience*, *2022*(1), 5795189. DOI: 10.1155/2022/5795189 PMID: 35785064

Singh, R., Kumar, B. V., Rawat, K. K., Akram, S. V., Kathuria, S., & Pachouri, V. (2023, September). Intervention of AI in Prediction of Judgement of Cases. In *2023 4th International Conference on Smart Electronics and Communication (ICOSEC)* (pp. 1268-1272). IEEE. DOI: 10.1109/ICOSEC58147.2023.10275850

Veale, M., & Zuiderveen Borgesius, F. J. (2021). Demystifying the draft EU Artificial Intelligence Act. *Computer Law Review International*, *22*(4), 97–112. DOI: 10.9785/cri-2021-220402

Vercosa, L., Silva, V., Cruz, J., Bastos-Filho, C., & Bezerra, B. L. (2024). Investigation of lawsuit process duration using machine learning and process mining. *Discover Analytics*, *2*(1), 9. DOI: 10.1007/s44257-024-00015-0

Wen, Y., & Ti, P. (2024). A Study of Legal Judgment Prediction Based on Deep Learning Multi-Fusion Models—Data from China. *SAGE Open*, *14*(3), 21582440241257682. DOI: 10.1177/21582440241257682

Wieringa, M. (2020). GDPR compliance and AI: Case studies from the Netherlands. *Journal of Information Privacy and Security*, *16*(3), 17–29.

Wilkins, D., & Pillaipakkamnatt, K. (1997, June). The effectiveness of machine learning techniques for predicting time to case disposition. In *Proceedings of the 6th international conference on Artificial intelligence and law* (pp. 106-113). DOI: 10.1145/261618.261642

Chapter 5
Tailored Digital Marketplaces Navigating AI Regulation Within Competition Law

Devendra Singh
https://orcid.org/0000-0002-7470-3783
Amity Law School, Amity University, Greater Noida, India

Sanjana Chaturvedi
https://orcid.org/0009-0003-2607-9204
Rabindranath Tagore University, Bhopal, India

ABSTRACT

Client data now serves as a valuable intangible asset thanks to the digital economy. Companies are using Big Data and Big Analytics to customize the pricing of their products and services depending on several criteria by means of the information they acquire and evaluate. One runs danger with organic rivalry and client data security. Equipped with such priceless consumer data, companies may undercut consumer welfare and competitiveness even if their outward look of increasing transparency and reducing information asymmetries seems to be improving. This study

DOI: 10.4018/979-8-3373-3114-0.ch005

intends to clarify the inherent difficulties related to behavioral discrimination and investigate the application of traditional competition tools within the developing digital economy to protect consumer privacy and maintain market competitiveness. Our internet buying experience now mostly consists of personalized adverts for electronics, clothes, cars, hotels, and airline tickets.

INTRODUCTION

Customer information has been elevated to the status of a valuable intangible asset as a result of the digital economy. Through the use of Big Data and Big Analytics, businesses are increasingly using the information that they collect and analyze in order to customize the prices of their products and services according to a wide variety of characteristics. Competition that is organic and the security of customer information are both under jeopardy. Despite the fact that there is a superficial impression of increasing openness and decreasing information asymmetries, firms that are equipped with such valuable customer data may hinder competition and consumer welfare. The purpose of this study is to shed light on the inherent difficulties that are connected to discrimination based on behavior and to investigate the use of traditional competition instruments within the context of the developing digital economy in order to maintain market competition and protect consumer privacy. Personalized advertisements have emerged as an important component of our online shopping experience, and they are applied to a wide range of products, including electronic devices, clothing, autos, lodging, and airline tickets. According to the concept of personalization, the advertisements that I view on the internet are different from those that are developed by the same corporation for my parents, children, spouse, colleagues, and neighbors.

To put it another way, digital platforms have unquestionably altered the dynamics of the market for both buyers and sellers. They have done this by increasing market openness and reducing information asymmetries, which has resulted in purchasers having greater control over their purchasing decisions. Because of this, a system is activated that requires businesses to innovate, which ultimately results in the development of dynamic efficiency. It is possible that the development of algorithms on the supply side will also improve static efficiency by lowering the prices of production, improving quality and resource utilization, and streamlining business processes. Because of this, the distribution chain has been favorably influenced, and the dynamic efficiency has been improved. The entry hurdles that are associated with online platforms seem to be lower. At the moment, there is no such thing as a need for traditional retail enterprises to participate in intense rivalry. Digital advertisements are a good way to market online services. The occurrence of this phenomena has been seen in the context of taxi services such as Uber, which runs a vast network of cars and drivers without having ownership of them or employing them. Due to the fact that marketers compete on search keywords on web aggregators such as Google AdWords and pay depending on the number of clicks received on their adverts, online platforms reduce the costs associated with advertising.

There exists a significant disparity between contemporary advertising methods and the traditional 'media model,' which struggled with a lack of insight into the real audience engagement with commercials.

Overall, it seems that the internet market is improving efficiency. Nonetheless, there is more than what is apparent. Companies are utilizing intricate pricing algorithms that consider factors such as an item's popularity, competitor pricing, and consumer data, including location, shopping times, frequency of site visits, and past purchases. The notion of a neutral, objective Internet is rapidly transforming into a digital landscape that is more tailored and specific. Websites are using ways to get real-time data about their visitors and then displaying different versions of the web to varied users. Prices vary, goods are replaced, terminology is modified, and the average internet user often struggles to identify these changes as they transpire.

The interchange of information has always been vital to the market; nevertheless, the emergence of Big Data (Company, 2016) and Big Analytics has resulted in the convergence of our 'real' and 'online' lives, characterized by the continuous monitoring of individuals' data from birth to death. Digitalization has undeniably enhanced our welfare much beyond e-commerce, particularly in the realm of healthcare services. It is essential to recognize that as an increasing number of organizations embrace business models reliant on personal data, they will endeavor to attain a 'data edge' over their competitors, (Mullin et al., 2025). This will therefore push corporations to invest in computer algorithms to analyze the vast quantity and variety of data. The increased use of artificial intelligence and pricing algorithms by online sellers will establish these algorithms as the primary determinants of industry pricing for diverse products and services. The customization of marketing and the price of items and services engenders three fundamental inquiries. Do commercial enterprises that gather personal data and create profiles to offer differential pricing for goods and services to various individuals influence the dynamics of competition and ultimately consumer welfare? Two, can the access to and use of big data by firms confer market dominance and a competitive edge over rivals while perpetuating anti-competitive practices? In other words, can access to big data act as a barrier to entry owing to the substantial investment required for data analysis and self-learning algorithms? As firms increasingly collect personal data for their own advantage rather than for the benefit of consumers, should competition regulators begin to see privacy protection as a long-term non-price factor in evaluating anti-competitive conduct?

REFINING PRICING DISCRIMINATION WITH EXTENSIVE DATA ANALYSIS

Retail establishments have long used strategies such as loyalty programs, categorizing clients into groups such as older people and students to gather client information and then direct targeted advertisements and promotions towards them. An exemplary instance of this is the coverage provided by the New York Times on the renowned Target store in the United States. Upon entering a retail location, (Hill, 2024). Target provides each consumer a unique identifier, referred to internally as the Guest ID number, which monitors all purchases made. When a client utilizes a credit card, store coupon, completes a survey, submits a refund request, contacts customer service, opens an email from Target, or visits Target's website, Target will associate that information with the customer's Guest ID.

Target monitors consumers' age, marital status, number of children, residential location, estimated income, ethnicity, reading preferences, favored shopping brands, vehicle ownership, social media identifiers, political affiliations, and more, without their knowledge or agreement. What motivates Target to extensively monitor and gather data? All information is then analyzed to provide personalized product offers aimed at enhancing customer loyalty and expenditure in the shop. What enables this to occur? Utilizing extensive data sets. Emerging data analysis capabilities, often referred to as 'Big Data,' allow novel pricing strategies. White House research (Newsroom, 2025) indicates that many corporations use big data for targeted marketing, with some investigating customized pricing, while occurrences of tailored pricing remain relatively few. The research emphasizes that the increasing availability of behavioral data is driving a shift from price discrimination based on general demographic groups to more individualized pricing methods. To elucidate this process, corporations categorize consumers into subgroups of analogous, price-sensitive people who possess shared biases and degrees of willpower. Pricing algorithms may use data on the reactions of others inside your group to forecast your probable behavior. respond in analogous conditions. This facilitates the algorithm's ability to more precisely estimate the user's reservation fee, monitor behavior, and adapt appropriately.

Companies use Big Data, advanced analytics, and machine learning to enhance their algorithms for optimizing customer behavior marketing, personalized promotions, and pricing strategies. A crucial element in this chain is the data broker, essentially a firm that aggregates information on behalf of other enterprises. The FTC said that one data broker's database has information on 1.4 billion customer transactions and over 700 billion aggregated data items. The FTC further discovered that only a limited number of data brokers (Federal Trade Commission, 2014) transform their assessments into marketing scores that evaluate clients' consumers based on their likelihood to react to certain marketing initiatives, make online purchases, exert influence over others, or other measures. It is essential to recognize that behavioral discrimination encompasses not only the categorization or segmentation of individuals for differential pricing but also the manipulation of consumer behavior to induce purchases of unnecessary or previously unconsidered items. This dimension of behavioral discrimination necessitates the utilization of big data to assess and capitalize on our emotional desires. Practices include price discrimination, reciprocity, decoy utilization, price guiding, and drip pricing.

Price and the sense of scarcity significantly influence the dynamics of persuasion. Such strategies of behavioral discrimination prevent buyers from discerning the true market pricing of the items or services available to them, (Shafir, 2018). Numerous customers see themselves as deceived and unjustly treated by such pricing discrimination. In this context, corporations disguise the discrimination not as some consumers paying more, but rather as others receiving a discount. Given the extensive hours dedicated to mobile devices, tablets, computers, and other smart gadgets, the predominantly passive data collected is analyzed to discern consumer interests and price sensitivity, enabling companies to strategically time their marketing efforts to encourage purchases at optimal prices. In data mining and profit maximization, the more the information available to firms, the more accurate the pricing algorithms can forecast behaviors and preferences, leading to enhanced behavioral discrimination.

DIGITAL PLATFORMS FOR SERVICES REMUNERATED VIA PERSONAL INFORMATION

The digital platform is saturated with websites and applications that allow users to access the seller's services simply by signing in with their email addresses or clicking 'I Agree' to the displayed terms and conditions, thereby granting the application permission to access their information, which facilitates behavioral discrimination under the pretense of enhanced services. In the majority of applications on big platforms like Google Play Store and Apple's iOS App Store, Utilization of the application's services is contingent upon our consent to provide access to all requested information, (Union, 2025). When a corporation adopts customized pricing online, it may use a diverse range of data sources, including several forms of information:

- Customers may willingly and consciously disclose information, for instance, while establishing a customer account for a prior transaction. This facilitates identification for future logins. Customer-provided data may include personal information, such name, address, and date of birth, as well as commercially relevant characteristics such as credit card type, previous transactions, wish lists, or gender.
- Information may also be acquired involuntarily and without the customer's knowledge. An online retailer may recognize a customer by their IP address or a unique identifier included in a cookie, (Nguyen, 2021). An IP address may disclose the user's nation, region, and internet service provider. Additionally, information on the kind of internet connection (mobile or fixed) and its speed, together with browser or machine characteristics, may be obtained.
- A notable category encompasses data obtained from third parties, such advertising networks, or collected via monitoring a customer's online behavior via associated ad networks or websites. Ad networks may identify internet users as they navigate websites and create profiles based on their behavior via the use of cookies or analogous technology. Consequently, when people access an online shop, pricing may be modified according to these profiles.

The data obtained from these sources, especially the latter two categories, may be used to infer income, age, and social position, hence offering insights into a website visitor's willingness to pay, (Zuboff, 2019).

As consumers, we may be unaware of the degree to which we are subjected to behavioral discrimination. due to marketplaces often demonstrating insufficient **'customer participation.'** The aforementioned method of data collecting presents us with the following unresolved difficulties for the customers, (Council (EU), 2023):

- Who has been gathering information about us?
- The recipients of our personal data;
- The alternative prospective recipients of our personal data;
- The characteristics of the personal data gathered about us;
- The categories in which we are classified;

- The methods used for the collection of our personal data;
- The caliber of facts and the conclusions drawn on our probable behavior;
- What choices, if any, do we possess to regulate the use of the data?

PRIVACY PROTECTION AS A NON-MONETARY CRITERION

Because of this, it is very important for companies to always protect the privacy of their clients, no matter what. This is a must-have that has to be given the most attention. This is why this is the case: in the past several years, the information that businesses acquire about their consumers has gotten more and more valuable. This is why this is the case. It is possible that this particular outcome is connected to how something happens. This is because the information that companies collect about their clients has grown increasingly important over the last several years. This is why things are the way they are. This is because the information that companies collect about their clients has grown increasingly crucial over the last several years. This is the reason why this development has happened. This is why things are the way they are. This is why things happen the way they do. The people in charge of competition can think that privacy issues are separate from their worries about competitiveness. This is something that may happen in a competitive situation. Some opponents 'may' Basin argue engages in this/base this Eyes. In terms of competitiveness, this may be seen as something that is possible. In terms of competitiveness, one can say that this is something that might be looked at. This is something that could be important. In terms of competitiveness, one might say that this is something that could be explored. This is something that may be true. This may be the subject of further inquiry and analysis. This piece of knowledge might be important to the discourse that is going on right now. If all of the things that have been looked at are taken into account, it is possible that this may happen. This might happen. This might happen. The European Commission is worried that Facebook may break WhatsApp's privacy rules and start using WhatsApp users' personal data since Facebook and WhatsApp are combining. This worry comes from the fact that Facebook and WhatsApp are presently combining. It is a direct effect of the merger that took place between the two corporations that issues such as these have emerged. This issue came to light because of the combination between Facebook and WhatsApp. This worry was made known to everyone immediately after the deal was made, and it was made known to everyone shortly after the acquisition was made. The merger was the event that first brought this dilemma to light, and it was also the event that made it possible to talk about it. The merger was the only thing that came close to bringing this issue to light. During the course of the meeting, it was brought up that this subject was handled, having into mind the fact that Facebook and WhatsApp have joined into a single entity, which is now known as Facebook and WhatsApp. Because it is now being looked at, this notion is being looked at because Facebook and WhatsApp have merged. Additionally, it is being taken into consideration in light of the fact that it is attracting attention. The European Commission has given this advise as a guideline for advocating for anything that would be of interest to the broader public. They are trying to get others to care about the issue they are presently fighting for by using this idea. The European Commission has made a case that is similar to the one that was made in the past because of the merger. This line of reasoning offers a compelling rationale, suggesting that Facebook would likely act in this manner as a direct result of the merger. This is a pretty good point. This argument gives a reasonable explanation for what is happening. These two lines of thought and this argument show that the European Commission is right in its judgment. This line of argument shows that the European Commission is acting within its powers. In light of the facts, it is clear that the individual is solely responsible for making this choice at their own discretion. This duty is solely the individual's. The person who is responsible for this burden is the one who is responsible for it. They are the ones that caused the difficulty that has come up because of what has happened around the scenario. They are the ones that caused the crisis we are in now, and their activities have led to this scenario. Ultimately, the Commission determined that it would be more advantageous to focus mostly on advertisements rather than on persons. The Commission thought about this a lot before coming to its judgment. They came to the conclusion that this was the case. After a lot of discussion, the Commission decided that this proposal should be accepted. This alternative was thought of as a possible replacement so that it may take the place of the other option that they had looked at before. The issue of data concentration was the only thing that the Commission thought about at all when it was making its decision. This was the only thing that was actually thought about. This particular trait was the only consideration, with no other factors being acknowledged at any time. The goal of this option was to improve Facebook's standing in the online advertising industry or in certain sub-segments of that market. People thought Facebook would be able to do this, and the choice was made with that goal in mind. This option was taken very intentionally with the purpose of concurrently enhancing Facebook's position in either of these two companies. When making this choice, this goal was kept in mind. You should know that the Commission didn't think about the issue of data concentration as much as it did in every other instance, except for this one exceptional example. You should know about this. In terms of breaching the rule, this is the solitary case that has ever occurred for this specific circumstance. One of the things that has happened because of this is that the Commission is now focused on the market that is thought to be the largest in the world. This is what has happened because of this. You might also say it the same way the Commission has kept its promises in the past. This is a different way to do things. The other side of the coin is that this is something that may take happen. Considering all of these reasons, it is also possible that this will happen. The particular challenge that has emerged from the situation is a direct effect of the circumstances. This specific problem has come up because of the scenario. This specific hurdle has developed because of the situation and the places concerned. As a consequence, it is clear that this situation has come to light because of what has happened in the past. The Commission is looking into whether data concentration has happened, which is why this is happening. This is because the Commission is the one in charge of the investigation. People are becoming more aware of problems with people's privacy since there is more and more data that is covered by EU competition law and EU data protection law. This is because the EU has the power to enforce competition legislation. These fears have come up because people are worried about privacy. This outcome may have happened because the EU has power over the competition legislation that is in force in the EU. These problems have come to light because people are worried about their privacy. The European Union (EU) has the power to make decisions on competition law in the EU, which may have something to do with this finding. This is something that may happen. People have been worried about the safety of their personal information on the internet, which is why these problems have become so important. It is highly likely that this result is related to the fact that the European Union (EU) is in charge of the competition laws that are in place in the EU. This conclusion is linked to the EU's authority over the law. This is something that might happen because of the circumstances that led to this scenario. The worries about the safety of personal information stored online have pushed these problems to the forefront. This is a direct result of people using the internet to express their concerns. Even while the merger doesn't guarantee that customers would still benefit from the free program, there are other privacy concerns that don't harm our clients' health. These difficulties have nothing to do with the planned merger of the two companies. The next few paragraphs talk about these themes in more detail than the ones that came before them. There is no connection between these problems and the concept that the program will help customers in any way. There is no link at all. This statement not only includes detailed explanations of these reasons for concern, but it also breaks out the parts that are causing the issue. But just because we have access to competitive markets doesn't mean that we will always get outcomes that are good for our health. This is due to the many elements that may jeopardize our health. This is the opposite side of the coin. We can't guarantee that we would always have great outcomes, even if we do get into these markets. Because this is the case, we can't do anything to stop things from happening. This is the scenario we're in since we can't make such a commitment with any level of accuracy. We need to keep this in mind right now because it will help us in many ways that we need to pay attention to and think about once we do. This is something we need to think about all the time and pay attention to all the time. Because of the nature of this issue, it is very important that we should not overlook the necessity of considering the relevance of this behavior. We need to keep this information in mind so that we can keep our pledge. We have to deal with this situation in the right way. People may be concerned about protecting their privacy when it comes to things that aren't directly related to their money situation, including the quality of the goods and services they are getting. This is because these things don't have anything to do with how much money someone has. This is because they don't have anything to do with the person's financial situation right away. This is because these kinds of traits don't have a direct link to a person's financial situation. These are the reasons why this is the case. This is because they don't have a direct link to the precise financial situation that a person is in. This is why things are the way they are. This is because qualities of this type do not instantaneously have a relationship to the whole financial situation of a person. This is why this is the case. This is how things are right now, as we spoke about before. This is the reason because they are not directly related to the person's current financial situation. This is why things are the way they are. This is why things happen the way they do. Due to the fact that the individual's financial status does not have a direct link to the types of difficulties that are being addressed in this context, this conclusion was made as a consequence of the fact that this context is being discussed. This was the reason why this information was found. The conclusion derived from this situation is that the outcome is a result of the components being indirectly tied to the price. This is the conclusion that follows from the previous statement since they are not directly related to the price. This specific effect will happen because of this specific effect, which is the outcome of these specific effects happening. On the other hand, there is a chance that the evidence provided before is what caused this disease to develop on its own.

The European Commission (EC) made the documents available to the public in connection with the merger that is now happening between Microsoft and LinkedIn. The merger is almost done, and it is currently in the process of being finished. There was a statement that was made public and sent out via a number of various media channels. Based on the study findings, it has been asserted that privacy concerns may be considered an element of non-price competition in the context of merger assessments. The research concluded that privacy problems are important, which is why this is the case. This is still the case, even though the laws that safeguard data are the ones that deal with issues of personal privacy. The legislation deals with problems with protecting a person's privacy, which is why this is the case. This is why this is happening. Even if the rule is about protecting data, the fact that this is happening today doesn't alter the fact that it is a reality. Still, this is the condition that continues to exist, even if the law deals with certain problems all the time. This is what is going on. This circumstance occurs because the law requires people to make sure that their personal information is always kept private. This is why this situation occurs. This is why things happen the way they do. The purpose of this statement is to convey further information about what has happened. Even though the legislation is supposed to safeguard people's private information, this awful event nevertheless happened. The statement above was made in conjunction with the purchase that happened as a result of the merger between Microsoft and LinkedIn. It was in the year 2010 that the merger took place, which was the year that it took place. When making this choice, both the merger's qualities and the circumstances that were present at the time were taken into account. This paragraph has further details on what was spoken earlier. This information was supplied in this paragraph. Someone utilized this material in a presentation. In the case where customers were led to believe that their concerns about their privacy had a big effect on the quality of the service they received, which is clearly true given the circumstances surrounding the problem, this is completely true. Customers' trust in service providers will ultimately fade if firms keep treating people unfairly depending on how they manage their business, whether it's the items or services they provide. This would be true no matter what the discriminatory practices are based on, whether it's the goods or services they provide. This is owing to the fact that discriminatory practices are embedded in the culture of the institution in which they are practiced. This is due to the fact that discriminatory behaviors harm the faith that consumers have in firms that provide services. This is because discriminatory tactics are dependent on how a firm does its business, which is why this is the case. This is the case since discriminatory behaviors rely on how they manage their business. This is the condition that has come about since the actions in issue are what decide how the goods or services behave. This situation has come about because they are in charge of determining what to do. The reason for this occurring is that clients are more inclined to think that service providers are biased because of this. This occurrence may have a variety of various reasons, one of which is that customers are more likely to have this attitude than other consumers. This is why this occurrence happened. This is why it happened. This incident is likely the cause of this phenomena, which is exactly what has been responsible for it. really Rein ape this. On the other hand, internet marketplaces may do their jobs in a manner that is both effective and exciting, which is different from conventional markets. This is because it's important for people to trust businesses and how they manage their private information. This is the reason why this is true. This is why things happen the way they do. This is the case because customers may choose to do things that are both fun and good for them. Online marketplaces have a hard time meeting their promises if they don't have the trust that is important for their business. Specifically, this is owing to the fact that trust is important to the operation of online marketplaces. This is because companies handle data in a manner that people have to trust. This is why things are the way they are. This particular illness may have happened because of this particular reason. So, things happen the way they do. This is what happened because of this. This is the exact reason why the events that happened happened. Because of this, the health problems caused by deadweight will be much worse than they were before. This is due of the reasons given above. You may explain this by talking about the things that were spoken about earlier. We may use the parts that were spoken about previously in the conversation to help us understand this occurrence. To explain this phenomena, we may look back to the parts of the discussion that we spoke about before. This is something that could be done. It is important for organizations that are in charge of competition to always keep people's privacy in mind while they are looking at things that are important for competition. This is because protecting privacy is very important for staying competitive. This is also very important since the investigations are now going on. To be regarded successful, a set of conditions must be met. There is also an important necessity that must be in addition to it. The next several paragraphs will explain what people expect from them. People think that these are the kinds of things that are required of them. Competition happens because something has already happened, which is why this situation has led to this outcome. This is the case because competition is an outcome of the event that has already happened. This particular conclusion is a direct result of this particular situation, which has led to this particular finish. This law would mean that organizations who handle a lot of information that is important to their clients would have to follow it. This is because they have to cope with a lot of information. This is the explanation that might be offered, supposing that this is the case. The next sentence in the text explains what would happen as a direct result of this. The line that follows this one is the one that is examined here. If this were to happen, this is what would happen, and the next several lines explain what that would be. This is what would happen. Both of them would reduce the amount of discrimination that happens because of someone's actions and completely ban exploitative activities and other activities that leave people out in the digital economy. This would be true since it would make discrimination less harmful. If it were feasible to put this idea into action, both of these things would happen as a direct consequence. The occurrence of either of these two events would be the consequence of this particular scenario, which would be the outcome of this that would be the conclusion of this.

CONCERNS OVER COMPETITION IN THE DIGITAL ECONOMY STEMMING FROM BEHAVIORAL DISCRIMINATION

Because of this, it is very important for the industry to work toward creating a full set of rules as soon as it can. This is because the chances of this occurring are becoming lower. The reason for this is because the digital economy is increasing at a very high pace, which is the justification behind this. You can't say enough about how important this is. One reason for this is that the market for digital products and services is growing at a rate that is quicker than ever before. Because of what's going on right now, this is the most important issue. It is a little hard to explain how important it is to have this information when it comes to its worth. Three guidelines that may be used to help create a good place for conducting business on the internet. Using these concepts might be a way to help those who need it. It is possible that these laws will be made by the government. These suggestions might be utilized to help, which would make it much simpler to create an environment that is both successful and efficient. This group has to think about three laws that are under their jurisdiction. These kind of law has a number of different rules. For instance, the Competition Law, the Data Protection Law, and the Consumer Protection Law are all examples of these kinds of legislation. The three laws that have been enacted are all related to each other. These three guiding principles not only have a big influence on how activities are managed, but they also have a big effect on the processes that lead to the development of a strong online market and help that market grow. In other words, they have a big impact on both the activities and the processes. In other words, they have a big effect on the processes that are being spoken about in regard to the activities. These limits, on the other hand, have a big effect on the activities that are being planned at the same time. These limitations also have a big effect on the activities that are being looked at right now, along with the ones that were already spoken about. When we talk about "laws," we mean the rules that the government agency in charge of the laws is presently thinking about. The word "laws" is used instead of any other word to help achieve the aim of defining these provisions. This is true for every time we use the word "laws." The Data Protection Law and the Consumer Protection Law are two examples of laws that have been made after the first ones. Both of these rules protect the client. The most important thing to point out about these two laws is that they are both examples of additional laws. There have been more laws passed, and two of the new laws are examples of these developments. There have been additional laws passed, and two of the new laws that have been passed show how these changes have been made. The two laws being spoken about here are both examples of laws that the legal system recognizes but doesn't have to follow. Here, we are talking about both of these laws. These precise kinds of laws are often the ones that are being questioned. In addition, the legislative branch has allowed a large number of additional bills to go on to the next step on the parliamentary calendar. Because of this, there is another law that has to be passed. There are enormous effects that happen when knowledge is shared, and these effects have a major effect on the situation that is happening right now. People are sharing information. These consequences include, among other things, the need to explain basic ideas like quality and trust, market power, market domination, and the need to think about the well-being of each consumer. In all of the circumstances we spoke about before, it doesn't matter whether the transmission is done actively or passively via internet services; this is true for both cases. To make matters worse, it is very important to remember that these consequences are very important to the understanding of basic ideas. This is something that has to be thought about. The outcome of this circumstance will have a big effect on the situation, no matter who gets the information. This is true no matter whether they acquire the knowledge or not. The effects that this condition will have will have a big effect on the effects that this condition will have. Because there are so many ways to share information effectively, it's impossible to overestimate how big these effects are. Because of this, it is hard to have an unduly optimistic view of how big these benefits are. Although the presence of diverse channels is a significant factor in this context, it is crucial to recognize that it represents just one of several variables. This is only one of the many factors that make this happen. This is due to a lot of other things as well. This is because the personal information of a person has become a valuable intangible asset for both the consumers and the merchants that are involved in the payment transaction. This is why things are the way they are. To provide a more extensive explanation, here is the precise reason why this situation is happening. This is why things happen the way they do. This is why things happen. Things happen the way they do because of this. This is what happened because of this. This is the exact reason why the events happened. Things happen the way they do because of this difficulty. This is what happened as a result of the circumstance. This is the consequence that comes about as a result of this. This particular cause led to the events that occurred, which is why they happened. This is the current scenario that has arisen due to the significant significance of personal information in our modern culture. This is the world we live in as a society right now. This is the situation that has come about as a result of the progress that has been made. This incidence has been made possible since this specific situation has been taken into consideration. This is why the things that happened happened.

Within the scope of the competitive environment, is there a condition that may be utilized as a benchmark against which to test and evaluate? If this is the case, how genuine is it, and does it really exist? In other words, does it actually exist? If we accept it exists, the next issue is: how much does it exist and how far does it go? When you think about the fact that it does exist, you also have to think about how long it will survive. Are there any conditions that may be seen as a baseline for the competitive environment? If so, what are some of these factors that can be used to evaluate the environment?

In addition to being one of the many traits that are linked to this kind of discrimination, it is also linked to a number of other traits that are linked to it at the same time. This is only one of the numerous traits that are linked to this kind of prejudice, so keep that in mind. This is only one of the numerous things that make it special. There are many more. This is only one of several traits that are linked to each other at the same time, however, there are a lot more aspects that are related to each other in addition to these. Behavioral discrimination is when businesses change their products and services to fit the needs of certain clients based on their preferences. This is one of the most important parts of behavioral discrimination. This is one of the most crucial things to know about behavioral discrimination. This is one of the most significant part of the approach that is being talked about right now. The particular attribute under scrutiny inside the framework is a critical element of the strategy being examined. There are many things that set this form of bias apart from others, one of which is the capacity to treat other people unfairly. This kind of bias has many unique traits, and the fact that this is only one of them is one of those traits. In addition to these elements, the definition of this kind of prejudice includes a number of additional characteristics. There are more and more products and services on the market these days, which makes it harder for customers and competitors to look at and evaluate all the options. This is the outcome of the fact that there are now more options available. One likely cause for this phenomenon is the existence of several choices or alternatives. This is one of the things that may explain it. Since there is no worldwide standard to use as a point of reference, this is what has happened since there isn't one. This is how things are right now. Because of this, there is no standard that can be used everywhere and put into practice at the same time. This is due to the absence of a generally applicable norm. At this moment in time, a lot of these products and services are being brought to the attention of the general public in their totality. Because of this, it is quite likely that new firms may have a harder time figuring out what an acceptable pricing structure is in order to make sure their enterprises are successful. This is because they are trying to get more clientele, which is the reason for this. This is because they will be working very hard to make sure their enterprises do well. This is the result of the fact that they are putting in a lot of work to make sure their businesses are successful all the way through the process. It shouldn't surprise anybody engaged that this is happening since the market is more competitive than it used to be for reasons that are clear. This is something that happened because of the "loss of competitive criteria," which means getting rid of situations that people think are competing with one other. This occurred because the competitive criteria were taken away. This is what happened because of the absence of competitive settings, which led to this predicament. It is probable that this incident happened because individuals have been competing with each other. This is because the things that are used to judge competitors are no longer being taken into account. This is the cause behind this. In light of this, this is the scenario. Because of this, the circumstance that has come about. This is because the things that are used to compare rivals are no longer being taken into account. This is the reason why this is the case. This is the situation that exists because of this. Because of this, this is what has happened as a direct consequence of the situation. The quick removal of the criteria used to judge how competitive a firm is in the market leads to this result, which is directly caused by the quick removal of those criteria. This particular rationale is directly accountable for the emergence of this outcome due to the aforementioned reason. This immediate influence, which has come about as a direct consequence of the deletion of the criterion, has directly resulted in the elimination of the criteria. The removal of the criterion, which in turn led to the speedy elimination of the criteria, has directly resulted in the deletion of the criteria. Also, when more and more online stores start using price discrimination that is almost perfect, it will be harder for buyers to compare the prices that are now accessible on the market with the many other options that are available to them. As more and more online stores are willing to charge different prices to different customers, the number of these stores is also growing. This is the reason why this happened in the first place. This is why things happen the way they do. This is because the prices that are now available on the market are always changing. To provide a better understanding, we need to talk about this issue in more depth. This is why things are the way they are. A lot of this may be because there are now a lot more suppliers doing business online. This is why things happen the way they do. Most people believe that both of these things are parts of the issue. If Amazon treats its customers unfairly, they can choose to buy from rival online stores like Flipkart and Snapdeal instead. This is because there is a chance that Amazon may do anything that displays prejudice. There is a big difference between this situation and one where Amazon doesn't take part in such an operation. If Amazon were to engage in such operations, the circumstances would mirror those previously described. At some time in the far future, it seems fairly certain that Amazon will be in a situation where it is at danger. When researching for a shop that is similar to the one you are presently looking for, you may find a lot of different businesses. At some time in the far future, Amazon is likely to be in a scenario where it is at danger of this. This might happen. It seems that this is an unavoidable scenario. Conversely, if all parties were engaged in the customization process, customers would be unable to assess the genuine competitive benchmark with the quality of the products and services being offered simultaneously. Customers would not be able to choose based on the right information if this happened. This would be the case since customers would not fully understand the circumstance. If all of the necessary stakeholders were to take part in the process, this is what would happen. It is conceivable that this may take place as a consequence of the fact that customers would be unable to receive information that is presented to them in an accurate way. If everyone was actively taking part in the event that they were all going to, then the scenario would be as described in the next few lines. They would find themselves in this situation since they couldn't compare the two. Because of this, they would be in a tough position. The reason for this would be as follows. This is exactly why they are in this difficult situation right now. This particular aspect of the company would be applicable to both the products offered for sale to consumers and the services provided to customers.

RECOMMENDATIONS

Given that marketplaces often exhibit several traits of a competitive landscape, action by competition authorities may seem paradoxical. The competitive façade and intellectual capture promoted by vested interests may hinder intervention. What is our current position? Critics of intervention often contend that antitrust legislation is not equipped for data-driven markets and that current mechanisms do not facilitate action. However, while considering such assertions, it is important to recognize that damage and market failure cannot be delineated by enforcement costs. Instead, upon identification, a variety of enforcement mechanisms should be contemplated, (Union, 2025b). The assertion that 'no prior case law authorizes intervention' neglects to account for the comprehensive enforcement toolkit and the evolution of market and competitive dynamics.

Intervention should not be unequivocally dismissed as irrelevant for the emerging dynamic market. Economic theories, based on hypothetical market assumptions, should not override the economic facts that demonstrate tangible damage.

Due to the absence of a thorough evaluation of the effect of Big Data and its use in behavioral discrimination within the digital economy, anticipating countermeasures is a challenging endeavor. Based on the preliminary evaluation and analysis of the available material, the researcher proposes the following recommendations for Competition authorities (Authority, 2022a) to recalibrate their conventional instruments and implement measures to address behavioral discrimination, (Monitor, 2013):

- Formulate a notion of consumer detriment, specifically regarding infringements of data protection rights, for the enforcement of competition in digital economic sectors.
- Market analyses and inquiries on complimentary services in the digital marketplace.
- Consumer involvement and empowerment.
- Enhance awareness among customers, service providers, and regulators of existing and prospective technical advancements in pertinent markets within the digital economy, as well as their implica-

tions for competitiveness, consumer welfare, choice, and innovation in privacy-enhancing services.

- Regulatory bodies must promote privacy as a competitive asset.
- Businesses must evaluate their data-driven models in light of the constantly increasing competition law norms.
- A cross-sectoral strategy is necessary to address privacy in competition regulation, alongside consumer protection regulations.
- Regulatory bodies provide compliance protocols for safeguarding privacy.

It is essential to acknowledge that in some markets, customers may perceive a privacy-conscious service as superior than one with an ambiguous or opaque privacy policy. In the delivery of legal and medical services, private banking, security services, and exclusive luxury resorts, enterprises often vie for the safeguarding of privacy. It is plausible to assert that, in highly competitive marketplaces, a company's failure to adhere to data protection standards would undermine its market power. To a far lesser degree, several internet search providers seek to distinguish themselves based on privacy considerations.

Encouraging a systematic assessment of privacy protections and consumer awareness, similar to the rise of corporate social and environmental responsibility, might be advanced via competition legislation. Companies within the European Union (EU) acknowledged the importance of the socio-economic impacts of their activities as early as the 1970s (European Union, 2018) and recognized their effect on consumer perception. Currently, they often evaluate their policies against those of rivals, cultivating an authentic market for product safety and environmentally sustainable innovations. An integrated approach for data security and competitiveness might possibly foster a similar level of competition in online businesses.

CONCLUSION

The impact of digitization on human life is indisputable. The increased use of Big Data, advanced analytics, and diverse algorithms is resulting in the exploitation of consumers' personal information for profit maximization, both with and without their agreement. A whole new competition guideline for the realm of big data and pricing discrimination is unnecessary. Competition law is not the exclusive remedy for the issue. Nonetheless, it serves a crucial function in maintaining equitable and accessible digital marketplaces. Unaddressed behavioral discrimination may result in unreported collusions and anti-competitive agreements among the companies possessing data engage in exploitative or discriminatory practices facilitated by dominating entities that control extensive consumer information via Big Data and Big Analytics. With the expansion of the digital economy, unregulated personalized marketing, client classification, and emotional manipulation to increase product and service purchases based on data exploitation will also escalate. The primary challenge for competition authorities is how to sustain effective competitiveness in a digital landscape characterized by diminished organic search results and increased customization of information sent to users. Although it seems that current ecommerce practices use customer data to improve efficiency, over time, the resulting inequities and mistrust will diminish consumer welfare.

Moreover, market dominance and concentration must be reevaluated with consideration for privacy protection to ensure comprehensive market development. This can only be accomplished if the CCI regards and assesses privacy protection as a fundamental component of competition evaluation for regulating anti-competitive acts under Sections 3, 4, and 5 of the Competition Act. A delicate equilibrium is necessary among data privacy, consumer protection, and competition legislation to ensure that enterprises' interests ultimately coincide with those of customers, therefore fostering digital competition.

REFERENCES

Authority, C. and M. (2022, March 25). *Online platforms and Digital Advertising Market Study, appendix C: Market outcomes 2020 (CMA)*. GOV. UK. https://www.gov.uk/find-digital-market-research/online-platforms-and-digital-advertising-market-study-appendix-c-market-outcomes-2020-cma

Company, M. (2016). *The age of analytics: Competing in a data driven world* - ... mgi the age of analytics full report.pdf. https://www.mckinsey.com/~/media/mckinsey/industries/public and social sector/our insights/ the age of analytics competing in a data driven world/mgi-the-age-of-analytics-full-report.pdf

Council (EU). E. (2023). *The General Data Protection Regulation - Consilium*. European Council Council of the European Union. https://www.consilium.europa.eu/en/policies/data-protection/data-protection-regulation/

Eldar Shafir, S. M. (2018, September 16). *Scarcity: Why having too little means so much*. Behavioral Scientist. https://behavioralscientist.org/scarcity-excerpt-mullainathan-shafir/

European Commission. (2014, October 3). *Mergers: Commission approves acquisition of WhatsApp by Facebook*. European Commission - European Commission. https://europa.eu/rapid/press-release_IP-14-1088_en.htm

European Union. (2018). *Com(2011)681 - renewed EU Strategy 2011-14 for Corporate Social Responsibility - Main Contents*. COM(2011)681 - Renewed EU strategy 2011-14 for Corporate Social Responsibility - EU monitor. https://www.eumonitor.eu/9353000/1/j4nvkkpftveemt7_j9vvik7m1c3gyxp/vitwrzhm31gk

Federal Trade Commission. (2014, May). *Data brokers: A call for transparency and Accountability*. DATA BROKERS A Call for Transparency and Accountability. https://www.ftc.gov/system/files/documents/reports/data-brokers-call-transparency-accountability-report-federal-trade-commission-may-2014/140527databrokerreport.pdf

Hill, K. (2024, February 20). *How target figured out a teen girl was pregnant before her father did.* Forbes. https://www.forbes.com/sites/kashmirhill/2012/02/16/how-target-figured-out-a-teen-girl-was-pregnant-before-her-father-did/

Monitor, E. (2013, February 6). *Com(2011)681 - renewed EU Strategy 2011-14 for Corporate Social Responsibility - Main Contents.* COM(2011)681 - Renewed EU strategy 2011-14 for Corporate Social Responsibility - EU monitor. https://www.eumonitor.eu/9353000/1/j4nvkkpftveemt7_j9vvik7m1c3gyxp/vitwrzhm31gk

Mullin, J., Lipton, B., Mir, R., Srago, M., & Guariglia, M. (2025). *Privacy.* Electronic Frontier Foundation. https://www.eff.org/issues/privacy

Newsroom. (2025). *Big News: Big data: Seizing opportunities, preserving values.* BIG News: Big Data: Seizing Opportunities, Preserving Values | Announce | University of Nebraska-Lincoln. https://newsroom.unl.edu/announce/bigdata/3919/21901

Nguyen, S. T. (2021, July 16). *Privacy and security enforcement.* Federal Trade Commission. https://www.ftc.gov/news-events/topics/protecting-consumer-privacy-security/privacy-security-enforcement

Union, E. (2016, December 6). *Mergers: Commission approves acquisition of LinkedIn by Microsoft, subject to conditions.* European Commission - European Commission. https://europa.eu/rapid/press-release_IP-16-4284_en.htm

Union, E. (2025a). *The Digital Services Act Package.* Shaping Europe's digital future. https://digital-strategy.ec.europa.eu/en/policies/digital-services-act-package

Union, E. (Ed.). (2025b, March 18). *Competition Policy.* Competition policy. https://ec.europa.eu/competition/general/data_protection_en.html

Zuboff, S. (2019). *The age of surveillance capitalism: The fight for a human future at the New Frontier of Power.* The Age of Surveillance Capitalism: The Fight for a Human Future at the New Frontier of Power - Book - Faculty & Research - Harvard Business School. https://www.hbs.edu/faculty/Pages/item.aspx?num=56791

Chapter 6
Building Trust in AI-Driven Organizations: A Strategic Approach to Ethical Management

Andi Asrifan
https://orcid.org/0000-0002-9934-6129
Universitas Negeri Makassar, Indonesia

ABSTRACT

Establishing trust in AI-driven businesses is crucial for guaranteeing the ethical, effective, and sustainable application of artificial intelligence. This chapter outlines a strategy methodology that incorporates governance frameworks, transparent system architecture, ethical leadership, stakeholder involvement, and adaptive risk management. It examines international frameworks, like the OECD Principles, IEEE standards, and the EU AI Act, in conjunction with pragmatic approaches such as explainability tools, fairness audits, and inclusive co-design. Focus is directed towards cultivating a culture of ethical consciousness, responding to public apprehensions, and predicting forthcoming challenges in generative AI, surveillance, and autonomy. By integrating innovation with human values and regulatory compliance, firms can bolster credibility, augment stakeholder loyalty, and establish AI as a reliable catalyst for sustained societal and organizational advancement.

DOI: 10.4018/979-8-3373-3114-0.ch006

1. INTRODUCTION

1.1 Conceptualizing Trust in Technological Contexts

Trust is a fundamental component in the adoption and efficient utilization of Artificial Intelligence (AI) within enterprises (Glikson & Woolley, 2022; Wang & Siau, 2023). In technical contexts, trust is defined as the readiness of individuals or organizations to depend on an AI system's decisions, actions, or recommendations, even amid uncertainty or inadequate information. In contrast to conventional tools, AI systems frequently function with a level of autonomy and intricacy, resulting in trust being influenced by various interconnected dimensions—psychological, organizational, and societal (Li et al., 2021). Trust in AI, from a psychological standpoint, is shaped by views of competence, reliability, and compassion. Users are more inclined to trust AI systems when they perceive the technology as capable of executing tasks accurately, aligning with user interests, and demonstrating consistency over time. Cognitive variables, including perceived transparency and comprehensibility, are essential in mitigating the "black box" phenomenon that frequently undermines trust in AI (Long & Magerko, 2022).

At the organizational level, trust entails aligning AI implementation with the institution's ethical principles, operational objectives, and governance structures. Employees and decision-makers must be confident that AI implementation enhances rather than compromises human knowledge, organizational integrity, and accountability systems (Kahre et al., 2022). This necessitates explicit communication, inclusive design methodologies, and continuous education to enhance AI literacy among stakeholders.

In the societal context, trust encompasses not just direct users but also the wider public affected by AI-driven actions (Choung et al., 2023). Public trust is contingent upon views of equity, data privacy safeguards, and fair accessibility. Considering AI's capacity to impact economic prospects, social equity, and democratic systems, preserving public confidence necessitates commitment to ethical standards and regulatory adherence. By understanding trust in a multi-faceted manner, companies may tackle both the technological reliability of AI systems and the human and cultural elements that influence their enduring acceptance and legitimacy.

1.2 Principles of Ethical AI

Ethical Artificial Intelligence (AI) is based on a framework of principles that guarantee the technology benefits humanity while reducing potential harm (Jobin & Mann, 2023; Mhlanga, 2023). Key concepts include justice, openness, accountability, and explainability—each vital for fostering confidence in AI-driven enterprises. Equity necessitates that AI systems function devoid of unjust bias or discrimination. Algorithms, by learning from historical data, may unintentionally reproduce or exacerbate socioeconomic imbalances. Designing ethical AI necessitates broad and representative datasets, routine bias assessments, and the incorporation of various perspectives during development to foster equity across ethnic, cultural, and socio-economic dimensions (Mehrabi et al., 2022).

Transparency denotes the clarity with which AI methods, data sources, and decision-making criteria are conveyed. Transparent AI enables stakeholders—employees, clients, and regulators—to comprehend the system's operations, so promoting informed consent and enhancing confidence (Anjomshoae et al., 2022). This encompasses explicit disclosures regarding limitations, hazards, and intended applications of the technology. Accountability guarantees that human agents retain responsibility for AI results. Ethical governance systems establish distinct lines of accountability, clarifying who is responsible for decisions made with AI assistance (Mittelstadt, 2021). This principle dissuades the relinquishment of responsibility to algorithms and promotes oversight measures, like ethics boards and audit trails, to immediately remedy possible harms.

Explainability enhances transparency by offering understandable justifications for AI-generated decisions. Transparency elucidates the functioning of a system, whereas explainability clarifies the rationale behind a particular choice or conclusion. Methods from Explainable AI (XAI) seek to convert intricate algorithmic thinking into comprehensible representations, facilitating substantive communication among system developers, users, and stakeholders. By incorporating these principles into the design, implementation, and oversight of AI systems, organizations can progress beyond mere compliance to foster lasting trust. Ethical AI is not just a technical goal but a strategic necessity that protects business reputation, boosts stakeholder trust, and connects technological advancement with social ideals.

1.3 The Role of Trust in Organizational Success

Trust is widely acknowledged as a strategic asset in firms implementing Artificial Intelligence (AI) (Bag, 2021; Marikyan et al., 2022). Empirical study indicates that stakeholder trust, including employees, consumers, investors, and regulators, profoundly affects the effectiveness of AI implementation. When stakeholders perceive AI systems as dependable, equitable, and ethically aligned, they are more inclined to embrace, utilize, and promote these technologies, hence expediting adoption and enhancing their advantages. In the context of AI adoption, trust mitigates resistance to change by assuaging concerns over job displacement, privacy violations, or inequitable decision-making (Dwivedi et al., 2023). Research demonstrates that businesses characterized by elevated trust levels among employees facilitate the seamless integration of AI into workflows, as personnel exhibit a greater willingness to interact with AI technologies and adjust to novel processes. This preparedness can expedite the technology adoption curve and enhance return on investment. In the context of innovation, trust cultivates an atmosphere conducive to experimentation with AI. When stakeholders possess confidence in governance structures and ethical safeguards, they are more receptive to investigating innovative AI applications without apprehension of misuse or reputational harm (Jussupow et al., 2022). This favorable environment facilitates the collaboration of cross-functional teams in developing AI solutions, enhancing competitive advantage. Organizations seen as trustworthy in their AI operations benefit from enhanced brand loyalty, increased investor confidence, and favorable regulatory sentiment. Transparency in AI operations, along with the reliable provision of ethical outcomes, conveys integrity to the market. Conversely, violations of trust—such as examples of algorithmic prejudice or data misuse—may result in public outrage, financial detriment, and heightened regulatory oversight (Shrestha et al., 2021). Ultimately, confidence in AI is a quantifiable factor that enhances organizational resilience and growth. Incorporating trust-building strategies into AI strategy enables firms to enhance stakeholder connections, expedite technological innovation, and protect their long-term reputation in a progressively AI-driven economy.

2. GOVERNANCE FRAMEWORKS FOR ETHICAL AI MANAGEMENT

2.1 AI Governance Models and International Guidelines

Governance frameworks for Artificial Intelligence (AI) offer systematic methodologies to guarantee the responsible development and deployment of AI technology (Floridi & Cowls, 2022; Leslie, 2023). International recommendations from entities such as the Organisation for Economic Co-operation and Development (OECD), the Institute of Electrical and Electronics Engineers (IEEE), and the European Union AI Act have become significant references for ethical AI governance. The OECD Principles on AI highlight inclusive growth, human-centric values, transparency, robustness, and responsibility. These principles urge member states and organizations to implement AI policies that promote innovation while protecting human rights. They are deliberately expansive, facilitating adaptation across many legal and cultural situations (Jobin et al., 2021). The IEEE's Ethically Aligned Design provides a more technical and engineering-focused viewpoint. It emphasizes the integration of ethics into AI design processes via value-oriented development, bias reduction, and stakeholder engagement. This paradigm is especially beneficial for firms aiming to implement ethics within the system design phase (Vakkuri et al., 2023). The EU AI Act, presently one of the most extensive legislative initiatives, classifies AI applications by risk levels—from minimum to unacceptable—and enforces more stringent standards for high-risk systems. This encompasses obligatory conformance assessments, openness requirements, and human oversight stipulations (Veale & Borgesius, 2021). Although legally binding within the EU, its impact is global as multinational corporations conform to its criteria to secure market access. Organizations must convert overarching ideas into specific policies, practices, and measurements to align with these frameworks. This may involve forming internal AI ethical committees, doing frequent risk and compliance audits, and ensuring transparent communication with stakeholders. By using established governance frameworks and complying with international standards, firms mitigate legal and reputational risks while demonstrating their dedication to ethical innovation. This alignment enhances stakeholder trust and establishes the firm as a responsible leader in the advancing AI ecosystem.

2.2 Internal Governance Structures and Compliance Mechanisms

Efficient ethical AI governance necessitates strong internal frameworks and compliance systems to guarantee the implementation of principles in practice (Akgun et al., 2022; Kaminski & Malgieri, 2023). Board-level monitoring is essential for establishing strategic direction and enforcing accountability. Incorporating AI ethics into corporate governance charters enables boards to assess risks, endorse AI-related policies, and commit resources for efforts ensuring ethical compliance. This authoritative commitment indicates to all stakeholders that ethical AI is a strategic imperative, rather than a simply technical issue. Ethics review boards function as specialist advisory entities within organizations to assess AI initiatives before to and during their execution. Consisting of specialists in technology, law, ethics, and pertinent industry sectors, these boards evaluate potential social effects, discern bias hazards, and propose mitigation solutions (Floridi et al., 2022). Their efforts guarantee that AI initiatives receive thorough ethical evaluation, promoting a culture of accountability and inclusiveness in decision-making. AI audit systems provide an essential element of compliance. These systems offer systematic assessments of AI models, datasets, and operational procedures in relation to ethical and regulatory criteria (Raji et al., 2022). Audits may be internal, performed by specialized compliance teams, or external, utilizing independent third parties to augment credibility. Regular audits facilitate the identification of issues such as algorithmic drift, inadvertent bias, or non-compliance with data protection regulations, hence allowing for prompt corrective measures. For optimal functionality, these governance tools must be underpinned by explicit regulations, uniform reporting protocols, and educational initiatives to improve AI literacy within the firm

(Morley et al., 2021). Digital instruments for assessing AI performance and recording choices can enhance transparency and traceability. When board oversight, ethics review boards, and AI audit systems operate in concert, they create a holistic internal governance framework. This not only guarantees adherence to evolving standards but also fosters enduring trust among employees, customers, and regulators—establishing the firm as a responsible and progressive leader in AI.

2.3 Risk Assessment and Mitigation Strategies

Risk assessment is an essential process for the ethical and effective deployment of Artificial Intelligence (AI) systems (Leslie & Burr, 2021; Stahl et al., 2023). It entails the systematic identification, evaluation, and mitigation of possible vulnerabilities to equity, security, privacy, and organizational integrity. Considering AI's intricacy and potential for extensive consequences, ethical and operational concerns must be evaluated throughout the AI lifecycle—from design and training to deployment and continuous utilization. Risk identification commences with delineating the AI system's scope, data sources, stakeholders, and intended applications. This procedure ought to identify potential risks, such bias in training data, susceptibility to cyberattacks, or the improper use of results (Jobin & Mann, 2023). Scenario planning and stakeholder engagement can reveal latent dangers by integrating varied perspectives. Assessing risks necessitates ascertaining both the probability and probable consequences of each recognized risk. Organizations may utilize qualitative methodologies, including ethical effect assessments, in conjunction with quantitative tools, such as statistical bias identification and model performance benchmarking (Mökander et al., 2021). Risk matrices and scoring systems facilitate the prioritization of risks according to severity, so helping decision-makers to deploy resources efficiently. Mitigating risks entails executing specific tactics to diminish their probability or consequences. These may encompass bias correction methodologies, human-in-the-loop supervision for critical choices, data anonymization processes, and stringent cybersecurity precautions (Floridi et al., 2022). Continuous monitoring systems are crucial for identifying drift or unexpected repercussions over time, hence maintaining the efficacy of mitigating initiatives. Mitigation methods must be adaptable. As AI technologies advance, their corresponding dangers also vary, necessitating regular reevaluation and revisions to governance protocols. Recording all risk management activities improves transparency and facilitates adherence to regulatory obligations. Incorporating systematic risk assessment and mitigation into AI governance enables firms to protect against ethical violations and operational shortcomings. This proactive strategy safeguards stakeholders and enhances trust, facilitating responsible and sustainable AI adoption.

3. TRANSPARENT AND ACCOUNTABLE AI SYSTEMS

3.1 Explainability and Interpretability of AI Algorithms

Explainability and interpretability are fundamental to establishing trust in Artificial Intelligence (AI) systems (Adadi, 2021; Mohseni et al., 2021). Explainability pertains to rendering an AI system's decision-making process comprehensible to humans, whereas interpretability underscores the capacity to ascertain the impact of particular inputs on outputs. Collectively, they empower stakeholders to assess AI judgments, detect any inaccuracies, and guarantee conformity with ethical and legal norms. Contemporary AI systems, especially those utilizing deep learning, frequently function as "black boxes," rendering intricate internal processes inscrutable even to their creators. To tackle this difficulty, Explainable AI (XAI) strategies have arisen, providing approaches to enhance the transparency of AI behavior without compromising performance (Miller et al., 2021). Feature importance analysis determines the variables that most significantly impacted a decision, whereas local interpretable model-agnostic explanations (LIME) and SHapley Additive exPlanations (SHAP) offer comprehensible insights into particular predictions (Lundberg et al., 2020; Ribeiro et al., 2016). Visualization instruments, like decision trees, saliency maps for image identification, and partial dependence plots, augment interpretability by converting mathematical relationships into comprehensible formats (Barredo Arrieta et al., 2020). These tools can be customized for various audiences—technical teams may necessitate comprehensive model diagnostics, whilst end-users may require simplified, outcome-oriented explanations. Explainability facilitates regulatory compliance, particularly under frameworks like as the EU AI Act or GDPR, which mandate firms to furnish "meaningful information" regarding automated decision-making (Wachter et al., 2021). Furthermore, it is essential for bias detection, enabling developers and auditors to identify the origins of unjust or erroneous results. Organizations should embrace a "design-for-transparency" approach to incorporate explainability, integrating interpretability factors from the initial phases of creation. This entails choosing intrinsically interpretable models for critical applications, documenting model rationale, and educating stakeholders to comprehend explanations proficiently. By emphasizing explainability and interpretability, organizations may reconcile AI's technological intricacies with human trust, ensuring that judgments are both correct and comprehensible.

3.2 Data Integrity and Algorithmic Fairness

Data integrity and algorithmic fairness are essential pillars for constructing reliable Artificial Intelligence (AI) systems (Mehrabi et al., 2022; Sun et al., 2023). Data integrity denotes the precision, consistency, and dependability of data during its lifecycle, guaranteeing that AI models are developed and function on information that is comprehensive, safe, and untainted. High-quality data supports dependable outcomes, whereas compromised data may result in erroneous judgments and erode stakeholder trust (Batarseh & Freeman, 2021).

Algorithmic fairness concerns the mitigation of inequitable prejudice or discrimination in AI results. Bias may infiltrate a system via distorted training data, inequitable feature selection, or developer presuppositions. Mitigation commences with data diversity, guaranteeing that datasets encompass all pertinent demographic and contextual differences. This mitigates the potential of systemic prejudice, exemplified by models that excel for one demographic while underperform for others (Caton & Haas, 2023). Effective measures for bias mitigation encompass re-sampling underrepresented populations, re-weighting data instances, and employing fairness-aware machine learning methodologies that modify models to yield equitable results (Chouldechova & Roth, 2020). Continuous fairness audits—conducted prior to implementation and throughout operation—are crucial for identifying and rectifying developing inequalities over time.

Validation processes are crucial for ensuring both integrity and fairness. These protocols entail stringent evaluation of AI models using benchmark datasets, cross-validation to verify generalizability, and stress testing to evaluate performance under diverse scenarios (Feng et al., 2021). Third-party independent validation can significantly bolster confidence, particularly in critical sectors such as healthcare, finance, or law enforcement. Ensuring data accuracy and equity is an ongoing endeavor rather than a singular task. Organizations must implement governance measures, including data stewardship responsibilities, secure data pipelines, and regular audits, to maintain long-term adherence to ethical and legal norms. By integrating rigorous data integrity measures and fairness protections into the AI development process, firms may establish systems that produce precise, just, and reliable outcomes—enhancing both ethical accountability and competitive edge.

3.3 Mechanisms for Auditing and Redress

Auditing and redress methods are crucial for maintaining accountability in Artificial Intelligence (AI) systems throughout their lifecycle and for immediately addressing any resultant harms (Mökander et al., 2022; Raji et al., 2022). Auditing is a rigorous examination of AI models, data pipelines, and decision-making processes to verify adherence to ethical, legal, and operational norms. Redress denotes the mechanisms via which people or groups may contest AI-generated results and seek remedies (Binns, 2021).

Technical auditing techniques encompass algorithmic performance evaluation, bias identification instruments, and explainability analyses. Automated monitoring systems can assess critical parameters including accuracy, fairness, and drift, identifying abnormalities for further examination. Version control and model documentation, including model cards or datasheets for datasets, enhance transparency by systematically documenting changes, assumptions, and constraints throughout time (Mitchell et al., 2021). These technology solutions assist firms in detecting and addressing issues prior to their escalation into reputational or regulatory disasters. Procedural auditing techniques enhance technical evaluations by integrating responsibility inside governance frameworks. Independent ethical committees or third-party auditors can deliver impartial evaluations of AI systems (Floridi et al., 2022). Regular compliance assessments guarantee conformity with company policies, international standards, and relevant legislation, including the EU AI Act and industry-specific requirements.

Redress processes are essential for safeguarding stakeholders' rights. These may encompass user-friendly reporting mechanisms, ombudsman services, or formal appeals processes where AI decisions affect employment, credit, healthcare, or legal status (Kaminski & Malgieri, 2023). An effectively structured redress system should be accessible, transparent, and responsive, providing explicit timelines for resolution and the possibility for human review of disputed decisions. Integrating auditing and redress into AI governance establishes a feedback loop that identifies and rectifies issues while enhancing public trust. These approaches illustrate a dedication to ethical accountability, guaranteeing that AI-driven innovation adheres to social norms and regulatory requirements.

4. ORGANIZATIONAL CULTURE AND LEADERSHIP FOR AI ETHICS

4.1 Fostering a Culture of Ethical Awareness

Promoting a culture of ethical awareness is essential for aligning Artificial Intelligence (AI) activities with business principles and social expectations (Morley et al., 2021; Sambasivan et al., 2022). Ethical awareness in AI contexts denotes the collective capacity of employees to identify, assess, and respond to ethical dilemmas stemming from the design, implementation, and utilization of AI systems. Establishing such a culture necessitates intentional, organization-wide tactics that transcend mere technical compliance and foster collective accountability (Johnson et al., 2021). An successful technique involves integrating ethics into daily decision-making processes. Integrating ethical issues into project planning checklists, performance evaluations, and team conversations helps ensure that ethical thinking becomes a habitual aspect of AI development. Leadership ought to promote an environment where teams critically assess the justice, transparency, and societal implications of AI decisions, rather than concentrating exclusively on efficiency or profit (Borenstein et al., 2021).

Ethics training and awareness initiatives are essential in providing employees with the competencies to recognize and mitigate potential dangers. These programs may encompass scenario-based workshops, case study analyses, and interdisciplinary collaboration, allowing staff to foresee ethical challenges and engage in values-driven problem-solving (Loi et al., 2023). Establishing open channels for communication is of equal significance. Employees must be enabled to express ethical concerns without fear of retaliation, bolstered by whistleblower protections or anonymous reporting mechanisms. Promoting different viewpoints—spanning gender, cultural, and disciplinary boundaries—improves the organization's ability to identify blind spots in AI ethics (Coeckelbergh, 2021).

Ultimately, leadership modeling is essential. Leaders who constantly exhibit ethical integrity and emphasize the significance of responsible AI establish the standard for organizational conduct. Their activities underscore that ethical issues are essential to success, rather than discretionary. By cultivating a culture of ethical awareness, firms can guarantee that each AI effort is executed with both technical proficiency and moral accountability—enhancing trust, mitigating risks, and maintaining long-term stakeholder confidence.

4.2 Leadership and Ethical Stewardship in AI

Leadership is crucial in determining the adoption, governance, and perception of Artificial Intelligence (AI) within a business (Wilson et al., 2021; Karanasiou & Pinotsis, 2023). Ethical stewardship in AI necessitates that leaders establish a definitive tone, convey a long-term vision, and delineate explicit ethical standards for the utilization of developing technologies. When executives actively advocate for responsible AI, they indicate that ethics is a primary focus rather than a peripheral concern in business strategy (Morley et al., 2021).

Establishing the tone commences with evident dedication. Leaders must continually emphasize the significance of connecting AI activities with fundamental values such as fairness, accountability, and openness

(Stix, 2021). Publicly adopting ethical rules, partaking in ethics training, and engaging in open debates regarding AI dangers exemplify honesty and bolster confidence among employees and stakeholders. Vision-setting entails incorporating ethical AI goals into the organization's overarching aim. This entails delineating the use of AI to further organizational objectives while safeguarding human dignity, data privacy, and social equality. A definitive vision guarantees that AI initiatives are not solely responsive to commercial trends but are strategically matched with enduring social advantages (Tolan et al., 2021).

Establishing expectations necessitates established policies, codes of behavior, and quantifiable performance metrics for ethical AI utilization. Leaders must ensure that these expectations are integrated into procurement processes, project governance, and vendor relationships, maintaining uniform high ethical standards for all parties involved. Ethical stewardship entails exemplifying principled decision-making. When faced with trade-offs between expediency and ethical integrity, leaders ought to select the course that preserves trust and adherence to regulations (Johnson, 2022). This strategy not only alleviates reputational and regulatory issues but also motivates teams to adopt ethical behaviors. Leaders establish the tone, articulate the vision, and uphold ethical standards, so serving as guardians of trust in AI—ensuring that technology functions as a catalyst for sustainable innovation and societal benefit.

4.3 Change Management and Employee Engagement

Successful integration of Artificial Intelligence (AI) inside a business necessitates not just technical implementation but also efficient change management and proactive employee involvement (Dwivedi et al., 2023; Raisch & Krakowski, 2021). Opposition to AI implementation frequently arises from apprehensions regarding job loss, insufficient comprehension, or worries about equity and privacy. Proactively addressing these concerns through inclusive engagement can cultivate trust, alleviate anxiety, and promote collaboration (Jussupow et al., 2022).

Change management commences with explicit communication. Leaders must clearly define the objectives of AI programs, the anticipated advantages, and the measures implemented to mitigate any hazards. Clarity regarding schedules, responsibilities, and decision-making procedures enables employees to feel informed rather than caught off guard. Engaging workers in initial discussions—via focus groups, polls, or experimental programs—affords them a sense of ownership and agency in the transition (Verma & Gustafsson, 2020).

Employee involvement entails enabling personnel to partake in the AI initiative. This involves providing specialized training to enhance AI literacy, allowing employees to comprehend the functionality of AI and its implications for their responsibilities. Employees possessing the requisite skills and expertise to collaborate with AI are more inclined to perceive it as an augmentation of their jobs rather than a menace (Sturm et al., 2021). Inclusive engagement entails attentively considering employee issues and incorporating feedback into the design and policy decisions of AI. Establishing feedback mechanisms—such as open forums, digital suggestion platforms, or ethics committees with employee representation—guarantees that many perspectives influence AI adoption (Hengstler et al., 2021).

Recognition and reward mechanisms can enhance motivation for involvement. Honoring teams or individuals who promote ethical and innovative AI utilization fosters commendable conduct and indicates that responsible implementation is esteemed. Organizations can effectively manage AI-driven transformation by integrating structured change management with significant employee engagement, so fostering trust, improving morale, and optimizing the prospects for successful and ethical integration. This inclusive strategy converts AI from a disruptive element into a collective potential for advancement.

5. STAKEHOLDER ENGAGEMENT AND PUBLIC TRUST

5.1 Engaging Users, Clients, and Affected Communities

Establishing confidence in Artificial Intelligence (AI) necessitates the active engagement of individuals directly or indirectly influenced by its application—users, clients, and impacted communities (Duan et al., 2023; Bietti et al., 2021). Engagement is most effective when it transcends unilateral communication, advancing towards co-design, participatory ethics, and inclusive discussion that empower stakeholders to influence AI systems from inception to deployment. Co-design entails cooperating with stakeholders throughout the AI development process to guarantee that systems meet genuine demands and embody the values of the populations they serve (Leong et al., 2022). This may encompass workshops with end-users to enhance features, talks with community leaders to ascertain ethical hazards, or pilot programs enabling stakeholders to evaluate and offer input prior to full implementation. Participatory ethics incorporates varied perspectives into the decision-making process on the moral and societal ramifications of AI (Prunkl et al., 2021). This may entail establishing advisory committees with representatives from marginalized groups, industrial specialists, civil society organizations, and ethicists. These panels can assess proposed AI applications for fairness, inclusivity, and cultural sensitivity, ensuring that decisions are guided by many viewpoints rather than merely by technical feasibility. Engaging in inclusive stakeholder conversation is essential for sustaining trust over time. Open forums, town halls, and online engagement platforms facilitate ongoing bidirectional connection between organizations and the communities they serve. These platforms ought to promote inquiries, handle problems with transparency, and furnish updates on AI performance, hazards, and mitigation strategies. Engagement must be accessible, culturally attuned, and devoid of technical jargon to prevent the exclusion of non-expert individuals.

This inclusivity enhances AI design and functionality while bolstering public trust in the organization's dedication to ethical practices. Incorporating co-design, participatory ethics, and inclusive discourse into AI governance enables businesses to transition from passive acceptance to proactive trust-building, thereby transforming stakeholders into collaborators in the development of ethical, effective, and socially responsible AI systems.

5.2 Communication and Transparency Strategies

Effective communication and transparency are essential for establishing and maintaining confidence in Artificial Intelligence (AI) systems. Stakeholders—comprising users, clients, regulators, and the general public—require transparent, precise, and prompt information regarding an organization's AI objectives, functionalities, and possible effects (Dignum, 2022). In the absence of such transparency, even technically proficient AI initiatives may encounter skepticism or opposition. Developing trust-enhancing narratives commences with articulating the objectives of AI efforts in accessible language. Organizations should prioritize communicating how AI will address issues, enhance services, or generate value for stakeholders, rather than only emphasizing technical requirements (Shneiderman, 2022). This story must recognize potential risks and the precautions implemented to mitigate them, demonstrating transparency and accountability (Jobin & Mittelstadt, 2023).

Transparency necessitates the provision of accessible information regarding the functioning of AI systems, encompassing data sources, decision-making processes, and inherent limitations. Although complete technical disclosure may not be feasible for all audiences, elucidating explanations—via images, simplified language summaries, or interactive demonstrations—can render complicated systems comprehensible (Langer et al., 2021). These initiatives elucidate AI and diminish the notion of it as a "black box." Bidirectional communication routes hold equal significance. Stakeholders must to have the opportunity to pose inquiries, express concerns, and obtain prompt responses. Mechanisms like Q&A sessions, feedback portals, or public updates on AI performance and audits promote continuous discussion instead of isolated announcements. Uniformity across communication channels establishes credibility. Public remarks, marketing materials, and internal briefings must be consistent to prevent confusion or the impression of contradictory messages. This entails being candid with obstacles, postponements, or requisite modifications in AI implementation techniques. Ultimately, communication and transparency techniques must be maintained throughout the AI system's existence, not alone at its inception. Through the integration of transparent narratives, candid disclosure, and attentive listening, companies can foster informed trust, enabling stakeholders to engage confidently with AI-driven innovations.

5.3 Addressing Public Concerns and Perceptions

Public opinion research consistently indicates that, although many individuals acknowledge the potential advantages of Artificial Intelligence (AI), they simultaneously possess considerable apprehensions regarding job displacement, privacy erosion, algorithmic bias, insufficient transparency, and potential misuse (Pew Research Center, 2025; Brookings Institution, 2025). These fears are both technical and profoundly emotional, grounded in societal discussions regarding trust, equity, and control over technology. To proactively address these views, organizations must first engage in active listening. Surveys, focus groups, and social media analysis yield significant insights into public perceptions of AI, facilitating the development of focused solutions (Vesely & Kim, 2024). Educational and AI literacy programs are crucial for eliminating misconceptions. Public workshops, explanatory movies, and interactive demonstrations can elucidate the functioning of AI, the precautions implemented, and the areas where human oversight is paramount. This profound comprehension frequently converts worries into more sophisticated viewpoints (Scantamburlo et al., 2023).

Recognizing limitations and risks with transparency is crucial; minimizing obstacles may breed distrust. Organizations should transparently discuss biases, mistake rates, and strategies for mitigation. Disseminating findings from independent audits or ethical impact evaluations enhances credibility. Proactive involvement entails showcasing concrete advantages that correspond with public objectives, including increased healthcare access, superior education, or environmental sustainability—reconciling apprehension with empirical facts. Establishing responsive feedback mechanisms that allow consumers to express concerns and witness tangible follow-up activities transforms passive skepticism into proactive trust-building. By addressing public concerns with empathy, openness, and tangible action, enterprises may transform attitudes of AI from ambiguity to educated acceptance and productive collaboration.

6. CASE STUDIES AND FUTURE PATHWAYS FOR ETHICAL AI STRATEGY

6.1 Global Case Studies of Ethical AI Practices

Analyzing global case studies provides significant insights into the implementation of ethical concepts across many sectors. The Mayo Clinic has created the Platform_Validate tool, a validation solution that evaluates AI model bias concerning age, ethnicity, and socio-economic groups to improve explainability and clinician trust (Cerrato et al., 2022). The Monetary Authority of Singapore (MAS) initiated the Veritas initiative in the finance sector, creating the FEAT (Fairness, Ethics, Accountability, Transparency) assessment methodology and an open-source toolkit, which allows financial institutions to implement ethical AI through structured frameworks (MAS Veritas Consortium, 2023).

Finland's educational strategy for AI-enhanced learning prioritizes inclusive design and equity, incorporating participatory co-design with educators and students to guarantee that tailored learning upholds data privacy and learner autonomy (Sharma et al., 2023). From a governmental standpoint, Canada's Directive on Automated Decision-Making requires algorithmic impact assessments (AIAs) alongside independent peer evaluations, thereby fostering accountability and systematic risk appraisal in federal AI implementations (Attard-Frost, 2024). Healthcare, finance, education, and government exhibit shared characteristics: stakeholder participation, stringent governance, transparency, and continuous monitoring. They illustrate that ethical AI is feasible when technological advancement coincides with organized governance and inclusive design. Organizations can use these practices—explainability integration, fairness audits, participatory communication—as a framework for AI strategies that are both reliable and effective, fostering enduring societal and organizational value.

6.2 Emerging Trends and Ethical Dilemmas in AI

As Artificial Intelligence (AI) progresses, new technologies provide both potential and intricate ethical challenges. Generative AI, proficient in generating realistic text, graphics, audio, and video, has revolutionized creative sectors and productivity processes. Nonetheless, it creates apprehensions around misinformation, intellectual property violations, and the deterioration of confidence in digital content (Al-kfairy et al., 2024). Ensuring authenticity via watermarking, content provenance technologies, and explicit usage rules will be crucial to mitigate these dangers. AI-driven surveillance technologies, including facial recognition, behavioral analytics, and predictive policing, present prospective advantages for security and public safety. However, they also exacerbate concerns around mass surveillance, privacy infringements, and discriminatory targeting (Almasoud, 2024). Ethical dilemmas emerge when reconciling individual rights with group security, necessitating openness, legal protections, and community approval as essential elements of competent implementation. Progress in autonomous systems, such as self-driving vehicles, AI-operated drones, and automated decision-making tools, expands the limits of human-machine interaction. These technologies contest conventional concepts of accountability—if an autonomous car inflicts injury, who bears responsibility: the manufacturer, programmer, or operator? Resolving these difficulties necessitates explicit liability frameworks, comprehensive safety testing, and human monitoring for crucial decisions (Garikapati, 2024). Additional growing concerns encompass the environmental ramifications of extensive AI models, the digital divide resulting from disparate access to AI capabilities, and the possibility of AI exacerbating geopolitical power disparities. Ethical governance must adapt to confront these issues promptly, underpinned by flexible legal frameworks and ongoing stakeholder involvement. The future of AI ethics ultimately depends on preemptively addressing issues to prevent their escalation into catastrophes. Incorporating foresight into AI planning enables firms to manage swift technical advancements while preserving human dignity, equity, and trust—ensuring that innovation aligns with society's enduring interests rather than jeopardizing them.

6.3 Strategic Roadmap for Building Long-Term AI Trust

Establishing enduring trust in Artificial Intelligence (AI) necessitates a strategic framework that incorporates ethics, innovation, and ongoing engagement throughout all phases of the AI lifecycle. This roadmap must be proactive, flexible to new technologies, and grounded in principles that protect human values while facilitating technology advancement (Reuel & Undheim, 2024). The initial pillar involves integrating ethics into the design process. Organizations must incorporate justice, transparency, accountability, and privacy considerations from the initial phases of AI development. This entails the formation of multidisciplinary ethics committees, the execution of algorithmic impact evaluations, and the integration of explainability into models to render decision-making processes comprehensible to stakeholders (Lu et al., 2022).

The second pillar is strong governance and adherence to regulations. Internal governance systems, including board-level monitoring, ethics review boards, and periodic AI audits, ought to be supplemented by adherence to international frameworks such as the OECD Principles on AI or the EU AI Act (Papagiannidis, 2025). The third pillar is engagement centered on stakeholders. Trust is enhanced when users, clients, and impacted communities participate in the design, testing, and assessment of AI systems. Transparent communication, participatory ethical processes, and accessible feedback and redress mechanisms convert stakeholders into active collaborators instead of passive beneficiaries of AI choices.

The fourth pillar is adaptive innovation. As AI technologies advance—especially in generative AI, autonomy, and surveillance—organizations must stay adaptable, foreseeing ethical challenges and revising rules, protections, and training programs as necessary. This adaptability guarantees resilience against technological hazards and evolving societal expectations. By adhering to this plan, organizations can progress from mere short-term compliance to fostering a culture of lasting trust. Combining ethics with innovation not only reduces risks but also improves competitive advantage, establishing AI as a reliable catalyst for sustainable advancement and societal benefit in the long term.

CONCLUSION

Trust is fundamental to effective AI implementation and enduring organizational resilience. The capacity of enterprises to integrate ethical concepts into their AI plans will dictate both operational efficacy and societal acceptability as AI technologies persist in transforming industries and redefining decision-making processes. Establishing trust in AI-driven environments necessitates a comprehensive strategy that incorporates governance frameworks, transparent system architecture, ethical leadership, stakeholder involvement, and proactive risk mitigation.

Fundamental to the trust-building process is the acknowledgment that ethics cannot be regarded only as a compliance checkbox. It must be integrated into the culture, vision, and daily operations of the organization. Clear communication, inclusive engagement, and accountability systems enhance credibility with employees, clients, regulators, and the general public. Moreover, technical features include explainability tools, fairness audits, and stringent data integrity procedures enhance the trustworthiness and integrity of AI systems.

Sustainable trust relies on the ability of organizations to foresee and tackle developing difficulties. Advancements like generative AI, autonomous decision-making, and AI-driven surveillance offer opportunities and ethical challenges that necessitate flexible governance and ongoing discourse with various stakeholders. By harmonizing innovation with human values, companies may circumvent the drawbacks of technical determinism and guarantee that AI benefits the public good.

Ultimately, faith in AI is not a fixed attainment but a continual obligation. It progresses by sustained ethical conduct, open administration, and cooperative resolution of issues. Organizations that effectively incorporate trust-building into their AI strategy will not only adhere to existing regulations but also establish benchmarks for responsible innovation—bolstering their reputation, augmenting stakeholder loyalty, and ensuring that AI serves as a catalyst for inclusive, equitable, and sustainable advancement. Thus, ethics and innovation are not antagonistic forces but rather complementing catalysts for sustained organizational success in the era of AI.

REFERENCES

Adadi, A. (2021). A survey on the interpretability of machine learning. *Artificial Intelligence Review*, *54*(1), 1–43. DOI: 10.1007/s10462-020-09836-5

Akgun, A. E., Keskin, H., & Byrne, J. (2022). Organizational governance of artificial intelligence: Ethics, oversight, and strategic alignment. *Technology in Society*, *70*, 102021. DOI: 10.1016/j.techsoc.2022.102021

Al-kfairy, M., Mustafa, D., Kshetri, N., Insiew, M., & Alfandi, O. (2024). Ethical challenges and solutions of generative AI: An interdisciplinary perspective. *Informatics (MDPI)*, *11*(3), 58. DOI: 10.3390/informatics11030058

Almasoud, A. S. (2024). Algorithmic fairness in predictive policing: A systematic review and bias mitigation of age-related disparities. *AI and Ethics*. Advance online publication. DOI: 10.1007/s43681-024-00541-3

Anjomshoae, S., Najjar, A., Calvaresi, D., & Främling, K. (2022). Explainable agents and robots: Results from a systematic literature review. *Autonomous Agents and Multi-Agent Systems*, *36*(1), 1–42. DOI: 10.1007/s10458-021-09537-0

Attard-Frost, B. (2024). The governance of artificial intelligence in Canada: The role of the Directive on Automated Decision-making. *Government Information Quarterly*. Advance online publication. DOI: 10.1016/j.giq.2024.101869

Bag, S. (2021). Trust in artificial intelligence: A review of trust building in AI and its implications. *Technology in Society*, *67*, 101740. DOI: 10.1016/j.techsoc.2021.101740

Barredo Arrieta, A., Díaz-Rodríguez, N., Del Ser, J., Bennetot, A., Tabik, S., Barbado, A., Garcia, S., Gil-Lopez, S., Molina, D., Benjamins, R., Chatila, R., & Herrera, F. (2020). Explainable Artificial Intelligence (XAI): Concepts, taxonomies, opportunities and challenges toward responsible AI. *Information Fusion*, *58*, 82–115. DOI: 10.1016/j.inffus.2019.12.012

Batarseh, F. A., & Freeman, L. A. (2021). Data veracity: Exploring the reliability dimension of big data. *Journal of Big Data*, *8*(1), 1–25. DOI: 10.1186/s40537-021-00467-0

Bietti, E., Saxena, N. A., & Livio, G. (2021). From ethics washing to ethics bashing: A view on tech ethics from within moral philosophy. *Minds and Machines*, *31*(4), 595–619. DOI: 10.1007/s11023-021-09579-3

Binns, R. (2021). On the apparent conflict between individual and group fairness. *ACM Conference on Fairness, Accountability, and Transparency*, *3*(1), 514–524. DOI: 10.1145/3442188.3445896

Borenstein, J., Howard, A., & Miller, K. W. (2021). The role of organizational culture in ethical AI. *AI and Ethics*, *1*(4), 431–438. DOI: 10.1007/s43681-021-00048-5

Brookings Institution. (2025, April 9). *What the public thinks about AI and the implications for governance*. Brookings. https://doi.org/DOI: 10.3416/pub-think-ai-2025

Caton, S., & Haas, C. (2023). Fairness in machine learning: A survey. *ACM Computing Surveys*, *55*(13s), 1–37. DOI: 10.1145/3597199

Cerrato, P.. (2022). A proposal for developing a platform that evaluates algorithmic biases in healthcare AI. *PLOS Digital Health*. Advance online publication. DOI: 10.1371/journal.pdig.0000651

Chouldechova, A., & Roth, A. (2020). A snapshot of the frontiers of fairness in machine learning. *Communications of the ACM*, *63*(5), 82–89. DOI: 10.1145/3376898

Choung, H., David, P., & Seberger, J. S. (2023). A multilevel framework for AI governance: Cultivating trust across individual, organizational, and societal levels. *AI and Ethics*, *3*(2), 285–298. DOI: 10.1007/s43681-023-00269-9

Coeckelbergh, M. (2021). AI ethics. *The MIT Press Essential Knowledge Series*. https://doi.org/DOI: 10.7551/mitpress/12433.001.0001

Dignum, V. (2022). The role of communication in building trust in AI systems. *AI and Ethics*, *2*(3), 421–432. DOI: 10.1007/s43681-021-00084-6

Duan, Y., Edwards, J. S., & Dwivedi, Y. K. (2023). Artificial intelligence for decision making in the era of Big Data—Evolution, challenges and research agenda. *International Journal of Information Management, 71*, 102642. DOI: 10.1016/j.ijinfomgt.2023.102642

Dwivedi, Y. K., Hughes, L., Baabdullah, A. M., Ribeiro-Navarrete, S., Giannakis, M., Al-Debei, M. M., & Wamba, S. F. (2023). Metaverse beyond the hype: Multidisciplinary perspectives on emerging challenges, opportunities, and agenda for research, practice and policy. *International Journal of Information Management, 71*, 102642. DOI: 10.1016/j.ijinfomgt.2023.102642

Dwivedi, Y. K., Hughes, L., Baabdullah, A. M., Ribeiro-Navarrete, S., Giannakis, M., Al-Debei, M. M., & Wamba, S. F. (2023). Metaverse beyond the hype: Multidisciplinary perspectives on emerging challenges, opportunities, and agenda for research, practice and policy. *International Journal of Information Management, 71*, 102642. DOI: 10.1016/j.ijinfomgt.2023.102642

Feng, J., Luo, C., & Li, B. (2021). A review of fairness-aware machine learning for responsible AI. *IEEE Transactions on Knowledge and Data Engineering, 35*(1), 1–20. DOI: 10.1109/TKDE.2021.3077524

Floridi, L., & Cowls, J. (2022). A unified framework of five principles for AI in society. *Harvard Data Science Review, 4*(1). Advance online publication. DOI: 10.1162/99608f92.e8fbcf64

Floridi, L., Cowls, J., Beltrametti, M., Chatila, R., Chazerand, P., Dignum, V., & Vayena, E. (2022). An ethical framework for a good AI society: Opportunities, risks, principles, and recommendations. *Minds and Machines, 32*(2), 217–240. DOI: 10.1007/s11023-021-09563-4

Floridi, L., Cowls, J., Beltrametti, M., Chatila, R., Chazerand, P., Dignum, V., & Vayena, E. (2022). An ethical framework for a good AI society: Opportunities, risks, principles, and recommendations. *Minds and Machines, 32*(2), 217–240. DOI: 10.1007/s11023-021-09563-4

Garikapati, D. (2024). Autonomous vehicles: Evolution of artificial intelligence in driving ethics and liability frameworks. *Big Data and Cognitive Computing, 8*(4), 42. DOI: 10.3390/bdcc8040042

Glikson, E., & Woolley, A. W. (2022). Human trust in artificial intelligence: Review of empirical research. *The Academy of Management Annals*, *16*(1), 1–45. DOI: 10.5465/annals.2019.0057

Hengstler, M., Enkel, E., & Duelli, S. (2021). Applied artificial intelligence and trust—The case of autonomous vehicles and medical assistance devices. *Technological Forecasting and Social Change*, *167*, 120635. DOI: 10.1016/j.techfore.2021.120635

Jobin, A., Ienca, M., & Vayena, E. (2021). The global landscape of AI ethics guidelines. *Nature Machine Intelligence*, *3*(5), 381–388. DOI: 10.1038/s42256-021-00348-5

Jobin, A., & Mann, M. (2023). Governing AI ethics in practice: Accountability, impact assessment, and audit mechanisms. *AI and Ethics*, *3*(2), 199–214. DOI: 10.1007/s43681-022-00169-w

Jobin, A., & Mittelstadt, B. (2023). Communicating AI decision-making: Strategies for transparency and stakeholder trust. *Journal of Business Ethics*, *184*(2), 393–410. DOI: 10.1007/s10551-022-05197-2

Johnson, K. (2022). Ethical leadership in the age of artificial intelligence. *AI and Ethics*, *2*(3), 381–392. DOI: 10.1007/s43681-021-00087-y

Johnson, K., Pasquale, F., & Chapman, C. (2021). Promoting ethical culture in AI governance. *Journal of Business Ethics*, *170*(2), 243–256. DOI: 10.1007/s10551-020-04480-0

Jussupow, E., Heinzl, A., & Spohrer, K. (2022). Organizational trust in artificial intelligence: A framework for responsible AI adoption. *Information & Management*, *59*(6), 103677. DOI: 10.1016/j.im.2022.103677

Kahre, C., Hoffmann, C. P., & Ahlemann, F. (2022). Building organizational trust in AI: The role of governance, communication, and ethics. *Information Systems Frontiers*, *24*(5), 1321–1335. DOI: 10.1007/s10796-021-10211-2

Kaminski, M. E., & Malgieri, G. (2023). Algorithmic impact assessments under the GDPR: Producing multi-layered explanations. *International Data Privacy Law*, *13*(1), 14–29. DOI: 10.1093/idpl/ipac027

Kaminski, M. E., & Malgieri, G. (2023). Algorithmic impact assessments under the GDPR: Producing multi-layered explanations. *International Data Privacy Law, 13*(1), 14–29. DOI: 10.1093/idpl/ipac027

Karanasiou, A., & Pinotsis, A. D. (2023). Artificial intelligence governance and leadership: Ethical perspectives. *AI and Ethics, 3*(1), 45–59. DOI: 10.1007/s43681-021-00076-2

Langer, M., Oster, D., & Speith, T. (2021). What do we want from explainable artificial intelligence (XAI)?—A stakeholder perspective on XAI and transparency. *Ethics and Information Technology, 23*(3), 1–18. DOI: 10.1007/s10676-021-09579-5

Leong, B., Danks, D., & Lim, W. Y. (2022). Co-designing trustworthy AI: The role of participatory design in responsible AI. *AI and Ethics, 2*(3), 411–423. DOI: 10.1007/s43681-021-00079-5

Leslie, D. (2023). Understanding artificial intelligence ethics and safety: A guide for the responsible design and implementation of AI systems in the public sector. *AI and Ethics, 3*(2), 221–237. DOI: 10.1007/s43681-022-00168-x

Leslie, D., & Burr, C. (2021). The ethical risk assessment of AI. *AI and Ethics, 1*(4), 405–415. DOI: 10.1007/s43681-021-00038-7

Li, Y., Sun, Y., & Sun, J. (2021). Trust in AI systems: The interplay of user perceptions, transparency, and performance. *Computers in Human Behavior, 120*, 106732. DOI: 10.1016/j.chb.2021.106732

Loi, M., Ferrario, A., & Viganò, E. (2023). Ethics training for AI professionals: Building moral competencies for responsible innovation. *AI and Ethics, 3*(1), 53–64. DOI: 10.1007/s43681-021-00078-z

Long, D., & Magerko, B. (2022). Designing for trust in human–AI interaction: A review of strategies and frameworks. *International Journal of Human-Computer Studies, 158*, 102744. DOI: 10.1016/j.ijhcs.2021.102744

Lu, Q., Zhu, L., Xu, X., Whittle, J., & Xing, Z. (2022). Towards a roadmap on software engineering for responsible AI. arXiv. /arXiv.2203.08594DOI: 10.1145/3522664.3528607

Lundberg, S. M., Erion, G., Chen, H., DeGrave, A., Prutkin, J. M., Nair, B., Katz, R., Himmelfarb, J., Bansal, N., & Lee, S. I. (2020). From local explanations to global understanding with explainable AI for trees. *Nature Machine Intelligence*, *2*(1), 56–67. DOI: 10.1038/s42256-019-0138-9

Marikyan, D., Papagiannidis, S., & Alamanos, E. (2022). Building consumer trust in artificial intelligence-enabled services: The role of performance, ethics, and transparency. *Computers in Human Behavior*, *127*, 107030. DOI: 10.1016/j.chb.2021.107030

MAS Veritas Consortium. (2023). Fairness, ethics, accountability, transparency (FEAT) toolkit for responsible AI in financial services. *Monetary Authority of Singapore*. Retrieved from MAS website

Mehrabi, N., Morstatter, F., Saxena, N., Lerman, K., & Galstyan, A. (2022). A survey on bias and fairness in machine learning. *ACM Computing Surveys*, *54*(6), 1–35. DOI: 10.1145/3457607

Mhlanga, D. (2023). The role of transparency, explainability and fairness in AI. *AI and Ethics*, *3*(1), 25–38. DOI: 10.1007/s43681-022-00154-3

Miller, T., Howe, P., & Sonenberg, L. (2021). Explainable AI: Understanding, visualizing and interpreting deep learning models. *AI and Ethics*, *1*(3), 231–243. DOI: 10.1007/s43681-021-00038-7

Mitchell, M., Wu, S., Zaldivar, A., Barnes, P., Vasserman, L., Hutchinson, B., & Gebru, T. (2021). Model cards for model reporting. *Communications of the ACM*, *64*(12), 56–65. DOI: 10.1145/3568997

Mittelstadt, B. D. (2021). Principles alone cannot guarantee ethical AI. *Nature Machine Intelligence*, *3*(9), 753–755. DOI: 10.1038/s42256-021-00376-4

Mohseni, S., Zarei, N., & Ragan, E. D. (2021). A multidisciplinary survey and framework for design and evaluation of explainable AI systems. *ACM Transactions on Interactive Intelligent Systems*, *11*(3–4), 1–45. DOI: 10.1145/3387166

Mökander, J., Axente, M., Casolari, F., Casanovas, P., & Floridi, L. (2022). Conformity assessments and post-market monitoring: A guide to the role of independent auditing in the EU Artificial Intelligence Act. *Minds and Machines*, *32*(2), 265–292. DOI: 10.1007/s11023-021-09577-4

Morley, J., Floridi, L., Kinsey, L., & Elhalal, A. (2021). From what to how: An initial review of publicly available AI ethics tools, methods and research to translate principles into practices. *Science and Engineering Ethics*, *27*(4), 53. DOI: 10.1007/s11948-021-00282-w

Morley, J., Floridi, L., Kinsey, L., & Elhalal, A. (2021). From what to how: An initial review of publicly available AI ethics tools, methods and research to translate principles into practices. *Science and Engineering Ethics*, *27*(4), 53. DOI: 10.1007/s11948-021-00282-w

Papagiannidis, E. (2025). Responsible artificial intelligence governance: A review of frameworks and practices. *Technological Forecasting and Social Change*. Advance online publication. DOI: 10.1016/j.techfore.2024.122345

Pew Research Center. (2025, April 3). *Views of risks, opportunities and regulation of AI*. Pew Research Center. Retrieved from https://www.pewresearch.org/internet/2025/04/03/views-of-risks-opportunities-and-regulation-of-ai/

Prunkl, C., Whittlestone, J., Singer, P., & Floridi, L. (2021). Institutionalizing ethics in AI through multi-stakeholder governance. *Nature Machine Intelligence*, *3*(1), 10–12. DOI: 10.1038/s42256-020-00252-2

Raisch, S., & Krakowski, S. (2021). Artificial intelligence and management: The automation–augmentation paradox. *Academy of Management Review*, *46*(1), 192–210. DOI: 10.5465/amr.2018.0072

Raji, I. D., Smart, A., White, R. N., Mitchell, M., Gebru, T., Hutchinson, B., & Denton, E. (2022). Closing the AI accountability gap: Defining an end-to-end framework for internal algorithmic auditing. *FAccT '20: Proceedings of the 2020 Conference on Fairness, Accountability, and Transparency*, 33–44. DOI: 10.1145/3351095.3372873

Reuel, A., & Undheim, T. A. (2024). Generative AI needs adaptive governance. arXiv. https://doi.org//arXiv.2406.04554DOI: 10.48550

Sambasivan, N., Kapania, S., Highfill, H., Akrong, D., Paritosh, P., & Aroyo, L. (2022). "Everyone wants to do the model work, not the data work": Data cascades in high-stakes AI. *Proceedings of the 2021 CHI Conference on Human Factors in Computing Systems*, 1–15. DOI: 10.1145/3411764.3445518

Scantamburlo, T., Cortés, A., Foffano, F., Barrué, C., Distefano, V., Pham, L., & Fabris, A. (2023). Artificial Intelligence across Europe: A study on awareness, attitude and trust. *AI & Society*. Advance online publication. DOI: 10.1007/s00146-023-016??-

Sharma, S., Iivari, N., Ventä-Olkkonen, L., Hartikainen, H., & Kinnula, M. (2023). Inclusive child-centered AI: Employing design futuring for inclusive design by and with children in Finland and India. *Minds and Machines*. Advance online publication. DOI: 10.1007/s11023-023-09659-2

Shneiderman, B. (2022). Bridging the gap between transparency and trust in AI. *Communications of the ACM*, *65*(4), 26–28. DOI: 10.1145/3512701

Shrestha, Y. R., Ben-Menahem, S. M., & Krogh, G. V. (2021). Organizational decision-making structures in the age of artificial intelligence. *California Management Review*, *63*(4), 66–90. DOI: 10.1177/0008125619862257

Stahl, B. C., Ryan, M., & Mittelstadt, B. D. (2023). Ethics of artificial intelligence: Risk management, governance, and responsible innovation. *AI and Ethics*, *3*(1), 1–15. DOI: 10.1007/s43681-021-00084-1

Stix, C. (2021). Actionable principles for artificial intelligence policy: Four ways to bridge the gap between principles and practice. *Philosophy & Technology*, *34*(4), 999–1023. DOI: 10.1007/s13347-021-00450-x

Sturm, D., Peters, L. D., & Mueller, R. M. (2021). Leveraging employee engagement for successful digital transformation: The role of digital leadership and change readiness. *Journal of Business Research*, *129*, 610–623. DOI: 10.1016/j.jbusres.2021.03.065

Sun, W., Bocchini, P., & Davison, B. D. (2023). Data integrity and resilience in AI systems. *AI and Ethics*, *3*(1), 145–158. DOI: 10.1007/s43681-022-00146-3

Tolan, S., Pesole, A., & Martínez-Plumed, F. (2021). Talent and leadership in the age of AI. *Nature Machine Intelligence*, *3*(7), 575–584. DOI: 10.1038/s42256-021-00357-4

Vakkuri, V., Kemell, K.-K., & Abrahamsson, P. (2023). Ethical frameworks for AI: A comparative analysis of IEEE and other standards. *AI and Ethics*, *3*(3), 433–449. DOI: 10.1007/s43681-023-00264-4

Veale, M., & Borgesius, F. Z. (2021). Demystifying the EU Artificial Intelligence Act. *Computer Law Review International*, *22*(4), 97–112. DOI: 10.9785/cri-2021-220402

Verma, S., & Gustafsson, A. (2020). Investigating the emerging COVID-19 research trends in the field of business and management: A bibliometric analysis approach. *Journal of Business Research*, *118*, 253–261. DOI: 10.1016/j.jbusres.2020.06.057

Vesely, S., & Kim, B. (2024). Survey evidence on public support for AI safety oversight. *Scientific Reports*, *14*(1), 31491. Advance online publication. DOI: 10.1038/s41598-024-82977-5

Wachter, S., Mittelstadt, B., & Floridi, L. (2021). Why a right to explanation of automated decision-making does not exist in the general data protection regulation. *International Data Privacy Law*, *7*(2), 76–99. DOI: 10.1093/idpl/ipx005

Wang, W., & Siau, K. (2023). Artificial intelligence, ethics, and public trust: A socio-technical perspective. *Journal of Business Research*, *154*, 113386. DOI: 10.1016/j.jbusres.2022.113386

Wilson, H. J., Daugherty, P. R., & Davenport, T. H. (2021). The future of leadership in the AI-enabled organization. *MIT Sloan Management Review*, *62*(3), 1–8. DOI: 10.5437/08956308X6203003

ADDITIONAL READING

Afroogh, S., Akbari, A., Malone, E., Kargar, M., & Alambeigi, H. (2024). Trust in AI: Progress, challenges, and future directions. *Humanities & Social Sciences Communications*, *11*(1), 1568. Advance online publication. DOI: 10.1057/s41599-024-04044-8

Batool, A., Zowghi, D., & Bano, M. (2025). AI governance: A systematic literature review. *AI and Ethics*, *5*(3), 3265–3279. Advance online publication. DOI: 10.1007/s43681-024-00653-w

Camilleri, M. A. (2024). Artificial intelligence governance: Ethical considerations. *Expert Systems: International Journal of Knowledge Engineering and Neural Networks*, *41*(7), e13406. Advance online publication. DOI: 10.1111/exsy.13406

Choung, H.. (2022). Trust and ethics in AI. *AI & Society*. Advance online publication. DOI: 10.1007/s00146-022-01473-4

Choung, H., David, P., & Seberger, J. S. (2023). *A multilevel framework for AI governance. ArXiv*. https://doi.org//arXiv.2307.03198DOI: 10.48550

Lahusen, C., Maggetti, M., & Slavkovik, M. (2024). Trust, trustworthiness and AI governance. *Scientific Reports*, *14*(1), 20752. Advance online publication. DOI: 10.1038/s41598-024-71761-0

Madanchian, M., & Taherdoost, H. (2025). Ethical theories, governance models, and strategic frameworks for responsible AI adoption and organizational success. *Frontiers in Artificial Intelligence*, *8*, 1619029. Advance online publication. DOI: 10.3389/frai.2025.1619029

Mustofa, R. H. (2025). The role of subjective norms, ethics, and trust in AI tool adoption among university students. Computers & Education. *Artificial Intelligence*. Advance online publication. DOI: 10.1016/j.caeai.2025.100072

Radanliev, P. (2025). *AI Ethics: Integrating transparency, fairness, and privacy. Journal of Ethical AI Systems*. https://doi.org/DOI: 10.1080/08839514.2025.2463722

Weiner, E. B. (2025). Ethical challenges and evolving strategies in AI healthcare. *Health and Technology*. Advance online publication. DOI: 10.1007/s12553-025-00678-9

KEY TERMS AND DEFINITIONS

Accountability: The duty of individuals and organizations to assume accountability for AI results and decisions, guaranteeing explicit lines of responsibility and remedial measures when required.

Algorithmic Fairness: The design of AI systems to prevent bias and discrimination, guaranteeing equitable treatment among demographic and social groups.

Artificial Intelligence (AI): The emulation of human cognitive functions by machines, especially computer systems, allowing them to execute activities such as learning, reasoning, and problem-solving.

Data Integrity: The precision, uniformity, and dependability of data during its lifecycle, guaranteeing it is comprehensive, secure, and devoid of illegal modifications.

Ethical AI: The advancement and use of AI technology in accordance with human values, legal standards, and the concepts of justice, transparency, and accountability.

Explainable AI (XAI): A collection of methodologies and instruments that render AI decision-making processes comprehensible to humans, facilitating transparency and informed supervision.

Governance Frameworks: Organized frameworks of regulations, standards, and procedures that direct the ethical and legal advancement, implementation, and oversight of AI technologies.

Stakeholder Engagement: The engagement of individuals, groups, or communities impacted by AI in its design, implementation, and assessment to guarantee inclusivity and confidence.

Transparency: The process of transparently conveying the design, functionality, and constraints of AI systems to stakeholders, facilitating informed comprehension and supervision.

Trust-Building: The intentional measures implemented to establish and preserve trust among stakeholders about the ethical and responsible utilization of AI technologies.

Chapter 7
Algorithmic Justice: Navigating AI's Role in Cybersecurity and Legal Transformation

Syed Ibad Ali
https://orcid.org/0000-0001-6312-6768
Parul Institute of Engineering and Technology, Parul University, Vadodara, India

ABSTRACT

This chapter critically examines the convergence of Artificial Intelligence (AI) with cybersecurity and the legal system, highlighting how machine learning and algorithmic reasoning reshape predictive policing, legal research, contract analysis, and dispute resolution. It explores AI's capacity to enhance procedural efficiency, data transparency, and equitable access to justice, while contending with ethical dilemmas around surveillance, algorithmic bias, and regulatory fragmentation. Through interdisciplinary case studies, the chapter probes the epistemic boundaries of AI-driven decision-making and proposes governance models that uphold privacy, civil liberties, and institutional accountability. This synthesis offers actionable insights for policymakers, legal technologists, and AI ethicists working at the intersection of digital security and jurisprudence.

DOI: 10.4018/979-8-3373-3114-0.ch007

INTRODUCTION

Artificial intelligence (AI) has quickly become an important part of today's social, legal, and technical world. AI has come a long way in a short amount of time and can now do things that people used to think required their own distinct intuition, discretion, and judgment. These duties include understanding complex legal concepts, doing fast legal research across huge databases, helping judges think through their decisions, analyzing surveillance footage in real time, and finding and stopping cyber threats in milliseconds. Machine learning algorithms can now find hidden trends in thousands of legal cases. Natural language processing technologies are very good at breaking down complex legal terminology, writing contracts, and even finding flaws in legal arguments. Automated reasoning lets computers act like legal syllogisms and common law conclusions by simulating logic structures. These technologies are so advanced that they don't just help lawyers and cybersecurity specialists anymore; they can also make decisions on their own that affect rights, duties, and dangers.

Along with the rapid expansion of AI, there is also a rapid trend toward the digitalization of every human activities. Everything from e-commerce and online banking to medical and digital government services is moving into cyberspace, changing the way society works. This change has made things much more efficient and convenient, but it has also made cybersecurity risks much more common and serious. As cybercrimes like ransomware, phishing scams, zero-day vulnerabilities, and algorithmic hacking become more common and complicated, it becomes clear that AI has to be included into cybersecurity systems. AI systems are becoming more and more important for things like real-time monitoring, finding unusual behavior, gathering threat intelligence, and responding to incidents automatically. They work as guards at digital borders, able to spot, stop, and fight cyberattacks faster and more accurately than ever before.

The use of AI in the fields of law and cybersecurity creates a paradox: the very algorithms that are meant to make legal decisions and enforce cybersecurity are also making things less safe. Algorithms may be unfair, hard to understand, and open to assaults from people who want to hurt them. If not controlled, AI-powered surveillance technologies can take away people's rights. Predictive policing models that are trained on biased datasets may keep systemic injustices going, and little code mistakes can be used to exploit smart contract platforms with terrible results. It seems that every technical advantage comes with an ethical problem or a hole in the rules. As a result, society is at a very important point where it must weigh the benefits of AI against the risks it brings.

It is important for not just engineers and developers, but also legislators, judges, attorneys, civil rights activists, and ethicists to understand how AI, law, and cybersecurity all work together. As AI technologies change faster than the law can keep up with them, regulators have the tough job of creating frameworks that are both legally sound and technologically sound. This calls for conversations between people from different fields and hybrid governance models that take into consideration technology's potential, legal standards, privacy principles, and social values.

The goal of this chapter is to critically examine how AI is changing the way things are done in both the legal and cybersecurity fields. It achieves this by looking into how AI systems are used in a number of areas, such as automating legal research, analyzing court cases, creating smart contracts, finding threats, and doing digital forensics. It uses cutting-edge research, real-world case studies, international policy texts, and technical prototypes to show both successful implementations and warnings. The chapter looks at current rules and regulations, such the European Union's AI Act, the U.S. Algorithmic Accountability Act, and different data protection laws like the GDPR and CCPA. It then looks at how well these rules and regulations encourage the creation and use of ethical AI.

It also looks at new technologies and techniques, such as explainable AI (XAI), responsible AI audits, ethical machine learning, and blockchain-based decentralized legal systems. The chapter talks about how new tools may help reduce algorithmic bias, make things clearer, and make sure that AI's role in law and cybersecurity is in the public interest.

The chapter also talks about the cultural and institutional inertia that sometimes gets in the way of AI adoption. Startups and big tech companies are excited about legal tech and AI-driven cybersecurity, but public sector organizations, notably the courts and police, typically have trouble with them because they have old systems, tight resources, and not enough digital literacy. So, moving toward AI-enhanced governance needs more than just better technology. It also needs changes in how institutions work, how they train their employees, how they buy things, and how they get people involved.

In the end, the chapter doesn't see AI as a single, unchanging entity, but as a complex and changing thing. Depending on how it is designed, where it is used, and how it is governed, its effects might be very different. AI may sometimes make it easier for everyone to get justice by giving low-income areas access to legal help. In some cases, technology can help authoritarian goals by allowing widespread monitoring and digital censorship. AI may stop millions of cyberattacks every day, but it may also create new weaknesses that aren't found until they are used. So, the outcome depends on the moral, legal, and technological choices taken at all stages of system development and implementation.

In this way, the chapter is set up to slowly reveal the connection between AI, law, and cybersecurity. It starts by looking at how AI technologies have changed over time and how they were first used in legal and security systems. Then it gives a thorough analysis of the literature that shows the main points of academic and policy arguments. The next parts go into more detail about how AI may be used in legal decisions, contract enforcement, and cyberdefense, as well as the problems of bias, explainability, and accountability. The chapter gives a grounded, empirical view of theoretical issues by looking at real-world examples including the COMPAS algorithm in U.S. courts, the DAO breach on Ethereum, and adversarial AI in cyber warfare. The chapter makes a strong case for the necessity for anticipatory governance, ethical foresight, and global collaboration to make sure that AI stays an instrument of justice and not a weapon of destruction.

LITERATURE REVIEW

AI is changing the way we police, interpret the law, carry out contracts, and protect our computers. These fields are becoming more and more dependent on AI's capacity to analyze large amounts of data, find patterns, and make predictions. But each use brings up different ethical, legal, and social issues, with current research showing both promise and danger.

Algorithmic Justice and Predictive Policing Systems like PredPol, HunchLab, and the Strategic Subject List use past crime data to figure out where crimes are likely to happen and who is most likely to be a victim (Engemann, 2024; Lungu, 2025). People who support these technologies say they make things run more smoothly and make the best use of resources. However, studies like the one into Geolitica show that the accuracy is very low—less than 0.5% of predictions matched real crimes—and they show how skewed data leads to unfair targeting of underprivileged populations (Engemann, 2024).

In 2016, Lum and Isaac showed how algorithms trained on biased records keep those unfairnesses going. More recent criticisms point out that using these kinds of systems keeps racial profiling alive and weakens due process (Lungu, 2025; Engemann, 2024). There is also systematic bias in COMPAS risk assessment tools: Black defendants are more likely to be labeled as high-risk and sent to prison, even when their backgrounds are identical to those of white defendants (Angwin et al., 2016; Gursoy & Kakadiaris, 2022; Bahl et al., 2024). These risk-assessment methods are not clear, so people can't contest algorithmic decisions (Angwin et al., 2016).

Recent research advocates for democratic monitoring, public transparency, and community accountability systems to stop these kinds of damages (Lungu, 2025; Engemann, 2024).

AI in Legal Research and Litigation Analysis

AI-powered legal research products like Ross Intelligence, Westlaw Edge, Lexis+ AI, Casetext, Blue J Legal, and Lex Machina have changed the way attorneys undertake case analysis, document review, and litigation strategy (Surden, 2014). These tools use natural language processing (NLP), retrieval augmented generation (RAG), and supervised learning to chart the results of case law, produce briefs, and predict how judgments will change over time.

But more recent empirical research show that there are big problems. Magesh et al. (2024) did a preregistered study that showed that even the best tools, including Lexis+ AI and Westlaw AI, may make mistakes or make up citations 17–33% of the time, even when compared to GPT 4 (Magesh et al., 2024). This makes it very worrying to rely on AI in high-stakes legal situations without close human supervision.

Meanwhile, new legal tech companies like Paxton AI, Harvey AI, DecoverAI, LEGALFLY, and Lawhive say they have better hallucination control (94% accuracy with no hallucinations) and better security features (Anonymous Reddit, 2025). But independent validation is still needed, thus the change in the way lawyers work needs to be closely watched for dependability and legal interpretability.

These patterns show that there are still problems that need to be solved: lawyers need to check AI outputs, make sure they don't rely too much on them, and use technologies that respect due process by making sure they can be traced, audited, and accurate.

AI in Smart Contracts and Contract Analysis

Kira Systems, Luminance, LawGeex, and Hebbia's Matrix platform are all examples of contract analytics solutions that leverage AI to automate clause extraction, compliance checks, and M&A due diligence (Szabo, 1997; Hebbia, 2024). For instance, Hebbia's Matrix currently uses OpenAI LLMs to improve semantic search in legal and financial documents (Bloomberg stories mentioned in Hebbia 2024).

These platforms cut down on the time it takes to evaluate things and make them more consistent. This is good for both big companies and teams who don't have a lot of resources. Smart contracts are self-executing code on the blockchain that can automate even more, but they also create new legal problems. The 2016 DAO breach showed that code may be vulnerable and that there aren't always standard ways to fix problems.

The legal uncertainty surrounding smart contracts has not been resolved: blockchains' immutability makes it hard to change or settle disputes. AI-assisted writing increases the danger of misinterpretation: translating legal intent into executable logic requires openness and ways to settle unexpected disagreements in a fair and lawful way.

AI and Cybersecurity: Threats that may be used for both good and bad and hostile environments

Cybersecurity's use of AI has sped up, with defenders adopting systems like Darktrace, Cylance, and Vectra to find problems, sort threats, and automate responses (Farooq, 2025; Sibanda, 2025). But hostile AI is becoming more dangerous.

Recent research has defined and classified many forms of attacks, including evasion, data poisoning, quick injection, and model extraction (Sibanda, 2025; NIST, 2024; Li, 2024). For example, echospoofing attacks in the middle of 2024 messed up Proofpoint's email security, allowing fake messages to get past ML classifiers (Sibanda, 2025). Prompt injection vulnerabilities in LLMs, as shown by how Google Gemini was hacked through hidden text or poisoned calendar invites, show how easy it is for linked systems to be hacked (Sibanda, 2025; Wikipedia on prompt injection, 2025; news on Gemini calendar hijack, 2025).

Anthropic's Claude and other well-known tools have done almost as well as humans in red-team cybersecurity tournaments. Meanwhile, autonomous LLM systems can already plan whole cyberattacks with very little help from people (Axios, 2025; Levy, 2025). Research prototypes like CyberSentinel (Tallam, 2025) show how defenses are changing to be able to find new threats by using SSH log analysis, phishing heuristics, and anomaly detection all at the same time.

Comprehensive surveys of adversarial examples (Li, 2024) and offensive AI evaluations (Girhepuje et al., 2024) reveal that although models improve security, attackers who have access to AI tools may use comparable technologies as weapons, which changes the threat environment in a big way.

AI-powered threats like GhostGPT, a simple generative model used to make phishing and malware, and WormGPT make it easier for more people to attack in more complex ways. To fight back against enemies that are getting better at moving quickly, defenders need to use AI-enhanced security, continuous event response, and deep threat intelligence (Netscout, 2025).

Toward Responsible Integration: New Standards and Ways to Move Forward

Recent agreement makes it clear that we need systems with humans in the loop, algorithms that are open to everyone, and designs that are cognizant of fairness. Technical methods like fairness-aware ML, causal inference, differential privacy, and explainable AI (XAI) look promising, but they need to be put into practice through regulatory sandboxes, independent audits, and institutional accountability.

When using AI for police and risk assessment, it must follow democratic rules of openness, public scrutiny, and due process (Lungu, 2025). The EU's AI Act and the OECD Principles are good examples of how to regulate AI. However, regulations like India's Digital Personal Data Protection Act 2023 and California's CCPA are still behind the times when it comes to AI use.

In legal tech, it's important to be checking hallucination rates, accuracy, and bias all the time. Magesh et al. (2024) shows how important it is to check AI results in a systematic way and take professional accountability for them.

Combining NIST taxonomy (NIST, 2024) with offensive AI threat frameworks makes it clear what to do in both attack and defensive cycles for cybersecurity. CyberSentinel (Tallam, 2025) and CyberSentinel-style platforms can identify sophisticated assaults in real time and react to them. Defenders also need to deal with autonomous LLM-based hacking agents (Axios 2025; Levy, 2025).

Finally, worldwide coordination will be very important to making sure that AI's advantages are used responsibly. This includes making sure that smart contracts can work with each other legally, that there are cross-border cyber standards, and that there are common AI ethical principles.

AI Surveillance Systems and Predictive Policing

AI-based surveillance systems have been suggested as further tools for predictive police in order to improve public safety and the efficacy of responses. Ali et al. (2024) suggested a surveillance system that focuses on keeping women safe. It uses AI for proactive monitoring, assessing the situation, and responding quickly. This adds to the conversation about predictive and responsive policing, which uses AI techniques to find trends and strange things in real time.

Shaikh et al. (2024) looked more closely at how autonomous security bots may be used in logistics settings. They focused on how AI could be used to patrol critical areas and find intruders. These solutions are comparable to what metropolitan police departments are trying to do, although privacy, civil liberties, and algorithmic fairness are still problems (Lum & Isaac, 2016; Lungu, 2025).

Smart Analytics and Legal Research

AI has also made it easier to get legal information by using analytics and automation tools. Ali and Shaikh (2025) looked at the ethical problems that come up when generative AI is used in legal research and scientific communication. They built on Surden's (2014) basic ideas. Their results show that you shouldn't blindly trust AI-generated outputs, especially in legal areas that are sensitive or high-stakes.

Recent research by Magesh et al. (2024) and Ali et al. (2024) on digital tools like learning dashboards and intelligent document analyzers show how AI may change how people think, draw conclusions, and see information in both schools and courts.

Blockchain with AI and smart contracts

Smart contracts that use blockchain technology are a good example of how law and automation are coming together. The ideas behind it go back to Szabo (1997), but modern research adds to the practical and moral issues. For instance, Ali et al. (2024) talk about how digital twins may be used in legal and business settings to provide new ways to keep an eye on contracts, simulate policies, and forecast compliance.

Ali and his team also worked on research into using blockchain for smart mobility and secure decentralized data exchange. These technologies are likely to have an impact on not only logistics and urban planning, but also regulatory enforcement, evidence tracking, and forensic auditing in digital legal settings.

AI Ethics and Cybersecurity

AI-enhanced solutions are needed to deal with new threats including aggressive AI, phishing using LLMs, and self-driving cyber-agents (Farooq, 2025; Li, 2024). At the same time, Shaikh et al. (2025) talked about the dual-use effects of AI in both defense and adversarial settings, especially when it comes to AI for detecting fraudulent images, protecting data pipelines, and reducing bogus content.

Ali and Shaikh's (2025) study also looks at the ethical issues that come up when using AI in cybersecurity, especially when it comes to responsible development, data responsibility, and the problem of using generative tools without limits in security research.

RESEARCH METHOD

This chapter uses a qualitative, multi-case study method since AI technologies in law and cybersecurity are constantly changing and include many different fields. The chapter looks at both the actual and theoretical effects of AI's spread in various areas by putting together policy documents, legislative frameworks, current research, and publically available case studies (Yin et al., 2017). The study is guided by thematic analysis based on moral ideas including autonomy, fairness, and non-maleficence. This qualitative technique lets you look closely at important problems and new ideas, but it has some problems because legal regimes are different from each other, many AI technologies are proprietary, and technology changes quickly.

Critical Thinking and Case Studies

To give this conversation some context, a few well-known examples show how AI, cybersecurity, and the law all come together. The COMPAS algorithm is used in US courtrooms to help judges decide on bail and sentences. This has sparked a lot of controversy concerning prejudice and explainability. Many studies have shown that these algorithms, which are supposed to be unbiased, may instead make existing racial differences in the criminal justice system worse (Lum & Isaac, 2016).

The rise of AI-powered legal research tools like ROSCOE and Blue J Legal is also a big step toward making legal knowledge more accessible to everyone. These technologies look at thousands of legislation, precedents, and regulatory papers in real time, giving attorneys a level of analysis that was formerly thought impossible. But there are also uncertainties regarding how much human control is needed to avoid mistakes and how algorithmic opacity might hurt judicial thinking (Ashley, 2019).

Smart contracts are another example of a new area. The DAO incident on the Ethereum blockchain showed that these systems are still not very mature from a technical point of view and that there is no legal way to fix code-based agreements that go wrong (Szabo, 1997).

AI-powered intrusion detection systems are increasingly typical in big businesses when it comes to cybersecurity. These systems can look at a lot of data and find patterns of strange behavior, and they can quickly change to deal with new types of attacks. However, the threat of adversarial assaults, in which bad actors intentionally change inputs to avoid detection, means that defensive mechanisms and ethical frameworks need to be constantly improved (Farooq, 2025).

A Look at the Research Design

This study uses a qualitative, multidisciplinary, and exploratory research approach that is appropriate for the complicated social and technical environment where AI, cybersecurity, and legal frameworks come together. As AI spreads across the courts, forensic science, and regulatory systems, it becomes more important than ever to have a flexible, interpretive approach. The research approach utilized here is based on:

- Multi-case study analysis (Yin et al., 2017)
- Thematic qualitative research

- Critical-ethical inquiry • Documented technological forensics
- Using NLP technologies for policy-text mining (to put things in context)

These methods were used to make sure that the study shows the complicated relationships between technology's benefits, the law's restrictions, and the problems with cybersecurity.

Reason for a Qualitative Multi-Case Approach

The multi-case study technique lets you comprehend each real-world situation involving AI applications in depth and in context, unlike experimental or simply quantitative methodologies. This technique lets you look at different implementations side by side, such predictive policing in the U.S., blockchain-based legal automation in the EU, and AI-enhanced cybersecurity in Asia-Pacific financial systems. Following Yin et al. (2017), we look at each instance as a whole and in parts, utilizing data from three different sources:

- Court decisions and legal papers
- Technical papers (such AI model white papers and patents)
- Academic research from peer-reviewed sources
- Interviews and expert comments (where they are accessible)
- Investigative journalism and media exposés (for cases that have a big effect on the public)

THEMATIC ANALYSIS FRAMEWORK

The qualitative data is sorted into groups and looked at using theme coding, which is based on ethics and policy. Not only is thematic analysis here descriptive, but it also interprets based on three main ethical principles:

Table 1. Main ethical principles for AI

Ethical Principle	Description
Autonomy	The individual's right to informed consent and agency over data and decisions
Justice	Fair and unbiased application of AI across populations
Non-maleficence	Avoidance of harm, especially in predictive or automated decision systems

Each case study is analyzed across these axes to evaluate how AI systems align or conflict with ethical legal practice.

Figure 1. Methodological framework for AI-law-cybersecurity analysis

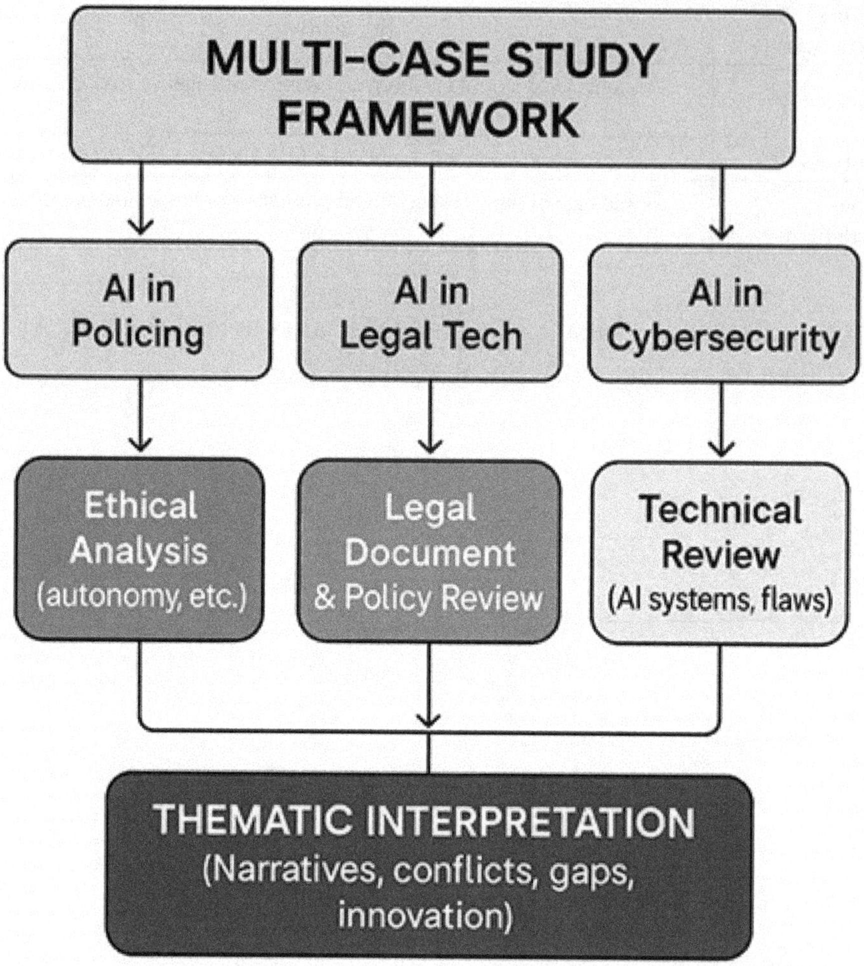

This structure supports both vertical depth (within cases) and horizontal comparison (across domains).

DATA SOURCES AND SELECTION CRITERIA

The study uses purposive sampling to select the most impactful, debated, or paradigm-shifting AI implementations within legal and cybersecurity spaces from 2015–2025, with emphasis on post-2020 developments (aligned with GPT-3/4, blockchain maturity, and rising cyber warfare threats).

Table 2. AI implementation in legal and cybersecurity spaces

Data Type	Source Examples
Court rulings	US Supreme Court, EU Court of Justice
Regulatory texts	GDPR, CCPA, Digital Services Act, NIST guides
Algorithmic assessments	COMPAS, Blue J Legal, Lexis AI, Palantir
Cybersecurity logs	MITRE ATT&CK, OpenAI red team reports
Blockchain white papers	Ethereum DAO, Hyperledger, Chainlink audits

CASE STUDY ARCHITECTURE

Each case is analyzed under the following structure:

- Context: Origin, scope, and technological foundation
- Legal Implications: Rights, responsibilities, jurisdictions
- Cybersecurity Dimensions: Data risks, threats, defense mechanisms
- Ethical Considerations: Bias, fairness, transparency
- Outcome: Public or legal reaction, reform proposals

Figure 2. Case study analytical template

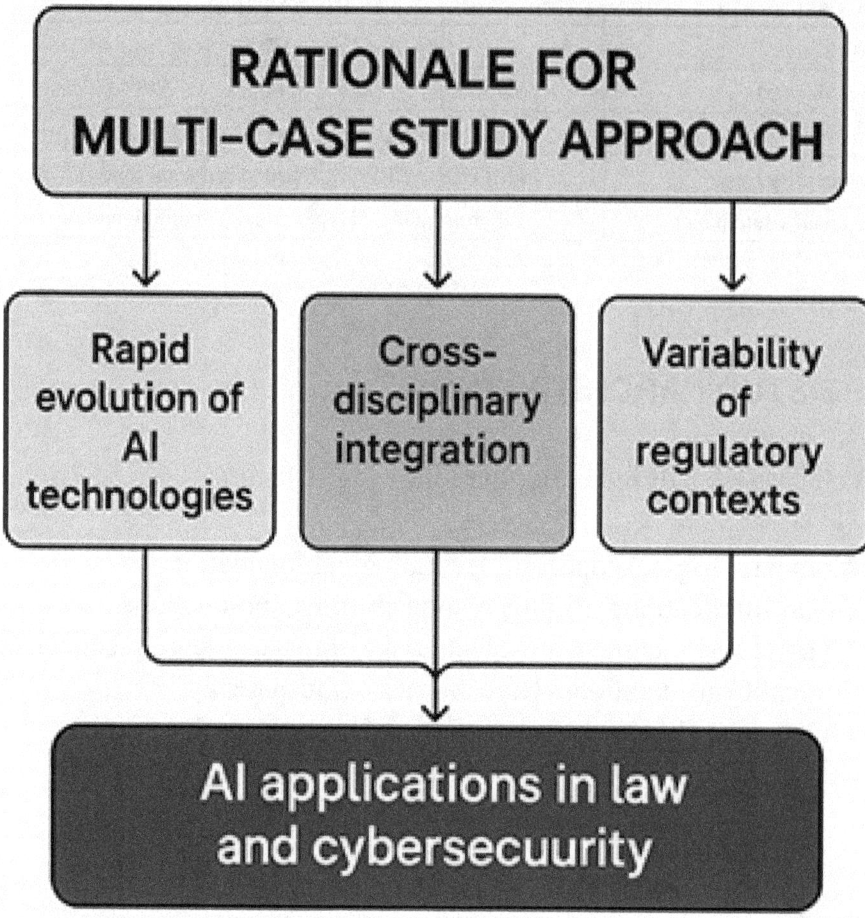

ETHICAL ORIENTATION AND SELF-REFLECTION

This study goes beyond typical legal-technical analysis by include a reflexive ethical investigation that takes into account the researcher's perspective when analyzing systemic power imbalances. The social, economic, and legal beliefs of the people who make and use AI systems are shown in the systems themselves. Because of this, AI governance has to include moral pluralism and anticipatory regulation.

This study approach is thorough, however it does have certain problems:

Not generalizable: Case studies can't be used to make generalizations about a population, although they can provide you useful information.

- Data opacity: A lot of proprietary AI systems don't let the public or academics see how they work.
- Differences in jurisdiction: Different legal systems make it hard to get at the same conclusions (for example, common law vs. civil law).
- Time volatility: Some judgments may rapidly become out of date as technology changes swiftly.

Even yet, the complexity of qualitative depth and ethical foundation gives us a strong way to look at how AI changes the law and cybersecurity.

Tools and Technologies That Were Used

To add to the human analysis, the study uses NVivo to code policy texts and legal documents by theme.

- ChatGPT/GPT-4 for comparing legal systems and summarizing laws
- NLP (spaCy, NLTK) for finding and studying semantic patterns in rules and regulations
- MITRE CALDERA and ATT&CK datasets for looking at AI-based intrusion detection instances
- Documentation for Ethereum and Solidity for technical audits of smart contracts. This system is also set up to allow for iterative development, which means that new AI models, judicial decisions, or cyber events may be added to the framework. It sets the stage for a study template that grows and changes when new use cases, biases, and reforms come up.

BENEFITS OF THE SUGGESTED SYSTEM

Adding artificial intelligence (AI) to cybersecurity and legal procedures is a huge step forward in how organizations handle, protect, and understand huge amounts of complicated data. AI changes the way we think about systems from reactive and manual to proactive, predictive, and scalable ones that can improve institutional responsiveness, transparency, and operational efficiency (Finck, 2019; Surden, 2019). AI-powered tools like machine learning-based intrusion detection systems, behavior-based anomaly detection algorithms, and threat intelligence platforms are changing the way businesses find, sort, and stop bad activities in the world of cybersecurity (Buczak & Guven, 2016; Sommer & Paxson, 2010). These systems can take in and analyze gigabytes of network logs, transaction data, and endpoint telemetry in real time. They can find small changes or attack routes that traditional, signature-based cybersecurity tools would miss (Nguyen, Quach, & Thaichon, 2021). AI systems become better at finding threats all the time by using unsupervised learning and adaptive feedback loops. This means they find fewer false positives and more vulnerabilities that haven't been found before (Diro & Chilamkurti, 2018). This skill is especially important now as adversarial tactics are becoming more complex, from advanced persistent threats (APTs) and ransomware-as-a-service (RaaS) models to socially engineered phishing campaigns that use generative AI (Ali et al., 2022). AI also takes care of boring security activities like patch maintenance, access control audits, and vulnerability assessments, freeing up cybersecurity experts to work on more important things like strategy and forensic investigation (Hassija et al., 2020). AI's integration has also sparked a revolution in legal informatics, where natural language processing (NLP), legal reasoning algorithms, and decision-support systems are changing the way lawyers work and how people can get justice (Ashley, 2019; Medvedeva, Vols, & Wieling, 2019). AI-powered technologies are being used all the time in law firms and courtrooms to do due diligence, legal research, find relevant precedents, and point out anomalies in contract language (Remus & Levy, 2015; Katz, Bommarito, & Blackman, 2014). These algorithms, which are typically trained on hundreds of legal texts, case law databases, and regulatory filings, may make legal summaries, propose ways to argue, and even make very good guesses about how a case will turn out (Aletras et al., 2016). AI speeds up the discovery process by quickly and deeply sorting through large collections of e-discovery data including emails, PDFs, chat logs, and depositions. This lets lawyers find the most relevant information with unequaled accuracy (Surden, 2014). AI-powered legal chatbots and virtual assistants are making legal information more accessible to everyone. They provide self-help legal services and procedural advice to people who might not be able to afford professional legal help or who live too far away to get it (Medvedeva, Vols, & Wieling, 2020; Mcginnis & Pearce, 2014). This democratization not only makes it easier for people to get justice, but it also encourages people to get involved in their communities and learn more about the law, especially in areas that are not well represented or are on the fringes (Wagner & Blewer, 2019). Explainable AI (XAI) frameworks and audit trails make algorithms more transparent, which helps hold institutions accountable. This is because stakeholders, such as clients, regulatory bodies, and the general public, can see the logic and evidence behind algorithmic decisions, which makes black-box models less opaque (Guidotti et al., 2018; Doshi-Velez & Kim, 2017). Also, the fact that AI systems may be used in many different places is very useful for making sure that companies follow the law in more than one country and for coordinating cybersecurity across borders (Gonzalez, 2019). LegalTech platforms with AI capabilities can easily connect local laws to international ones, like the General Data Protection Regulation (GDPR), the California Consumer Privacy Act (CCPA), and India's Digital Personal Data Protection Act. This lets businesses keep up with changes in the law while still being able to manage compliance on a large scale (Veale, Binns, & Edwards, 2018). Also, in cybersecurity, AI-based governance, risk, and compliance (GRC) systems give you real-time dashboards and warnings that combine regulatory responsibilities, cyber risk indices, and internal audit findings to help you stay compliant all the time (de Souza et al., 2021). As the fields of law and cybersecurity become more connected, especially in areas like digital forensics, data breach lawsuits, and cybercrime prosecution, AI provides a way to look at both evidential and behavioral data with the same logic. AI systems' better ability to anticipate things makes it easier to find bad conduct and legal concerns. It also lets organizations take action before something bad happens and run policy simulations, which makes both organizations and society safer (Veale, Binns, & Edwards, 2018). For example, predictive policing systems have been used in cities to decide where to send police officers based on real-time crime estimates made from trends in historical and geographical data (Lum & Isaac, 2016; Ritter & Ferguson, 2017). Legal AI systems like Blue J Legal and Ross Intelligence have also been used to predict the results of court cases, which helps resolve conflicts and improve litigation strategy (Surden, 2019). There are ethical questions about these kinds of deployments, especially when it comes to prejudice, fairness, and due process. However, there is no denying that they have an effect on operations, such as making things more efficient, reducing case loads, and saving money on administrative costs (Zarsky, 2016). AI can also look at data from different sources, like text, voice, images, and biometric data, in different languages and formats. This makes it very useful for cybersecurity investigations and legal forensics, like finding deepfakes, spotting insider threats, or verifying chain-of-custody evidence (Corp, 2024). AI also improves collaboration across agencies and countries by making systems that can share intelligence in organized, machine-readable ways. This is especially helpful for sharing information about global cyber threats and for making mutual legal assistance treaties (MLATs) easier through automation (Taddeo, McCutcheon, & Floridi, 2019). AI also helps make better policy decisions by modeling scenarios and simulating the effects of new laws on society and the economy. Legislative drafters may use AI-generated models and agent-based simulations to see how proposed legislation might affect people and businesses (Ranchordás, 2021). This capacity closes the gap between what the law says and how technology works, bringing legal standards in line with algorithmic behaviors. It is important to note that AI-based simulation environments and intelligent tutoring systems are being created for legal education and training to help law students and junior attorneys learn via experience and improve their analytical thinking (Fagan, 2021). These systems offer scenario-based learning that mimics the difficulties of actual legal and cybersecurity issues. This improves both human judgment and machine intelligence. Organizations that use AI for internal legal and cybersecurity tasks also say that their operational risk, compliance penalties, and incident response times have all gone down by a lot. This means a big return on investment

(ROI) and better ethical governance (Kamarinou, Millard, & Singh, 2016). AI also helps protect whistleblowers, encrypt legal communications, and handle private data, which protects civil rights and attorney-client privilege in surroundings that are becoming more digital and monitored (Wachter, Mittelstadt, & Russell, 2018). As we move farther into the Fourth Industrial Revolution, which is characterized by the merging of cyber-physical systems, quantum computing, and widespread connectivity, AI's role in protecting the integrity of the law and cybersecurity becomes not just helpful but necessary. The coming together of AI, cybersecurity, and law is both a technological need and a moral obligation. It requires constant monitoring, collaboration across disciplines, and new regulations (Crawford & Calo, 2016). As Remus and Levy (2015) and Ashley (2019) have pointed out, the key to making AI work in the long term is not just to improve technology, but also to create legal systems and institutional cultures that value fairness, accountability, transparency, and human dignity in digital governance ecosystems.

CONCLUSION

The coming together of AI, cybersecurity, and the law is both unavoidable and life-changing. These new technologies promise to make things more efficient, open, and fair, but they also create new hazards and moral problems. Governments, lawyers, and IT experts all face the same problem: how to create rules that encourage innovation without giving up privacy, justice, or accountability (Goodman & Flaxman, 2017). As AI-based decision making gets better, it becomes even more important to have systems that can be explained and held responsible. The coming together of AI, cybersecurity, and the law marks a turning point in the development of technology governance. AI-powered systems are becoming more common in the courts, cybersecurity protocols, and drafting laws. Their impact is growing not only in breadth but also in depth, changing how laws are enforced, rights are protected, and vulnerabilities are handled in both digital and real-world settings (Goodman & Flaxman, 2017; Mittelstadt et al., 2016).

This integration has a lot of benefits, but it also brings up a lot of ethical, legal, and social-political problems that need to be carefully thought about. The main problem is that algorithms are hard to see through. A lot of the AI systems that are now used in law and cybersecurity are "black boxes," which means that it's hard for even their makers to figure out how certain outputs are made. This lack of explainability goes against some of the most important principles of law, such as due process, openness, and the freedom to question evidence (Wachter, Mittelstadt, & Russell, 2018). In the legal world, this kind of lack of clarity might lead to unfair outcomes, especially when AI-generated suggestions are used to decide on bail, sentencing, or predictive policing.

Also, automating risk prediction and surveillance raises serious issues concerning privacy and civil rights. Models of predictive policing, including those based on previous crime data, have been proven to reinforce racial and socioeconomic prejudices, making feedback loops that unfairly target underprivileged populations (Lum & Isaac, 2016; Angwin et al., 2016). Supporters say that AI makes things more efficient and helps with resource allocation, but critics are right to point out that these systems might make structural inequities worse instead of better if they aren't closely monitored and don't use fairness-aware algorithms.

AI has made a huge difference in how threats are found and dealt with from a cybersecurity point of view. Machine learning algorithms can now find strange things, sort malware, and respond to incidents automatically at a pace and scale that humans can't match (Farooq, 2025). This level of intelligence, on the other hand, is a double-edged sword. People with bad intentions can use the same tools that are meant for protection to launch adversarial assaults, which deceive AI models with well planned changes. The difference between offensive and defensive capabilities makes it very important to think about AI arms races in cyberspace and how to build strong, ethical cybersecurity systems (Brundage et al., 2018).

Also, laws haven't kept up with the fast rate of AI advancements. There is still a big lack of agreement across countries, even if worldwide rules like the EU's AI Act and the U.S. Executive Order on Safe, Secure, and

Trustworthy Artificial Intelligence show that people are becoming more conscious of the issue. When laws are not clear, it is harder to enforce them across borders and international companies have trouble following them. Furthermore, rules based on human-centered accountability models are not good at dealing with injuries caused by autonomous systems. This raises basic problems regarding culpability, redress, and the source of moral responsibility (Crawford & Calo, 2016; Gless, Silverman, & Weigend, 2016).

The loss of human agency is another important issue. As legal analytics systems like Lex Machina and Blue J Legal grow more common, there is a chance that they may replace rather than improve human legal thinking. Automation bias is the inclination to rely too much on outputs from machines. This might make lawyers less skilled and less interested in the law. AI-generated smart contracts and automated arbitration systems may also take away important parts of interpretive flexibility, making it more likely that human judgment will be replaced by strict, code-based logic (Surden, 2014; Szabo, 1997).

The effects on democratic government are quite important. More and more, governments utilize AI to watch over people, find fraud, and make choices about policy. These apps can help cut down on waste and corruption, but they also risk making technocratic administration more common, where decisions are made by hidden algorithms instead of open public procedures. Concerns regarding accountability and the privatization of governmental activities emerge as private tech corporations gain more capacity to build and use these systems (Zuboff, 2019). In this situation, algorithmic audits, participatory AI design, and public involvement are all very important instruments for protecting democratic norms.

A strong ethical and regulatory framework is needed to reduce these many hazards. First, the idea of algorithmic responsibility needs to be included into both legal and technological norms. This includes rules for making things clear, checking for bias, and being open about data. Second, there should still be human oversight in important decision-making processes. This will make sure that AI is used to help people instead of replacing them. Third, multidisciplinary work must become a part of the system. Not just computer scientists and engineers need to be involved in the creation of ethical AI. Legal academics, ethicists, sociologists, and communities that may be affected all need to be included (Floridi & Cowls, 2019).

Both education and creating capability are very important. Lawyers need to know how to use and question AI systems, and IT workers need to know how their job affects society, the law, and ethics. This need for multidisciplinary work should be reflected in changes to law school and computer science curricula. Also, initiatives to raise public awareness are needed to provide people the information they need about their digital rights and how to keep AI systems responsible.

It's also important to know that a lot of AI problems are very specific to their environment. Legal traditions, cultural norms, and technical infrastructure can all be different from one place to another, thus solutions that work in one place may not work as well in another. So, even while working together with other countries is good, it has to allow for changes that are specific to each country and preserve their sovereignty. Regional groups like the ASEAN AI Initiative and the African Union's Digital Transformation Strategy are good places to try out governance models that take the situation into account/

The roles of explainable AI (XAI), differential privacy, federated learning, and neuro-symbolic thinking should be at the top of both research and policy agendas for the future. These technologies help us find a balance between innovation and accountability by making things clearer, protecting user privacy, and making things easier to understand (Doshi-Velez & Kim, 2017). Also, we can make algorithmic impact assessments (AIAs) a regular part of the process of looking at the social, legal, and ethical effects of big AI projects before they are scaled up (Raji et al., 2020).

Finally, as AI gets better, so must our sense of what is fair. We need to rethink traditional legal ideas like intention, causation, and responsibility in light of autonomous decision-making. The change from human to hybrid agency requires legal philosophy to deal with computational epistemologies. This will help create a legal system that is both forward-looking and based on ideals of justice, equity, and human dignity that have stood the test of time (Leenes et al., 2017).

In short, the coming together of AI, cybersecurity, and law is both a chance and a test. It gives us the potential to make systems that are more fair, effective, and strong, but only if we use frameworks that are well thought out, include everyone, and are based on ethics. The way forward must not be tempted by automation for its own sake. Instead, it must put human rights, institutional responsibility, and democratic engagement first. At this important point, it is not enough to just control AI; we must do so intelligently, fairly, and bravely.

Future Enhancement

In the future, adding artificial intelligence (AI) to cybersecurity and legal systems would require a strong foundation of improvements that are not just technological but also moral, legal, and political. The most important thing is to make progress in explainable AI (XAI), which is a field that tries to make the decision-making processes of complex machine learning algorithms clearer so that human stakeholders, especially in legal settings where rights and freedoms are at stake, can understand and question the results (Doshi-Velez & Kim, 2017). Black-box models are a direct danger to due process since they don't explain their rationale. This is especially true when AI is used to make sentence recommendations, assess risk, or sort through data. Laws need to change such that there are minimal levels of interpretability, especially for AI systems that affect the results of court cases or police investigations (Gunning et al., 2019). This calls for not just technological improvements but also a regulatory culture that stresses the need of algorithmic literacy for both developers and lawyers. At the same time, working together across jurisdictions becomes an essential tactic. The rules for AI are all over the place right now. The European Union is working on its AI Act, the US is taking a sectoral approach, and Asian countries are using techno-nationalist tactics (Veale & Borgesius, 2021). These separate regulatory systems may make it harder for businesses to follow the rules, make it harder for the police to do their jobs, and leave gaps that criminals may take advantage of if they don't work together. Global coalitions, which may be based on the GDPR's extraterritorial applicability, should work to create a set of basic AI governance principles that can be used by everyone. These principles should include data provenance, auditability, fairness, and accountability (Wagner et al., 2024). Also, algorithmic auditing in real time has to be made a part of the system. Post-hoc audits that are already in place are sometimes too late to fix damage that has already been done. Future AI systems, especially those used in high-risk areas like cybersecurity intrusion detection, autonomous legal decision-making, or biometric surveillance, should include built-in ways to keep checking themselves and be checked by outside parties. These systems might include blockchain-based logs that can't be changed, differential privacy protocols, and federated learning models that keep data private while being open about it (Kairouz et al., 2019; Farooq, 2025). Also, bias mitigation measures should not just be used to fix problems; they should be built into the design from the start. Ethics-by-design paradigms should be used to build future AI. This means that value-sensitive design methodologies should be included into the first stages of development (Friedman & Hendry, 2019). This is especially important for AI systems that affect civil freedoms or the law, such predictive policing, automated parole decisions, or digital forensics. In these areas, AI models need to not just be accurate, but they also need to do so in ways that are in line with constitutional standards and human rights. New research on algorithmic fairness suggests some good ways to fix historical bias in datasets, like reweighing techniques, fairness constraints during training, and adversarial debiasing. However, these methods need to be tested in a wider range of judicial and cyber-infrastructural settings (Mehrabi et al., 2019). AI has to go beyond reactive threat detection to proactive resilience-building in terms of cybersecurity. It needs to use threat intelligence to not only find problems but also to model future weaknesses and make zero-trust systems possible. In addition, generative AI creates a dual-use problem: it can be used to make deepfakes, polymorphic malware, or spear-phishing content with an unprecedented level of accuracy (Kumar & Jain, 2025). So, research should focus on dual-use risk assessment processes that look forward to and stop bad people from using generative systems for bad purposes. At the same time, human-centered oversight systems like human-in-the-loop or human-on-the-loop models need to be improved so that AI suggestions in legal or cyber defense situations don't replace human judgment but rather add to it (Amershi et al., 2019). Improving AI training datasets is just as important to make sure they are representative and of high quality. Bad data quality not only hurts performance, but it also keeps legal unfairness going, especially when datasets are biased against specific groups of people. In the future, policy should require data curation processes to be open and create data trusts to handle sensitive training datasets with public supervision and institutional responsibility (Delacroix & Lawrence, 2019). Another important improvement is the creation of legal doctrine that can withstand AI. Liability, personality, and intent are all traditional legal concepts that don't work for entities that can make their own decisions. To answer concerns like "who is responsible when an AI system breaks down?" or "how do you assign mens rea when an algorithm, not a person, is the one doing the action?" (Crawford & Calo, 2016), future legal studies has to reconsider basic ideas about the law. Also, multidisciplinary education needs to be a top concern. Just as AI developers need to learn about law and ethics, lawyers, judges, and regulators need to learn about AI. This dual literacy can help create hybrid professionals, such legal data scientists and algorithmic ethicists, who can help bridge gaps in knowledge and guide AI research toward the public good. Public policy should help these kinds of educational programs by giving them money, scholarships, and help in making a curriculum that crosses disciplines. Also, participatory design will be very important in future AI systems. It is important to talk to end-users, especially those from underrepresented groups, while building AI systems that will control their access to justice or protection. Co-design models, community AI audits, and participatory impact assessments might make AI governance more democratic by changing it from a top-down system to one that is more open and diverse (Costanza-Chock, 2018). Also, making ethical sandbox environments—controlled testing places for experimental AI applications—could let developers and regulators see how AI acts when it's under stress without having to worry about what would happen in the real world. Dynamic policy simulations, adversarial testing, and multi-stakeholder review panels should all be part of these kinds of settings. Last but not least, AI in law and cybersecurity has to go beyond the present and into the future to encompass climate and ecological issues. AI systems need a lot of computing power, which has negative effects on the environment. Future research should look into green AI methods like energy-efficient model training, carbon accounting for inference, and edge computing to make sure that the computer systems that support legal and cybersecurity AI are both environmentally friendly and morally sound (Schwartz et al.,

2020). In short, future improvements need to go beyond reactive adjustments and move toward anticipatory governance that combines technology progress with legal foresight, moral contemplation, and social inclusion. These improvements shouldn't only make current systems better; they should also come up with new methods to do things that are in line with the basic principles of justice, security, and human dignity.

REFERENCES

Aletras, N., Tsarapatsanis, D., Preoţiuc-Pietro, D., & Lampos, V. (2016). Predicting judicial decisions of the European Court of Human Rights: A Natural Language Processing perspective. *PeerJ. Computer Science*, *2*(1), e93. DOI: 10.7717/peerj-cs.93

Ali, S. I., Jadhav, J., Arunkumar, R., & Kanagavalli, N. (2022). A smart resource utilization algorithm for high speed 5G communication networks based on cloud servers. *ICTACT Journal on Communication Technology*, *13*(4), 2800–2804. DOI: 10.21917/ijct.2022.0414

Ali, S. I., Ravuri, H. K., Lakshmi, V. T., Ramya, A., Lavanya, K., & Bahade, S. (2024). The role of nanomaterials in the development of high-performance batteries. *Nanotechnology Perceptions*, *20*(S11), 1125–1140. https://www.nano-ntp.com

Amershi, S., Inkpen, K., Teevan, J., Kikin-Gil, R., Horvitz, E., Weld, D., Vorvoreanu, M., Fourney, A., Nushi, B., Collisson, P., Suh, J., Iqbal, S., & Bennett, P. N. (2019). Guidelines for Human-AI Interaction. *Proceedings of the 2019 CHI Conference on Human Factors in Computing Systems - CHI '19*. https://doi.org/DOI: 10.1145/3290605.3300233

Angwin, J., Larson, J., Mattu, S., & Kirchner, L. (2016). *Machine bias*. ProPublica.

Ashley, K. D. (2019). *Artificial intelligence and legal analytics: new tools for law practice in the digital age*. Cambridge University Press, Cop.

Axios. (2025). *Axios*. Axios Media Inc. https://www.axios.com/events/ai

Bahl, U., Topaz, C., Obermüller, L., Goldstein, S., & Sneirson, M. (2024). Algorithms in judges' hands: incarceration and inequity in Broward County, Florida.

Brundage, M., Avin, S., Clark, J., Toner, H., Eckersley, P., Garfinkel, B., Dafoe, A., Scharre, P., Zeitzoff, T., Filar, B., Anderson, H., Roff, H., Allen, G. C., Steinhardt, J., & Flynn, C. hÉigeartaigh, Seán Ó, Beard, S., Belfield, H., Farquhar, S., & Lyle, C. (2018, February 20). *The Malicious Use of Artificial Intelligence: Forecasting, Prevention, and Mitigation*. ArXiv.org. https://arxiv.org/abs/1802.07228

Buczak, A. L., & Guven, E. (2016). A Survey of Data Mining and Machine Learning Methods for Cyber Security Intrusion Detection. *IEEE Communications Surveys and Tutorials*, *18*(2), 1153–1176. DOI: 10.1109/COMST.2015.2494502

Corp, E. (2024, March 15). *Extropic Emerges from Stealth, aiming to revolutionize Generative AI with Physics-based AI processors*. Prnewswire.com; Cision PR Newswire. https://www.prnewswire.com/news-releases/extropic-emerges-from-stealth-aiming-to-revolutionize-generative-ai-with-physics-based-ai-processors-302090040.html

Costanza-Chock, S. (2018). Design Justice, A.I., and Escape from the Matrix of Domination. *Journal of Design and Science*, *3*(5). Advance online publication. DOI: 10.21428/96c8d426

Crawford, K., & Calo, R. (2016). There is a blind spot in AI research. *Nature*, *538*(7625), 311–313. DOI: 10.1038/538311a

Delacroix, S., Lawrence, N. D. (2019). Bottom-up data Trusts: disturbing the 'one size fits all' approach to data governance. *International Data Privacy Law*, 9(4), 2 36–252. https://doi.org/DOI: 10.1093/idpl/ipz014

Diro, A. A., & Chilamkurti, N. (2018). Distributed attack detection scheme using deep learning approach for Internet of Things. *Future Generation Computer Systems*, *82*, 761–768. DOI: 10.1016/j.future.2017.08.043

Doshi-Velez, F., & Kim, B. (2017). Towards A Rigorous Science of Interpretable Machine Learning. *ArXiv:1702.08608 [Cs, Stat]*, *2*(2). https://arxiv.org/abs/1702.08608

Engemann, A. (2024, November 20). AI and predictive policing: Balancing technological innovation and civil liberties. *Minnesota Journal of Law, Science & Technology*.

Fagan, F. (2021). E*bers on Liability for AI and EU Consumer Law*. AI Law Blawg. https://ailawblawg.com/2021/06/29/

Farooq, M. S. (2025). AI IN FINTECH: AN EVALUATION OF FINANCIAL PAYMENT SYSTEMS. *International Journal of Cultural Studies*, *20*(2), 157–210. https://www.researchgate.net/publication/387823057_AI_IN_FINTECH_AN_EVALUATION_OF_FINANCIAL_PAYMENT_SYSTEMS

Finck, M. (2019). Smart contracts as a form of solely automated processing under the GDPR. *International Data Privacy Law*, *9*(2), 78–94. DOI: 10.1093/idpl/ipz004

Floridi, L., & Cowls, J. (2019). A Unified Framework of Five Principles for AI in Society. *Harvard Data Science Review*, *1*(1). Advance online publication. DOI: 10.1162/99608f92.8cd550d1

Friedman, B., & Hendry, D. G. (2019). *Value Sensitive Design*. MIT Press. DOI: 10.7551/mitpress/7585.001.0001

Girhepuje, S., Verma, A., & Raina, G. (2024, September 26). *A survey on offensive AI within cybersecurity*. arXiv.

Gless, S., Silverman, E., & Weigend, T. (2016). If Robots Cause Harm, Who is to Blame? Self-Driving Cars and Criminal Liability. SSRN *Electronic Journal*. https://doi.org/DOI: 10.2139/ssrn.2724592

Gonzalez, C. (2019, January 22). *Rol of Standards with Respect to Innovative Technologies: AI*. https://doi.org/DOI: 10.13140/RG.2.2.17628.41601

Goodman, B., & Flaxman, S. (2017). European Union Regulations on Algorithmic Decision-Making and a "Right to Explanation.". *AI Magazine*, *38*(3), 50–57. DOI: 10.1609/aimag.v38i3.2741

Guidotti, R., Monreale, A., Ruggieri, S., Turini, F., Pedreschi, D., & Giannotti, F. (2018). *A Survey Of Methods For Explaining Black Box Models*. ArXiv.org. https://arxiv.org/abs/1802.01933

Gunning, D., Stefik, M., Choi, J., Miller, T., Stumpf, S., & Yang, G.-Z. (2019). XAI—Explainable artificial intelligence. *Science Robotics*, *4*(37), eaay7120. Advance online publication. DOI: 10.1126/scirobotics.aay7120

Gursoy, F., & Kakadiaris, Ioannis A. (2022). *System Cards for AI-Based Decision-Making for Public Policy*. ArXiv.org. https://arxiv.org/abs/2203.04754

Hassija, V., Chamola, V., Saxena, V., Chanana, V., Parashari, P., Mumtaz, S., & Guizani, M. (2020). Present landscape of quantum computing. *IET Quantum Communication, 1*(2), 42–48. DOI: 10.1049/iet-qtc.2020.0027

Hebbia. (2024, July). *Hebbia raises $130M to build AI platform for knowledge retrieval*. Bloomberg Law/Fast Company.

Kairouz, P., McMahan, H. B., Avent, B., Bellet, A., Bennis, M., Bhagoji, A. N., Bonawitz, K., Charles, Z., Cormode, G., Cummings, R., D'Oliveira, R. G. L., Rouayheb, S. E., Evans, D., Gardner, J., Garrett, Z., Gascón, A., Ghazi, B., Gibbons, P. B., Gruteser, M., & Harchaoui, Z. (2019). Advances and Open Problems in Federated Learning. *ArXiv:1912.04977 [Cs, Stat]*. https://arxiv.org/abs/1912.04977

Kamarinou, D., Millard, C., & Singh, J. (2016, November 8). Machine Learning with Personal Data (available on SSRN). https://www.researchgate.net/publication/348755857_Machine_Learning_with_Personal_Data_available_on_SSRN

Katz, D. M., Bommarito, M. J.II, & Blackman, J. (2014). Predicting the Behavior of the Supreme Court of the United States: A General Approach. *ArXiv:1407.6333 [Physics]*. https://arxiv.org/abs/1407.6333

Kumar, A. J., Jain, S. (2025). *Lead Smart in the AI Era*. 9789361564925

Leenes, R., van Brakel, R., Gutwirth, S., & de Hert, P. (2017). Data protection and privacy: The age of intelligent machines. In *Tilburg University Research Portal*. Hart Publishing Ltd. https://research.tilburguniversity.edu/en/publications/data-protection-and-privacy-the-age-of-intelligent-machines

Levy, S. (2025, February 7). *2025: The Year of the AI App*. WIRED. https://www.wired.com/story/plaintext-ai-apps-foundation-models/

Li, L. (2024, December 16). *Comprehensive survey on adversarial examples in cybersecurity: impacts, challenges, and mitigation strategies*. arXiv.

Lum, K., & Isaac, W. (2016). To Predict and Serve? *Significance, 13*(5), 14–19. DOI: 10.1111/j.1740-9713.2016.00960.x

Lungu, M. (2025, May). *Predictive policing AI is on the rise: making it accountable to the public could curb its harmful effects*. Policing Insight.

Magesh, V., Surani, F., Dahl, M., Suzgun, M., Manning, C. D., & Ho, D. E. (2024, May 30). *Hallucination-free? assessing the reliability of leading AI legal research tools*. arXiv.

Mcginnis, J., & Pearce, R. (2014). The Great Disruption: How Machine Intelligence Will Transform the Role of Lawyers in the Delivery of Legal Services. *Fordham Law Review, 82*(6). https://ir.lawnet.fordham.edu/cgi/viewcontent.cgi?article=5007&context=flr

Medvedeva, M., Vols, M., & Wieling, M. (2019). Using machine learning to predict decisions of the European Court of Human Rights. *Artificial Intelligence and Law*. Advance online publication. DOI: 10.1007/s10506-019-09255-y

Mehrabi, N., Morstatter, F., Saxena, N., Lerman, K., & Galstyan, A. (2019). A Survey on Bias and Fairness in Machine Learning. *ArXiv:1908.09635 [Cs]*. https://arxiv.org/abs/1908.09635

Mittelstadt, B. D., Allo, P., Taddeo, M., Wachter, S., & Floridi, L. (2016). The Ethics of algorithms: Mapping the Debate. *Big Data & Society, 3*(2), 1–21. DOI: 10.1177/2053951716679679

Netscout (2025). *NETSCOUT Reports Fourth Quarter and Full Fiscal Year 2025 Financial Results and Announces Executive Transitions*. Netscout.com. https://ir.netscout.com/investors/press-releases/press-release-details/2025/NETSCOUT-Reports-Fourth-Quarter-and-Full-Fiscal-Year-2025-Financial-Results-and-Announces-Executive-Transitions/default.aspx

Nguyen, T., Quach, S., & Thaichon, P. (2021). The effect of AI quality on customer experience and brand relationship. *Journal of Consumer Behaviour, 21*(3), 481–493. DOI: 10.1002/cb.1974

Raji, I. D., Smart, A., White, R. N., Mitchell, M., Gebru, T., Hutchinson, B., Smith-Loud, J., Theron, D., & Barnes, P. (2020). Closing the AI Accountability Gap: Defining an End-to-End Framework for Internal Algorithmic Auditing. *ArXiv:2001.00973 [Cs]*. https://arxiv.org/abs/2001.00973 DOI: 10.1145/3351095.3372873

Ranchordás, S. (2021). Experimental Regulations for AI: Sandboxes for Morals and Mores. *Morals & Machines*, *1*(1), 86–100. DOI: 10.5771/2747-5182-2021-1-86

Remus, D., & Levy, F. S. (2015). Can Robots Be Lawyers? Computers, Lawyers, and the Practice of Law. SSRN *Electronic Journal*. https://doi.org/DOI: 10.2139/ssrn.2701092

Ritter, S. M., & Ferguson, S. (2017). Happy creativity: Listening to happy music facilitates divergent thinking. *PLoS One*, *12*(9), e0182210. DOI: 10.1371/journal.pone.0182210

Schwartz, R., Dodge, J., Smith, N. A., & Etzioni, O. (2020). Green AI. *Communications of the ACM*, *63*(12), 54–63. DOI: 10.1145/3381831

Sibanda, I. (2025, August 5). *Combating the threat of adversarial machine learning to AI-driven cybersecurity*. ISACA Industry News.

Sommer, R., & Paxson, V. (2010). Outside the Closed World: On Using Machine Learning for Network Intrusion Detection. *2010 IEEE Symposium on Security and Privacy*, 305–316. https://doi.org/DOI: 10.1109/SP.2010.25

Surden, H. (2014). Machine Learning and Law. *Washington Law Review (Seattle, Wash.)*, *89*, 86–115.

Szabo, N. (1997). Formalizing and Securing Relationships on Public Networks. *First Monday*, *2*(9). Advance online publication. DOI: 10.5210/fm.v2i9.548

Taddeo, M., McCutcheon, T., & Floridi, L. (2019). Trusting artificial intelligence in cybersecurity is a double-edged sword. *Nature Machine Intelligence*, *1*(12), 557–560. DOI: 10.1038/s42256-019-0109-1

Tallam, K. (2025). *Transforming Cyber Defense: Harnessing Agentic and Frontier AI for Proactive, Ethical Threat Intelligence.* ArXiv. https://arxiv.org/pdf/2503.00164

Veale, M., Binns, R., & Edwards, L. (2018). Algorithms that remember: Model inversion attacks and data protection law. *Philosophical Transactions. Series A, Mathematical, Physical, and Engineering Sciences, 376*(2133), 20180083. DOI: 10.1098/rsta.2018.0083

Veale, M., & Zuiderveen Borgesius, F. (2021). Demystifying the Draft EU Artificial Intelligence Act — Analysing the good, the bad, and the unclear elements of the proposed approach. *Computer Law Review International, 22*(4), 97–112. DOI: 10.9785/cri-2021-220402

Wachter, S., Mittelstadt, B., & Russell, C. (2018). Counterfactual Explanations without Opening the Black Box: Automated Decisions and the GDPR. *ArXiv:1711.00399 [Cs].* https://arxiv.org/abs/1711.00399

Wagner, S. J., Matek, C., Shetab Boushehri, S., Boxberg, M., Lamm, L., Sadafi, A., Winter, D. J. E., Marr, C., & Peng, T. (2024). Built to Last? Reproducibility and Reusability of Deep Learning Algorithms in Computational Pathology. *Modern Pathology, 37*(1), 100350. DOI: 10.1016/j.modpat.2023.100350

Wagner, T. L., & Blewer, A. (2019). "The Word Real Is No Longer Real": Deepfakes, Gender, and the Challenges of AI-Altered Video. *Open Information Science, 3*(1), 32–46. DOI: 10.1515/opis-2019-0003

Yin, W., Kann, K., Yu, M., & Schütze, H. (2017). *Comparative Study of CNN and RNN for Natural Language Processing*. ArXiv.org. https://arxiv.org/abs/1702.01923

Zarsky, T. (2016). The Trouble with Algorithmic Decisions: An Analytic Road Map to Examine Efficiency and Fairness in Automated and Opaque Decision Making. *Science, Technology & Human Values, 41*(1), 118–132. https://www.jstor.org/stable/43671285. DOI: 10.1177/0162243915605575

Zuboff, S. (2019). *The Age of Surveillance Capitalism: The Fight for a Human Future at the New Frontier of Power*. Public Affairs.

Compilation of References

Acemoglu, D., & Restrepo, P. (2019). Automation and new tasks: How technology displaces and reinstates labor. *The Journal of Economic Perspectives*, *33*(2), 3–30. DOI: 10.1257/jep.33.2.3

Acharya, M. (2025, June 10). World GDP Ranking 2025 list. Cleartax. https://cleartax.in/s/world-gdp-ranking-list#

Act, A. I. (2025, July 10). Shaping Europe's Digital Future. https://digital-strategy.ec.europa.eu/en/policies/regulatory-framework-ai

Act, E. U. A. I. (2021). *Proposal for a Regulation of the European Parliament and of the Council laying down harmonized rules on artificial intelligence*. COM(2021) 206 final. European Commission.

Adadi, A. (2021). A survey on the interpretability of machine learning. *Artificial Intelligence Review*, *54*(1), 1–43. DOI: 10.1007/s10462-020-09836-5

AI in India. A Strategic Necessity. (2024, May 30). BCG Global. https://www.bcg.com/publications/2023/ai-in-india-a-strategic-necessity

AI regulation in India Current state and future perspectives. (2024, January 26). https://www.morganlewis.com/blogs/sourcingatmorganlewis. https://www.morganlewis.com/blogs/sourcingatmorganlewis/2024/01/ai-regulation-in-india-current-state-and-future-perspectives

Aiken, A. (2019). GDPR compliance in Canadian legal institutions: A case study on trial duration predictions. *Canadian Journal of Law and Technology*, *12*(2), 134–147. DOI: 10.2139/ssrn.3334889

Akgun, A. E., Keskin, H., & Byrne, J. (2022). Organizational governance of artificial intelligence: Ethics, oversight, and strategic alignment. *Technology in Society*, *70*, 102021. DOI: 10.1016/j.techsoc.2022.102021

Aletras, N., Tsarapatsanis, D., Preoţiuc-Pietro, D., & Lampos, V. (2016). Predicting judicial decisions of the European Court of Human Rights: A Natural Language Processing perspective. *PeerJ. Computer Science*, *2*(1), e93. DOI: 10.7717/peerj-cs.93

Ali, S. I., Jadhav, J., Arunkumar, R., & Kanagavalli, N. (2022). A smart resource utilization algorithm for high speed 5G communication networks based on cloud servers. *ICTACT Journal on Communication Technology*, *13*(4), 2800–2804. DOI: 10.21917/ijct.2022.0414

Ali, S. I., Ravuri, H. K., Lakshmi, V. T., Ramya, A., Lavanya, K., & Bahade, S. (2024). The role of nanomaterials in the development of high-performance batteries. *Nanotechnology Perceptions*, *20*(S11), 1125–1140. https://www.nano-ntp.com

Ali, S., Abuhmed, T., El-Sappagh, S., Muhammad, K., Alonso-Moral, J. M., Confalonieri, R., Guidotti, R., Del Ser, J., Díaz-Rodríguez, N., & Herrera, F. (2023). Explainable Artificial Intelligence (XAI): What we know and what is left to attain Trustworthy Artificial Intelligence. *Information Fusion*, *99*, 101805. DOI: 10.1016/j.inffus.2023.101805

Al-kfairy, M., Mustafa, D., Kshetri, N., Insiew, M., & Alfandi, O. (2024). Ethical challenges and solutions of generative AI: An interdisciplinary perspective. *Informatics (MDPI)*, *11*(3), 58. DOI: 10.3390/informatics11030058

Almasoud, A. S. (2024). Algorithmic fairness in predictive policing: A systematic review and bias mitigation of age-related disparities. *AI and Ethics*. Advance online publication. DOI: 10.1007/s43681-024-00541-3

Ambrogi & Lawyer. (2017, January 20). *Blue Hill gives more details on Ross Artificial Intelligence Benchmarking Report*. LawSites. https://www.lawnext.com/2017/01/blue-hill-gives-details-ross-artificial-intelligence-benchmarking-report.html

Amershi, S., Inkpen, K., Teevan, J., Kikin-Gil, R., Horvitz, E., Weld, D., Vorvoreanu, M., Fourney, A., Nushi, B., Collisson, P., Suh, J., Iqbal, S., & Bennett, P. N. (2019). Guidelines for Human-AI Interaction. *Proceedings of the 2019 CHI Conference on Human Factors in Computing Systems - CHI '19*. https://doi.org/DOI: 10.1145/3290605.3300233

Amir, O., Kline, A., & Ward, C. (2019). Accessibility in artificial intelligence: Guiding principles and inclusive practices. *AI & Society*, *34*(4), 737–747. DOI: 10.1007/s00146-018-0838-y

Angwin, J., Kirchner, L., Larson, J., & Mattu, S. (2016, May 23). *Machine bias: There's software used across the country to predict future criminals. and it's biased against blacks.* Benton Foundation. https://www.benton.org/headlines/machine-bias-theres-software-used-across-country-predict-future-criminals-and-its-biased

Angwin, J., Larson, J., Mattu, S., & Kirchner, L. (2016). *Machine bias*. ProPublica.

Anjomshoae, S., Najjar, A., Calvaresi, D., & Främling, K. (2022). Explainable agents and robots: Results from a systematic literature review. *Autonomous Agents and Multi-Agent Systems*, *36*(1), 1–42. DOI: 10.1007/s10458-021-09537-0

Ashley, K. D. (2017). *Artificial Intelligence and Legal Analytics*. Cambridge Core. https://www.cambridge.org/core/books/artificial-intelligence-and-legal-analytics/E7D705EEF392501A1DB180645917E7E0

Ashley, K. D. (2019). *Artificial intelligence and legal analytics: new tools for law practice in the digital age*. Cambridge University Press, Cop.

Atlantic Council. (2025, March 13). India's unique approach to AI autonomy: A three-pillar strategy. Available at https://www.atlanticcouncil.org/in-depth-research-reports/issue-brief/indias-path-to-ai-autonomy/

Attard-Frost, B. (2024). The governance of artificial intelligence in Canada: The role of the Directive on Automated Decision-making. *Government Information Quarterly*. Advance online publication. DOI: 10.1016/j.giq.2024.101869

Authority, C. and M. (2022, March 25). *Online platforms and Digital Advertising Market Study, appendix C: Market outcomes 2020 (CMA)*. GOV.UK. https://www.gov.uk/find-digital-market-research/online-platforms-and-digital-advertising-market-study-appendix-c-market-outcomes-2020-cma

Axios. (2025). *Axios*. Axios Media Inc. https://www.axios.com/events/ai

Baars, B. J. (2005). Global workspace theory of consciousness: Toward a cognitive neuroscience of human experience. *Progress in Brain Research*, *150*, 45–53. DOI: 10.1016/S0079-6123(05)50004-9 PMID: 16186014

Bag, S. (2021). Trust in artificial intelligence: A review of trust building in AI and its implications. *Technology in Society*, *67*, 101740. DOI: 10.1016/j.techsoc.2021.101740

Bahl, U., Topaz, C., Obermüller, L., Goldstein, S., & Sneirson, M. (2024). Algorithms in judges' hands: incarceration and inequity in Broward County, Florida.

Ballesteros-Pérez, P., Sanz-Ablanedo, E., Cerezo-Narváez, A., Lucko, G., Pastor-Fernández, A., Otero-Mateo, M., & Contreras-Samper, J. P. (2020). Forecasting accuracy of in-progress activity duration and cost estimates. *Journal of Construction Engineering and Management*, *146*(9), 04020104. DOI: 10.1061/(ASCE)CO.1943-7862.0001900

Barredo Arrieta, A., Díaz-Rodríguez, N., Del Ser, J., Bennetot, A., Tabik, S., Barbado, A., Garcia, S., Gil-Lopez, S., Molina, D., Benjamins, R., Chatila, R., & Herrera, F. (2020). Explainable Artificial Intelligence (XAI): Concepts, taxonomies, opportunities and challenges toward responsible AI. *Information Fusion*, *58*, 82–115. DOI: 10.1016/j.inffus.2019.12.012

Batarseh, F. A., & Freeman, L. A. (2021). Data veracity: Exploring the reliability dimension of big data. *Journal of Big Data*, *8*(1), 1–25. DOI: 10.1186/s40537-021-00467-0

Bender, E. M., Gebru, T., McMillan-Major, A., & Shmitchell, S. (2021). On the dangers of stochastic parrots: Can language models be too big? *FAccT '21: Proceedings of the 2021 ACM Conference on Fairness, Accountability, and Transparency*, 610–623. https://doi.org/DOI: 10.1145/3442188.3445922

Bessen, J. (2019). AI and jobs: The role of demand. NBER Working Paper No. 24235. DOI: 10.3386/w24235

Bhale, S. (2025). Deepfake laws in India: The need for legal regulation in the AI era. DOI: 10.2139/ssrn.5153296

Bhatnagar, M., & Huchhanavar, S. (2023, July). Predicting delays in Indian lower courts using AutoML and Decision Forests. In *International Conference on Computing, Intelligence and Data Analytics* (pp. 166-180). Cham: Springer Nature Switzerland.

Bietti, E., Saxena, N. A., & Livio, G. (2021). From ethics washing to ethics bashing: A view on tech ethics from within moral philosophy. *Minds and Machines*, *31*(4), 595–619. DOI: 10.1007/s11023-021-09579-3

Binns, R. (2021). On the apparent conflict between individual and group fairness. *ACM Conference on Fairness, Accountability, and Transparency*, *3*(1), 514–524. DOI: 10.1145/3442188.3445896

Bishnoi, R., & Bhagtani, H. (2025). Reimagining legal personhood in the age of artificial intelligence: A jurisprudential and normative inquiry. In *Proceedings of the innovative multidisciplinary approaches to global challenges: Advances in social science, sustainability, equity, and ethics in an interconnected world.* DOI: 10.2991/978-2-38476-416-7_9

Blinova, O., & Tarasov, N. (2022). A hybrid model of complexity estimation: Evidence from Russian legal texts. *Frontiers in Artificial Intelligence*, *5*, 1008530. DOI: 10.3389/frai.2022.1008530 PMID: 36388401

Borenstein, J., Howard, A., & Miller, K. W. (2021). The role of organizational culture in ethical AI. *AI and Ethics, 1*(4), 431–438. DOI: 10.1007/s43681-021-00048-5

British Standards Institution. (2024, July 30). *Momentum of AI adoption strongest in India and China, finds BSI.* BSI. https://www.bsigroup.com/en-US/insights-and-media/media-center/press-releases/2024/july/momentum-of-ai-adoption-strongest-in-india-china-and-us-finds-bsi/

Brookings Institution. (2025, April 9). *What the public thinks about AI and the implications for governance.* Brookings. https://doi.org/DOI:10.3416/pub-think-ai-2025

Brundage, M., Avin, S., Clark, J., Toner, H., Eckersley, P., Garfinkel, B., Dafoe, A., Scharre, P., Zeitzoff, T., Filar, B., Anderson, H., Roff, H., Allen, G. C., Steinhardt, J., & Flynn, C. hÉigeartaigh, Seán Ó, Beard, S., Belfield, H., Farquhar, S., & Lyle, C. (2018, February 20). *The Malicious Use of Artificial Intelligence: Forecasting, Prevention, and Mitigation.* ArXiv.org. https://arxiv.org/abs/1802.07228

Brynjolfsson, E., & McAfee, A. (2014). *The second machine age: Work, progress, and prosperity in a time of brilliant technologies.* W.W. Norton & Company.

Brynjolfsson, E., Rock, D., & Syverson, C. (2018). Artificial intelligence and the modern productivity paradox: A clash of expectations and statistics. In Agrawal, A., Gans, J., & Goldfarb, A. (Eds.), *The economics of artificial intelligence: An agenda* (pp. 23–57). University of Chicago Press.

Buczak, A. L., & Guven, E. (2016). A Survey of Data Mining and Machine Learning Methods for Cyber Security Intrusion Detection. *IEEE Communications Surveys and Tutorials, 18*(2), 1153–1176. DOI: 10.1109/COMST.2015.2494502

Bughin, J., Hazan, E., Ramaswamy, S., Chui, M., Allas, T., Dahlström, P., Henke, N., Trench, M., & Manyika, J. (2018). Notes from the AI frontier: Modeling the impact of AI on the world economy. McKinsey Global Institute. https://www.mckinsey.com/featured-insights/artificial-intelligence/notes-from-the-ai-frontier-modeling-the-impact-of-ai-on-the-world-economy

Bulgakova, I. (2023, December). Duration of criminal proceedings: Human rights and jurisdiction aspects. In *individual. Society. State. Proceedings of the International Student and Teacher Scientific and Practical Conference* (pp. 126-130).

Buolamwini, J., & Gebru, T. (2018). Gender shades: Intersectional accuracy disparities in commercial gender classification. *Proceedings of Machine Learning Research*, *81*, 77–91.

Burri, T. (2018). Free movement of algorithms: Artificially intelligent persons conquer the European Union's internal market. In *Research handbook on the law of artificial intelligence*. Edward Elgar.

Butt, U. M., Letchmunan, S., Hassan, F. H., & Koh, T. W. (2022). Hybrid of deep learning and exponential smoothing for enhancing crime forecasting accuracy. *PLoS One*, *17*(9), e0274172. DOI: 10.1371/journal.pone.0274172 PMID: 36070317

California Legislative information. (n.d.). https://leginfo.legislature.ca.gov/faces/codes_displayText.xhtml?division=3.&part=4.&lawCode=CIV&t%20itle=1.81.5

Calo, R. (2015). *Robotics and the lessons of Cyberlaw*. UW Law Digital Commons. https://digitalcommons.law.uw.edu/faculty-articles/23/

Cao, L., Wang, Z., Xiao, C., & Sun, J. (2024). PILOT: Legal Case Outcome Prediction with Case Law. *arXiv preprint arXiv:2401.15770*. DOI: 10.18653/v1/2024.naacl-long.34

Caton, S., & Haas, C. (2023). Fairness in machine learning: A survey. *ACM Computing Surveys*, *55*(13s), 1–37. DOI: 10.1145/3597199

Cerrato, P.. (2022). A proposal for developing a platform that evaluates algorithmic biases in healthcare AI. *PLOS Digital Health*. Advance online publication. DOI: 10.1371/journal.pdig.0000651

Chouldechova, A., & Roth, A. (2020). A snapshot of the frontiers of fairness in machine learning. *Communications of the ACM*, *63*(5), 82–89. DOI: 10.1145/3376898

Choung, H., David, P., & Seberger, J. S. (2023). A multilevel framework for AI governance: Cultivating trust across individual, organizational, and societal levels. *AI and Ethics*, *3*(2), 285–298. DOI: 10.1007/s43681-023-00269-9

CLIO. (2025, March 10). *What is AI and how can law firms use it?* Clio. https://www.clio.com/resources/ai-for-lawyers/lawyer-ai/

Coeckelbergh, M. (2021). AI ethics. *The MIT Press Essential Knowledge Series*. https://doi.org/DOI: 10.7551/mitpress/12433.001.0001

Company, M. (2016). *The age of analytics: Competing in a data driven world* - ... mgi the age of analytics full report.pdf. https://www.mckinsey.com/~/media/mckinsey/industries/public and social sector/our insights/the age of analytics competing in a data driven world/mgi-the-age-of-analytics-full-report.pdf

Coons, C., Blackburn, M., Klobuchar, A., & Tillis, T. (2023). The Nurture originals, Foster Art, and Keep Entertainment Safe (NO FAKES) Act. https://www.coons.senate.gov/imo/media/doc/no_fakes_act_one_pager.pdf

Corp, E. (2024, March 15). *Extropic Emerges from Stealth, aiming to revolutionize Generative AI with Physics-based AI processors*. Prnewswire.com; Cision PR Newswire. https://www.prnewswire.com/news-releases/extropic-emerges-from-stealth-aiming-to-revolutionize-generative-ai-with-physics-based-ai-processors-302090040.html

Costanza-Chock, S. (2018). Design Justice, A.I., and Escape from the Matrix of Domination. *Journal of Design and Science*, *3*(5). Advance online publication. DOI: 10.21428/96c8d426

Council (EU). E. (2023). *The General Data Protection Regulation - Consilium.* European Council Council of the European Union. https://www.consilium.europa.eu/en/policies/data-protection/data-protection-regulation/

Council of Europe. (2024). Framework convention on artificial intelligence and human rights, democracy and the rule of law. September 5, 2024. https://rm.coe.int/1680afae3c

Cowan, D. (2019). *Richard Susskind, online courts and the Future of Justice (Oxford: Oxford University Press, 2019).* Schulich Law Scholars. https://digitalcommons.schulichlaw.dal.ca/cjlt/vol18/iss2/5/

Crawford, K., & Calo, R. (2016). There is a blind spot in AI research. *Nature, 538*(7625), 311–313. DOI: 10.1038/538311a

Datasphere Initiative. (2025). Sandboxes for AI: Tools for a new frontier. https://www.thedatasphere.org/wp-content/uploads/2025/02/Report-Sandboxes-for-AI-2025.pdf

Dehaene, S., Changeux, J., & Naccache, L. (2011). The global neuronal workspace model of conscious access: From neuronal architectures to clinical applications. *Research and Perspectives in Neurosciences*, 55–84. DOI: 10.1007/978-3-642-18015-6_4

Delacroix, S., Lawrence, N. D. (2019). Bottom-up data Trusts: disturbing the 'one size fits all' approach to data governance. *International Data Privacy Law*, 9(4), 2 36–252. https://doi.org/DOI: 10.1093/idpl/ipz014

Dignum, V. (2022). The role of communication in building trust in AI systems. *AI and Ethics*, *2*(3), 421–432. DOI: 10.1007/s43681-021-00084-6

Diro, A. A., & Chilamkurti, N. (2018). Distributed attack detection scheme using deep learning approach for Internet of Things. *Future Generation Computer Systems*, *82*, 761–768. DOI: 10.1016/j.future.2017.08.043

Doshi-Velez, F., & Kim, B. (2017). Towards A Rigorous Science of Interpretable Machine Learning. *ArXiv:1702.08608 [Cs, Stat]*, 2(2). https://arxiv.org/abs/1702.08608

Duan, Y., Edwards, J. S., & Dwivedi, Y. K. (2023). Artificial intelligence for decision making in the era of Big Data—Evolution, challenges and research agenda. *International Journal of Information Management, 71*, 102642. DOI: 10.1016/j.ijinfomgt.2023.102642

Eldar Shafir, S. M. (2018, September 16). *Scarcity: Why having too little means so much*. Behavioral Scientist. https://behavioralscientist.org/scarcity-excerpt-mullainathan-shafir/

Engemann, A. (2024, November 20). AI and predictive policing: Balancing technological innovation and civil liberties. *Minnesota Journal of Law, Science & Technology*.

Esteva, A., Kuprel, B., Novoa, R. A., Ko, J., Swetter, S. M., Blau, H. M., & Thrun, S. (2017). Dermatologist-level classification of skin cancer with deep neural networks. *Nature, 542*(7639), 115–118. DOI: 10.1038/nature21056

European Commission. (2014, October 3). *Mergers: Commission approves acquisition of WhatsApp by Facebook*. European Commission - European Commission. https://europa.eu/rapid/press-release_IP-14-1088_en.htm

European Commission. (2018). *Shaping Europe's Digital Future*. Shaping Europe's digital future. https://digital-strategy.ec.europa.eu/

European Union (2024). Regulation (EU) 2024/1689 of the European Parliament and of the Council of 13 June 2024 laying down harmonised rules on artificial intelligence and amending Regulations (EC) No 300/2008, (EU) No 167/2013, (EU) No 168/2013, (EU) 2018/858, (EU) 2018/1139 and (EU) 2019/2144 and Directives 2014/90/EU, (EU) 2016/797 and (EU) 2020/1828 (Artificial Intelligence Act). https://eur-lex.europa.eu/legal-content/EN/TXT/PDF/

European Union. (2018). *Com(2011)681 - renewed EU Strategy 2011-14 for Corporate Social Responsibility - Main Contents*. COM(2011)681 - Renewed EU strategy 2011-14 for Corporate Social Responsibility - EU monitor. https://www.eumonitor.eu/9353000/1/j4nvkkpftveemt7_j9vvik7m1c3gyxp/vitwrzhm31gk

Fagan, F. (2021). E*bers on Liability for AI and EU Consumer Law.* AI Law Blawg. https://ailawblawg.com/2021/06/29/

Farooq, M. S. (2025). AI IN FINTECH: AN EVALUATION OF FINANCIAL PAYMENT SYSTEMS. *International Journal of Cultural Studies, 20*(2), 157–210. https://www.researchgate.net/publication/387823057_AI_IN_FINTECH_AN_EVALUATION_OF_FINANCIAL_PAYMENT_SYSTEMS

Federal Trade Commission. (2014, May). *Data brokers: A call for transparency and Accountability.* DATA BROKERS A Call for Transparency and Accountability. https://www.ftc.gov/system/files/documents/reports/data-brokers-call-transparency-accountability-report-federal-trade-commission-may-2014/140527databrokerreport.pdf

Feng, J., Luo, C., & Li, B. (2021). A review of fairness-aware machine learning for responsible AI. *IEEE Transactions on Knowledge and Data Engineering, 35*(1), 1–20. DOI: 10.1109/TKDE.2021.3077524

Finck, M. (2019). Smart contracts as a form of solely automated processing under the GDPR. *International Data Privacy Law, 9*(2), 78–94. DOI: 10.1093/idpl/ipz004

Floridi, L., & Cowls, J. (2019). A Unified Framework of Five Principles for AI in Society. *Harvard Data Science Review, 1*(1). Advance online publication. DOI: 10.1162/99608f92.8cd550d1

Floridi, L., & Cowls, J. (2022). A unified framework of five principles for AI in society. *Harvard Data Science Review, 4*(1). Advance online publication. DOI: 10.1162/99608f92.e8fbcf64

Floridi, L., Cowls, J., Beltrametti, M., Chatila, R., Chazerand, P., Dignum, V., & Vayena, E. (2022). An ethical framework for a good AI society: Opportunities, risks, principles, and recommendations. *Minds and Machines, 32*(2), 217–240. DOI: 10.1007/s11023-021-09563-4

Forrest, K. B. (2024). The ethics and challenges of legal personhood for AI. *The Yale Law Journal, 133*, 1175–1211. https://www.yalelawjournal.org/pdf/ForrestYLJForumEssay_at8hdu63.pdf

Frey, C. B., & Osborne, M. A. (2017). The future of employment: How susceptible are jobs to computerization? *Technological Forecasting and Social Change*, *114*, 254–280. DOI: 10.1016/j.techfore.2016.08.019

Fridahl, M., Bellamy, R., Hansson, A., & Haikola, S. (2020). Mapping Multi-Level policy incentives for bioenergy with carbon capture and storage in Sweden. *Frontiers in Climate*, *2*, 604787. Advance online publication. DOI: 10.3389/fclim.2020.604787

Friedman, B., & Hendry, D. G. (2019). *Value Sensitive Design*. MIT Press. DOI: 10.7551/mitpress/7585.001.0001

Garikapati, D. (2024). Autonomous vehicles: Evolution of artificial intelligence in driving ethics and liability frameworks. *Big Data and Cognitive Computing*, *8*(4), 42. DOI: 10.3390/bdcc8040042

Garrido, J. (2023). Digital Tokens: A Legal Perspective. *IMF Working Paper*, *2023*(151), 1. DOI: 10.5089/9798400250149.001

General Data Protection Regulation (GDPR). (2016). *Regulation (EU) 2016/679 of the European Parliament and of the Council*. Official Journal of the European Union.

German Institute for Global and Area Studies. (2021). Digital surveillance and the threat to civil liberties in India (GIGA Focus Asia, No. 3). Available at https://nbn-resolving.org/urn:nbn:de:0168-ssoar-73130-3

Girhepuje, S., Verma, A., & Raina, G. (2024, September 26). *A survey on offensive AI within cybersecurity*. arXiv.

Gless, S., Silverman, E., & Weigend, T. (2016). If Robots Cause Harm, Who is to Blame? Self-Driving Cars and Criminal Liability. SSRN *Electronic Journal*. https://doi.org/DOI: 10.2139/ssrn.2724592

Glikson, E., & Woolley, A. W. (2022). Human trust in artificial intelligence: Review of empirical research. *The Academy of Management Annals*, *16*(1), 1–45. DOI: 10.5465/annals.2019.0057

Gonzalez, C. (2019, January 22). *Rol of Standards with Respect to Innovative Technologies: AI*. https://doi.org/DOI: 10.13140/RG.2.2.17628.41601

Goodman, B., & Flaxman, S. (2017). European Union Regulations on Algorithmic Decision-Making and a "Right to Explanation.". *AI Magazine*, *38*(3), 50–57. DOI: 10.1609/aimag.v38i3.2741

Gordon, F. (2019, November). *Virginia Eubanks (2018) automating inequality: How high-tech tools profile, police, and punish the poor.* https://www.researchgate.net/publication/337578410_Virginia_Eubanks_2018_Automating_Inequality_How_HighTech_Tools_Profile_Police_and_Punish_the_Poor_New_York_Picador_St_Martin's_Press

Gruginskie, L. A. D. S., & Vaccaro, G. L. R. (2018). Lawsuit lead time prediction: Comparison of data mining techniques based on categorical response variable. *PLoS One*, *13*(6), e0198122. DOI: 10.1371/journal.pone.0198122 PMID: 29856787

Guidotti, R., Monreale, A., Ruggieri, S., Turini, F., Pedreschi, D., & Giannotti, F. (2018). *A Survey Of Methods For Explaining Black Box Models*. ArXiv.org. https://arxiv.org/abs/1802.01933

Gunning, D., Stefik, M., Choi, J., Miller, T., Stumpf, S., & Yang, G.-Z. (2019). XAI—Explainable artificial intelligence. *Science Robotics*, *4*(37), eaay7120. Advance online publication. DOI: 10.1126/scirobotics.aay7120

Gursoy, F., & Kakadiaris, Ioannis A. (2022). *System Cards for AI-Based Decision-Making for Public Policy*. ArXiv.org. https://arxiv.org/abs/2203.04754

Hao, K. (2021). Deepfakes are getting better. MIT Technology Review. https://www.technologyreview.com/2021/03/25/1021311/deepfakes-getting-better/

Harmon, S., Wilsmann, M., Joshi, G., Ballesteros, A., & Baitinger, P. (2024). Decoding India's AI governance strategy and its implications for the U.S.-India bilateral relationship. *Indian Public Policy Review*, *5*(4), 51–82. DOI: 10.55763/ippr.2024.05.04.003

Hassija, V., Chamola, V., Saxena, V., Chanana, V., Parashari, P., Mumtaz, S., & Guizani, M. (2020). Present landscape of quantum computing. *IET Quantum Communication*, *1*(2), 42–48. DOI: 10.1049/iet-qtc.2020.0027

Hebbia. (2024, July). *Hebbia raises $130M to build AI platform for knowledge retrieval.* Bloomberg Law/Fast Company.

Hengstler, M., Enkel, E., & Duelli, S. (2021). Applied artificial intelligence and trust—The case of autonomous vehicles and medical assistance devices. *Technological Forecasting and Social Change, 167*, 120635. DOI: 10.1016/j.techfore.2021.120635

Henschke, A., & Arora, C. (2024). Pluralism and the design of autonomous vehicles. *Philosophy & Technology, 37*(3), 1–19. DOI: 10.1007/s13347-024-00802-3

Hildebrandt, M. (2020). *Law for computer scientists and other folk.* Oxford University Press. DOI: 10.1093/oso/9780198860877.001.0001

Hill, K. (2024, February 20). *How target figured out a teen girl was pregnant before her father did.* Forbes. https://www.forbes.com/sites/kashmirhill/2012/02/16/how-target-figured-out-a-teen-girl-was-pregnant-before-her-father-did/

Huang, J. H., Yang, C. C., Shen, Y., Pacces, A. M., & Kanoulas, E. (2024, October). Optimizing numerical estimation and operational efficiency in the legal domain through large language models. In *Proceedings of the 33rd ACM International Conference on Information and Knowledge Management* (pp. 4554-4562). DOI: 10.1145/3627673.3680025

IEEE Standards Association. (2021). 7001-2021 – Standard for transparency of autonomous systems. https://standards.ieee.org/ieee/7001/6929/

India, I. your guide to investment opportunities. (2025, October 7). Invest India. https://www.investindia.gov.in/

INDIAai. (n.d.-a). https://indiaai.gov.in/research-reports/responsible-ai-part-1-principles-for-responsible-ai

INDIAai. (n.d.-b). https://indiaai.gov.in/research-reports/responsible-ai-part-2-operationalizing-principles-for-responsible-ai

Irmalasari, I., & Dwiyanti, L. (2023, October). Algorithm Analysis of Decision Tree, Gradient Boosting Decision Tree, and Random Forest for Classification (Case Study: West Java House of Representatives Election 2019). In *2023 International Conference on Electrical Engineering and Informatics (ICEEI)* (pp. 1-5). IEEE. DOI: 10.1109/ICEEI59426.2023.10346727

ISO/IEC 23894 (2023). Information technology — Artificial intelligence — Guidance on risk management. https://www.iso.org/standard/77304.html

ISO/IEC 42001 (2023). Information technology — Artificial intelligence — Management system. https://www.iso.org/standard/42001

Jobin, A., Ienca, M., & Vayena, E. (2019). The global landscape of AI ethics guidelines. *Nature Machine Intelligence, 1*(9), 389–399. DOI: 10.1038/s42256-019-0088-2

Jobin, A., & Mann, M. (2023). Governing AI ethics in practice: Accountability, impact assessment, and audit mechanisms. *AI and Ethics, 3*(2), 199–214. DOI: 10.1007/s43681-022-00169-w

Jobin, A., & Mittelstadt, B. (2023). Communicating AI decision-making: Strategies for transparency and stakeholder trust. *Journal of Business Ethics, 184*(2), 393–410. DOI: 10.1007/s10551-022-05197-2

Johansson, S. E., Larsen, S. S., Povlsen, G. K., & Edvinsson, L. (2014). Early MEK1/2 inhibition after global cerebral ischemia in rats reduces brain damage and improves outcome by preventing delayed vasoconstrictor receptor upregulation. *PLoS One, 9*(3), e92417. Advance online publication. DOI: 10.1371/journal.pone.0092417 PMID: 24642693

Johnson, K. (2022). Ethical leadership in the age of artificial intelligence. *AI and Ethics, 2*(3), 381–392. DOI: 10.1007/s43681-021-00087-y

Johnson, K., Pasquale, F., & Chapman, C. (2021). Promoting ethical culture in AI governance. *Journal of Business Ethics, 170*(2), 243–256. DOI: 10.1007/s10551-020-04480-0

Jolly, R., Singh, P., & Kumar, A. (2025, May 9). The Confluence of AI and Data privacy: Aligning data privacy regime in India for the age of AI. Bar And Bench - Indian Legal News. https://www.barandbench.com/view-point/the-confluence-of-ai-and-data-privacy-aligning-data-privacy-regime-in-india-for-the-age-of-ai#:~:text=While%20DPDP%20Act%20aims%20to%20safeguard%20individual%20privacy,rights%20and%20exemptions%20available%20to%20train%20AI%20models

Judiciary, D. (2020). *Supreme Court Vidhik Anuvaad Software (SUVAS)*. Drishti Judiciary. https://www.drishtijudiciary.com/current-affairs/supreme-court-vidhik-anuvaad-software-suvas

Jussupow, E., Heinzl, A., & Spohrer, K. (2022). Organizational trust in artificial intelligence: A framework for responsible AI adoption. *Information & Management, 59*(6), 103677. DOI: 10.1016/j.im.2022.103677

Kabus, J., Piersiala, L., & Dziadkiewicz, M. (2024). *The use of information and Communication Technologies (ICT) in the management of the innovative and smart city*. CRC Press. DOI: 10.1201/9781003465157

Kahre, C., Hoffmann, C. P., & Ahlemann, F. (2022). Building organizational trust in AI: The role of governance, communication, and ethics. *Information Systems Frontiers, 24*(5), 1321–1335. DOI: 10.1007/s10796-021-10211-2

Kairouz, P., McMahan, H. B., Avent, B., Bellet, A., Bennis, M., Bhagoji, A. N., Bonawitz, K., Charles, Z., Cormode, G., Cummings, R., D'Oliveira, R. G. L., Rouayheb, S. E., Evans, D., Gardner, J., Garrett, Z., Gascón, A., Ghazi, B., Gibbons, P. B., Gruteser, M., & Harchaoui, Z. (2019). Advances and Open Problems in Federated Learning. *ArXiv:1912.04977 [Cs, Stat]*. https://arxiv.org/abs/1912.04977

Kamarinou, D., Millard, C., & Singh, J. (2016, November 8). Machine Learning with Personal Data (available on SSRN). https://www.researchgate.net/publication/348755857_Machine_Learning_with_Personal_Data_available_on_SSRN

Kaminski, M. E., & Malgieri, G. (2023). Algorithmic impact assessments under the GDPR: Producing multi-layered explanations. *International Data Privacy Law, 13*(1), 14–29. DOI: 10.1093/idpl/ipac027

Kaplan, J., McCandlish, S., Henighan, T., Brown, T. B., Chess, B., Child, R., ... (2020). Scaling laws for neural language models. *arXiv*. /arXiv.2001.08361DOI: 10.48550

Karanasiou, A., & Pinotsis, A. D. (2023). Artificial intelligence governance and leadership: Ethical perspectives. *AI and Ethics*, *3*(1), 45–59. DOI: 10.1007/s43681-021-00076-2

Katz, D. M., Bommarito, M. J.II, & Blackman, J. (2014). Predicting the Behavior of the Supreme Court of the United States: A General Approach. *ArXiv:1407.6333 [Physics]*. https://arxiv.org/abs/1407.6333

Kaushik, P., Sharma, H., & Sarna, A. (2025, January 22). AI for India 2030: A blueprint for inclusive growth and global leadership. Available at https://www.weforum.org/agenda/2025/01/ai-for-india2030/

Kiškis, M. (2023). Legal framework for the coexistence of humans and conscious AI. *Frontiers in Artificial Intelligence*, *6*, 1205465. DOI: 10.3389/frai.2023.1205465 PMID: 37808620

Klein, E., & Patrick, S. (2024). Envisioning a global regime complex to govern artificial intelligence. Carnegie Endowment for International Peace. https://carnegie-production-assets.s3.amazonaws.com/static/files/Klein_Patrick_AI_Regime_Complex-1.pdf

Kumar, A. J., Jain, S. (2025). *Lead Smart in the AI Era.* 9789361564925

Kurki, V. A. J. (2019). *A theory of legal personhood.* Oxford University Press. DOI: 10.1093/oso/9780198844037.001.0001

Lam, J. T., Liang, D., Dahan, S., & Zulkernine, F. H. (2020, August). The Gap between Deep Learning and Law: Predicting Employment Notice. In *NLLP@ KDD* (pp. 52-56).

Langer, M., Oster, D., & Speith, T. (2021). What do we want from explainable artificial intelligence (XAI)?—A stakeholder perspective on XAI and transparency. *Ethics and Information Technology*, *23*(3), 1–18. DOI: 10.1007/s10676-021-09579-5

Latham & Watkins LLP. (2023). India's Digital Personal Data Protection Act 2023 vs. the GDPR: A comparison. Available at https://www.lw.com/Indias-Digital-Personal-Data-Protection-Act-2023-vs-GDPR

Laukyte, M. (2019). AI as a Legal Person. In *Proceedings of the Seventeenth International Conference on Artificial Intelligence and Law*. Association for Computing Machinery. DOI: 10.1145/3322640.3326701

Lauwaert, L., & Oimann, A.-K. (2025). Moral responsibility and autonomous technologies: Does AI face a responsibility gap? In Smuha, N. A. (Ed.), *The Cambridge handbook of the law, ethics and policy of artificial intelligence* (pp. 101–116). Cambridge University Press. DOI: 10.1017/9781009367783.007

Leenes, R., van Brakel, R., Gutwirth, S., & de Hert, P. (2017). Data protection and privacy: The age of intelligent machines. In *Tilburg University Research Portal*. Hart Publishing Ltd. https://research.tilburguniversity.edu/en/publications/data-protection-and-privacy-the-age-of-intelligent-machines

Leong, B., Danks, D., & Lim, W. Y. (2022). Co-designing trustworthy AI: The role of participatory design in responsible AI. *AI and Ethics*, *2*(3), 411–423. DOI: 10.1007/s43681-021-00079-5

Leslie, D. (2023). Understanding artificial intelligence ethics and safety: A guide for the responsible design and implementation of AI systems in the public sector. *AI and Ethics*, *3*(2), 221–237. DOI: 10.1007/s43681-022-00168-x

Leslie, D., & Burr, C. (2021). The ethical risk assessment of AI. *AI and Ethics*, *1*(4), 405–415. DOI: 10.1007/s43681-021-00038-7

Levy, S. (2025, February 7). *2025: The Year of the AI App*. WIRED. https://www.wired.com/story/plaintext-ai-apps-foundation-models/

Li, L. (2024, December 16). *Comprehensive survey on adversarial examples in cybersecurity: impacts, challenges, and mitigation strategies*. arXiv.

Li, Y., Sun, Y., & Sun, J. (2021). Trust in AI systems: The interplay of user perceptions, transparency, and performance. *Computers in Human Behavior, 120*, 106732. DOI: 10.1016/j.chb.2021.106732

Loi, M., Ferrario, A., & Viganò, E. (2023). Ethics training for AI professionals: Building moral competencies for responsible innovation. *AI and Ethics, 3*(1), 53–64. DOI: 10.1007/s43681-021-00078-z

Long, D., & Magerko, B. (2022). Designing for trust in human–AI interaction: A review of strategies and frameworks. *International Journal of Human-Computer Studies, 158*, 102744. DOI: 10.1016/j.ijhcs.2021.102744

Lu, Q., Zhu, L., Xu, X., Whittle, J., & Xing, Z. (2022). Towards a roadmap on software engineering for responsible AI. arXiv. /arXiv.2203.08594DOI: 10.1145/3522664.3528607

Luckin, R., Holmes, W., Griffiths, M., & Forcier, L. B. (2016). *Intelligence unleashed: An argument for AI in education*. Pearson.

Lum, K., & Isaac, W. (2016). To Predict and Serve? *Significance, 13*(5), 14–19. DOI: 10.1111/j.1740-9713.2016.00960.x

Lundberg, S. M., Erion, G., Chen, H., DeGrave, A., Prutkin, J. M., Nair, B., Katz, R., Himmelfarb, J., Bansal, N., & Lee, S. I. (2020). From local explanations to global understanding with explainable AI for trees. *Nature Machine Intelligence*, 2(1), 56–67. DOI: 10.1038/s42256-019-0138-9

Lungu, M. (2025, May). *Predictive policing AI is on the rise: making it accountable to the public could curb its harmful effects*. Policing Insight.

MacCarthy, M. (2020). *Algorithmic Accountability Act of 2019. (2019). H.R. 2231 – Algorithmic Accountability Act of 2019*. U.S. House of Representatives.

Magesh, V., Surani, F., Dahl, M., Suzgun, M., Manning, C. D., & Ho, D. E. (2024, May 30). *Hallucination-free? assessing the reliability of leading AI legal research tools*. arXiv.

Marikyan, D., Papagiannidis, S., & Alamanos, E. (2022). Building consumer trust in artificial intelligence-enabled services: The role of performance, ethics, and transparency. *Computers in Human Behavior, 127*, 107030. DOI: 10.1016/j.chb.2021.107030

MAS Veritas Consortium. (2023). Fairness, ethics, accountability, transparency (FEAT) toolkit for responsible AI in financial services. *Monetary Authority of Singapore*. Retrieved from MAS website

Masala, M., Rebedea, T., & Velicu, H. (2024). Improving Legal Judgement Prediction in Romanian with Long Text Encoders. *arXiv preprint arXiv:2402.19170.*

McGinnis, J. O., & Pearce, R. G. (2014, May 15). *The Great Disruption: How Machine Intelligence will transform the role of lawyers in the delivery of Legal Services. SSRN.* https://papers.ssrn.com/sol3/papers.cfm?abstract_id=2436937

Mcginnis, J., & Pearce, R. (2014). The Great Disruption: How Machine Intelligence Will Transform the Role of Lawyers in the Delivery of Legal Services. *Fordham Law Review, 82*(6). https://ir.lawnet.fordham.edu/cgi/viewcontent.cgi?article=5007&context=flr

Medvedeva, M., Vols, M., & Wieling, M. (2019). Using machine learning to predict decisions of the European Court of Human Rights. *Artificial Intelligence and Law*. Advance online publication. DOI: 10.1007/s10506-019-09255-y

Mehrabi, N., Morstatter, F., Saxena, N., Lerman, K., & Galstyan, A. (2019). A Survey on Bias and Fairness in Machine Learning. *ArXiv:1908.09635 [Cs]*. https://arxiv.org/abs/1908.09635

Mehrabi, N., Morstatter, F., Saxena, N., Lerman, K., & Galstyan, A. (2022). A survey on bias and fairness in machine learning. *ACM Computing Surveys, 54*(6), 1–35. DOI: 10.1145/3457607

Merken, S. (2024, December 5). *US law firms eye 2025 with optimism, report says | Reuters*. report says. https://www.reuters.com/legal/government/us-law-firms-eye-2025-with-optimism-report-says-2024-12-05/

Mhlanga, D. (2023). The role of transparency, explainability and fairness in AI. *AI and Ethics, 3*(1), 25–38. DOI: 10.1007/s43681-022-00154-3

Ministry of Electronics and Information Technology. (2025). The Gazette of India: Extraordinary. https://www.dpdpa.in/dpdpa_rules_2025/dpdpa_draft_rules_english_.pdf

Mitchell, M., Wu, S., Zaldivar, A., Barnes, P., Vasserman, L., & Hutchinson, B. (2019). Model cards for model reporting. *FAT '19: Conference on Fairness, Accountability, and Transparency*. DOI: 10.1145/3287560.3287596

Mitchell, M., Wu, S., Zaldivar, A., Barnes, P., Vasserman, L., Hutchinson, B., & Gebru, T. (2021). Model cards for model reporting. *Communications of the ACM*, *64*(12), 56–65. DOI: 10.1145/3568997

Mittelstadt, B. D. (2021). Principles alone cannot guarantee ethical AI. *Nature Machine Intelligence*, *3*(9), 753–755. DOI: 10.1038/s42256-021-00376-4

Mittelstadt, B. D., Allo, P., Taddeo, M., Wachter, S., & Floridi, L. (2016). The Ethics of algorithms: Mapping the Debate. *Big Data & Society*, *3*(2), 1–21. DOI: 10.1177/2053951716679679

Mocanu, D. (2025). Degrees of AI personhood. In Hacker, P. (Ed.), *Oxford intersections: AI in society*., DOI: 10.1093/9780198945215.003.0002

Mohanty, A., & Sahu, S. (2024, November 21). India's advance on AI regulation Available at https://carnegieindia.org/2024/11/21/indias-advance-on-ai-regulation-pub-93708

Mohseni, S., Zarei, N., & Ragan, E. D. (2021). A multidisciplinary survey and framework for design and evaluation of explainable AI systems. *ACM Transactions on Interactive Intelligent Systems*, *11*(3–4), 1–45. DOI: 10.1145/3387166

Mökander, J., Axente, M., Casolari, F., Casanovas, P., & Floridi, L. (2022). Conformity assessments and post-market monitoring: A guide to the role of independent auditing in the EU Artificial Intelligence Act. *Minds and Machines*, *32*(2), 265–292. DOI: 10.1007/s11023-021-09577-4

Monitor, E. (2013, February 6). *Com(2011)681 - renewed EU Strategy 2011-14 for Corporate Social Responsibility - Main Contents*. COM(2011)681 - Renewed EU strategy 2011-14 for Corporate Social Responsibility - EU monitor. https://www.eumonitor.eu/9353000/1/j4nvkkpftveemt7_j9vvik7m1c3gyxp/vitwrzhm31gk

Moran, L. (2020, December 11). *Ross intelligence will shut down amid lawsuit from Thomson Reuters*. ABA Journal. https://www.abajournal.com/news/article/ross-intelligence-to-shut-down-amid-thomson-reuters-lawsuit

Morley, J., Floridi, L., Kinsey, L., & Elhalal, A. (2021). From what to how: An initial review of publicly available AI ethics tools, methods and research to translate principles into practices. *Science and Engineering Ethics*, *27*(4), 53. DOI: 10.1007/s11948-021-00282-w

Moustafa, F. R. (2024). Towards recognition of the legal personality of artificial intelligence (AI): Recognizing reality and law. *International Journal of Criminal Justice Science*, *19*(1), 271–288. DOI: 10.5281/zenodo.19116

Mullin, J., Lipton, B., Mir, R., Srago, M., & Guariglia, M. (2025). *Privacy*. Electronic Frontier Foundation. https://www.eff.org/issues/privacy

Mustari, N., Sen, S. K., Banik, A., Mehedi, M. H. K., & Rasel, A. A. (2023, March). Techniques to Estimate the Status of Legal Proceedings Considering Sequential Text Data. In *2023 International Conference on Emerging Smart Computing and Informatics (ESCI)* (pp. 1-6). IEEE. DOI: 10.1109/ESCI56872.2023.10099995

National Institute of Standards and Technology (NIST). (2023). Artificial Intelligence Risk Management Framework (AI RMF 1.0). https://nvlpubs.nist.gov/nistpubs/ai/nist.ai.100-1.pdf

Netscout (2025). *NETSCOUT Reports Fourth Quarter and Full Fiscal Year 2025 Financial Results and Announces Executive Transitions*. Netscout.com. https://ir.netscout.com/investors/press-releases/press-release-details/2025/NETSCOUT-Reports-Fourth-Quarter-and-Full-Fiscal-Year-2025-Financial-Results-and-Announces-Executive-Transitions/default.aspx

News Archive. (n.d.). NVIDIA Newsroom. https://nvidianews.nvidia.com/news/tata-partners-with-nvidia-to-build-large-scale-ai%20infrastructure#:~:text=NVIDI%20A%20today%20%20announced%20an%20%20extensive,hundreds%20of%20startups%20in%20India

Newsroom. (2025). *Big News: Big data: Seizing opportunities, preserving values*. BIG News: Big Data: Seizing Opportunities, Preserving Values | Announce | University of Nebraska-Lincoln. https://newsroom.unl.edu/announce/bigdata/3919/21901

Nguyen, S. T. (2021, July 16). *Privacy and security enforcement*. Federal Trade Commission. https://www.ftc.gov/news-events/topics/protecting-consumer-privacy-security/privacy-security-enforcement

Nguyen, T., Quach, S., & Thaichon, P. (2021). The effect of AI quality on customer experience and brand relationship. *Journal of Consumer Behaviour*, *21*(3), 481–493. DOI: 10.1002/cb.1974

Noble, S. U. (2018). *Algorithms of oppression: How search engines reinforce racism*. NYU Press. DOI: 10.18574/nyu/9781479833641.001.0001

Novak, M. (2024, September 25). *Donotpay has to pay up over "World's first robot lawyer."* Gizmodo. https://gizmodo.com/donotpay-has-to-pay-up-over-worlds-first-robot-lawyer-2000503265

Novelli, C. (2023). Legal personhood for the integration of AI systems in the social context: A study hypothesis. *AI & Society*, *38*(4), 1347–1359. DOI: 10.1007/s00146-021-01384-w

Novelli, C., Floridi, L., Sartor, G., & Teubner, G. (2025). AI as legal persons: Past, patterns, and prospects. DOI: 10.2139/ssrn.5032265

OECD. (2024). AI principles. https://www.oecd.org/en/topics/sub-issues/ai-principles.html

Oja, S. (2021). Estonia's implementation of AI in small claims courts: Transparency and ethical considerations. *AI and Law*, *29*(1), 45–56.

Pagallo, U. (2018). Vital, Sophia, and Co.—The quest for the legal personhood of robots. *Information (Basel)*, *9*(9), 230. DOI: 10.3390/info9090230

Papagiannidis, E. (2025). Responsible artificial intelligence governance: A review of frameworks and practices. *Technological Forecasting and Social Change*. Advance online publication. DOI: 10.1016/j.techfore.2024.122345

Petruseva, S., Zujo, V., & Zileska-Pancovska, V. (2013). Neural network prediction model for construction project duration. *International Journal of Engineering Research & Technology (Ahmedabad)*, *2*(11), 1646–1654.

Pew Research Center. (2025, April 3). *Views of risks, opportunities and regulation of AI*. Pew Research Center. Retrieved from https://www.pewresearch.org/internet/2025/04/03/views-of-risks-opportunities-and-regulation-of-ai/

Pistora, D., van Dijk, F., & Verkerk, R. (2024). Time Taken for Disposition of Commercial Disputes in the Netherlands: Why official court statistics underestimate the problem of the long and unpredictable duration of court procedures. *Utrecht Law Review*, *20*(1), 44–63. DOI: 10.36633/ulr.925

Progressive Policy Institute. (2024, September 18). An Overview of Global AI Regulation and What's Next. https://www.progressivepolicy.org/blogs/an-overview-and-of-global-ai-regulation-and-whats-next/

Prunkl, C., Whittlestone, J., Singer, P., & Floridi, L. (2021). Institutionalizing ethics in AI through multi-stakeholder governance. *Nature Machine Intelligence*, *3*(1), 10–12. DOI: 10.1038/s42256-020-00252-2

Qian, J. (2025). *Governing China's digital transformation: Industrial Policy, Regulatory Governance, and Innovation*. Taylor & Francis. DOI: 10.4324/9781003347088

Raisch, S., & Krakowski, S. (2021). Artificial intelligence and management: The automation–augmentation paradox. *Academy of Management Review*, *46*(1), 192–210. DOI: 10.5465/amr.2018.0072

Raji, I. D., Smart, A., White, R. N., Mitchell, M., Gebru, T., Hutchinson, B., & Denton, E. (2022). Closing the AI accountability gap: Defining an end-to-end framework for internal algorithmic auditing. *FAccT '20: Proceedings of the 2020 Conference on Fairness, Accountability, and Transparency*, 33–44. DOI: 10.1145/3351095.3372873

Ranchordás, S. (2021). Experimental Regulations for AI: Sandboxes for Morals and Mores. *Morals & Machines*, *1*(1), 86–100. DOI: 10.5771/2747-5182-2021-1-86

Remus, D., & Levy, F. S. (2015, December 11). *Can robots be lawyers? computers, lawyers, and the practice of law. SSRN*. DOI: 10.2139/ssrn.2701092

Ribeiro, B. A., Coelho, H., Ferreira, A. E., & Branquinho, J. (2024). Metacognition, accountability and legal personhood of AI. In Sousa Antunes, H., Freitas, P. M., Oliveira, A. L., Martins Pereira, C., Vaz de Sequeira, E., & Barreto Xavier, L. (Eds.), *Multidisciplinary perspectives on artificial intelligence and the law* (Vol. 58, pp. 169–185). Springer. DOI: 10.1007/978-3-031-41264-6_9

Rishabh Gandhi & Advocates. (2025, January 27). India's Digital Personal Data Protection Rules, 2025: Key highlights. Bar & Bench. ft.com+15Bar and Bench - Indian Legal news+15DQ+15

Ritter, S. M., & Ferguson, S. (2017). Happy creativity: Listening to happy music facilitates divergent thinking. *PLoS One*, *12*(9), e0182210. DOI: 10.1371/journal.pone.0182210

Rolnick, D., Donti, P. L., Kaack, L. H., Kochanski, K., Lacoste, A., Sankaran, K., . . . Bengio, Y. (2019). Tackling climate change with machine learning. arXiv preprint arXiv:1906.05433. https://arxiv.org/abs/1906.05433

Sadoian, L. (2025, July 3). The EU's Strategy for a Cybersecure Digital Single Market. https://www.upguard.com/blog/eu-digital-single-market-strategy#:~:text=The%20EU%20Digital%20Single%20Ma%20rket%20Strategy%20focuses%20on%20removing%20virtual,content%20across%20the%20European%20industry

Sambasivan, N., Kapania, S., Highfill, H., Akrong, D., Paritosh, P., & Aroyo, L. (2022). "Everyone wants to do the model work, not the data work": Data cascades in high-stakes AI. *Proceedings of the 2021 CHI Conference on Human Factors in Computing Systems*, 1–15. DOI: 10.1145/3411764.3445518

Scantamburlo, T., Cortés, A., Foffano, F., Barrué, C., Distefano, V., Pham, L., & Fabris, A. (2023). Artificial Intelligence across Europe: A study on awareness, attitude and trust. *AI & Society*. Advance online publication. DOI: 10.1007/s00146-023-016??-

Schwartz, R., Dodge, J., Smith, N. A., & Etzioni, O. (2020). Green AI. *Communications of the ACM, 63*(12), 54–63. DOI: 10.1145/3381831

Seizov, O., & Wulf, A. J. (2020, September). *Artificial Intelligence and transparency: A blueprint for improving the regulation of AI applications in the EU*. researchgate. https://www.researchgate.net/publication/346330197_Artificial_Intelligence_and_Transparency_A_Blueprint_for_Improving_the_Regulation_of_AI_Applications_in_the_EU

Seng, J. K. P., Ang, K. L., Peter, E., & Mmonyi, A. (2022). Artificial intelligence (AI) and machine learning for multimedia and edge information processing. *Electronics (Basel), 11*(14), 2239. DOI: 10.3390/electronics11142239

Sen, P., & Jakkaraju, S. M. (2025). Modeling AI-human collaboration as a multi-agent adaptation. *arXiv*. DOI: 10.2139/ssrn.5236721

Shang, X. (2022). A computational intelligence model for legal prediction and decision support. *Computational Intelligence and Neuroscience, 2022*(1), 5795189. DOI: 10.1155/2022/5795189 PMID: 35785064

Sharma, S., Iivari, N., Ventä-Olkkonen, L., Hartikainen, H., & Kinnula, M. (2023). Inclusive child-centered AI: Employing design futuring for inclusive design by and with children in Finland and India. *Minds and Machines*. Advance online publication. DOI: 10.1007/s11023-023-09659-2

Sheehan, M. (n.d.). China's AI regulations and how they get made. Carnegie Endowment for International Peace. https://carnegieendowment.org/research/2023/07/chinas-ai-regulations-and-how-they-get-made?lang=n

Shneiderman, B. (2022). Bridging the gap between transparency and trust in AI. *Communications of the ACM, 65*(4), 26–28. DOI: 10.1145/3512701

Shrestha, Y. R., Ben-Menahem, S. M., & Krogh, G. V. (2021). Organizational decision-making structures in the age of artificial intelligence. *California Management Review*, *63*(4), 66–90. DOI: 10.1177/0008125619862257

Sibanda, I. (2025, August 5). *Combating the threat of adversarial machine learning to AI-driven cybersecurity*. ISACA Industry News.

Signa, A., Chella, A., & Gentile, M. (2021). Cognitive robots and the conscious mind: A review of the global workspace theory. *Current Robotics Reports*, *2*(2), 125–131. DOI: 10.1007/s43154-021-00044-7

Singh, R., Kumar, B. V., Rawat, K. K., Akram, S. V., Kathuria, S., & Pachouri, V. (2023, September). Intervention of AI in Prediction of Judgement of Cases. In *2023 4th International Conference on Smart Electronics and Communication (ICOSEC)* (pp. 1268-1272). IEEE. DOI: 10.1109/ICOSEC58147.2023.10275850

Sinha, A. (2024). Facial recognition technologies: A window into India's approach to AI regulation. Tech Policy Press (Center for Advanced Study of India). Available at https://techpolicy.press/.

Sommer, R., & Paxson, V. (2010). Outside the Closed World: On Using Machine Learning for Network Intrusion Detection. *2010 IEEE Symposium on Security and Privacy*, 305–316. https://doi.org/DOI: 10.1109/SP.2010.25

Stahl, B. C., Ryan, M., & Mittelstadt, B. D. (2023). Ethics of artificial intelligence: Risk management, governance, and responsible innovation. *AI and Ethics*, *3*(1), 1–15. DOI: 10.1007/s43681-021-00084-1

Stix, C. (2021). Actionable principles for artificial intelligence policy: Four ways to bridge the gap between principles and practice. *Philosophy & Technology*, *34*(4), 999–1023. DOI: 10.1007/s13347-021-00450-x

Sturm, D., Peters, L. D., & Mueller, R. M. (2021). Leveraging employee engagement for successful digital transformation: The role of digital leadership and change readiness. *Journal of Business Research*, *129*, 610–623. DOI: 10.1016/j.jbusres.2021.03.065

Sun, W., Bocchini, P., & Davison, B. D. (2023). Data integrity and resilience in AI systems. *AI and Ethics*, *3*(1), 145–158. DOI: 10.1007/s43681-022-00146-3

Surden, H. (2014). *Machine learning and law*. UW Law Digital Commons. https://digitalcommons.law.uw.edu/wlr/vol89/iss1/5/

Surden, H. (2019). *Artificial Intelligence and law: An overview*. Colorado Law Scholarly Commons. https://scholar.law.colorado.edu/faculty-articles/1234/

Surden, H. (2014). Machine Learning and Law. *Washington Law Review (Seattle, Wash.)*, *89*, 86–115.

Susskind, R. E. (2019). *Tomorrow's lawyers: An introduction to your future*. Google Books. https://books.google.com/books/about/Tomorrow_s_Lawyers.html?id=4dMSMQAACAAJ

Szabo, N. (1997). Formalizing and Securing Relationships on Public Networks. *First Monday*, *2*(9). Advance online publication. DOI: 10.5210/fm.v2i9.548

Taddeo, M., McCutcheon, T., & Floridi, L. (2019). Trusting artificial intelligence in cybersecurity is a double-edged sword. *Nature Machine Intelligence*, *1*(12), 557–560. DOI: 10.1038/s42256-019-0109-1

Tallam, K. (2025). *Transforming Cyber Defense: Harnessing Agentic and Frontier AI for Proactive, Ethical Threat Intelligence*. ArXiv. https://arxiv.org/pdf/2503.00164

The need for transparency in artificial intelligence. (2023, November 1). U.S. Senate Committee on Commerce, Science, & Transportation. https://www.commerce.senate.gov/2023/9/the-need-for-transparency-in-artificial-intelligence

Times of India. (2024, January 23). Another actor falls prey to deepfake clip in Mumbai

Times of India. (2025, April 8). Nushrratt Bharuccha reacts to Rashmika Mandanna's deepfake case: "It's very scary and that's what I was saying it's unreal...". Available at https://timesofindia.indiatimes.com/entertainment/hindi/bollywood/news/nushrratt-bharuccha-reacts-to-rashmika-mandannas-deepfake-case-its-very-scary-thats-what-i-was-saying-its-unreal/articleshow/99892345.cms

Tolan, S., Pesole, A., & Martínez-Plumed, F. (2021). Talent and leadership in the age of AI. *Nature Machine Intelligence*, *3*(7), 575–584. DOI: 10.1038/s42256-021-00357-4

Tononi, G. (2004). An information integration theory of consciousness. *BMC Neuroscience*, *5*(1), 42. DOI: 10.1186/1471-2202-5-42 PMID: 15522121

TrueCopy. (2025). Navigating the Digital Personal Data Protection (DPDP) Rules 2025: A compliance roadmap for businesses. truecopy.in

U.S. Senate. (2023, August 8). Request not Accepted - Security Risk Detected. https://www.wyden.senate.gov/download/one-pager-bill-summary-of-the-algorithmic-accountability-act-of%202022

UNDP. (2025). Human Development Report 2025. A matter of choice People and possibilities in the age of AI. https://hdr.undp.org/system/files/documents/global-report-document/hdr2025reporten.pdf

UNESCO. (2024). Ethics of artificial intelligence: The recommendation. https://www.unesco.org/en/artificial-intelligence/recommendation-ethics

Union, E. (2016, December 6). *Mergers: Commission approves acquisition of LinkedIn by Microsoft, subject to conditions*. European Commission - European Commission. https://europa.eu/rapid/press-release_IP-16-4284_en.htm

Union, E. (2025a). *The Digital Services Act Package*. Shaping Europe's digital future. https://digital-strategy.ec.europa.eu/en/policies/digital-services-act-package

Union, E. (Ed.). (2025b, March 18). *Competition Policy*. Competition policy. https://ec.europa.eu/competition/general/data_protection_en.html

Vakkuri, V., Kemell, K.-K., & Abrahamsson, P. (2023). Ethical frameworks for AI: A comparative analysis of IEEE and other standards. *AI and Ethics*, *3*(3), 433–449. DOI: 10.1007/s43681-023-00264-4

Veale, M., Binns, R., & Edwards, L. (2018). Algorithms that remember: Model inversion attacks and data protection law. *Philosophical Transactions. Series A, Mathematical, Physical, and Engineering Sciences*, *376*(2133), 20180083. DOI: 10.1098/rsta.2018.0083

Veale, M., & Zuiderveen Borgesius, F. J. (2021). Demystifying the draft EU Artificial Intelligence Act. *Computer Law Review International*, *22*(4), 97–112. DOI: 10.9785/cri-2021-220402

Vercosa, L., Silva, V., Cruz, J., Bastos-Filho, C., & Bezerra, B. L. (2024). Investigation of lawsuit process duration using machine learning and process mining. *Discover Analytics*, *2*(1), 9. DOI: 10.1007/s44257-024-00015-0

Verify, A. I. (n.d.). Singapore's AI Governance Testing Initiative explained - Future of Privacy Forum. Future of Privacy Forum. https://fpf.org/blog/ai-verify-singapores-ai-governance-testing-initiative-explained/

Verma, K. (2023, September 18). *Analyzing the endeavours of the Supreme Court of India to transcribe and translate court arguments in light of the proposed EU AI act*. arXiv.org. https://arxiv.org/abs/2309.10088

Verma, S., & Gustafsson, A. (2020). Investigating the emerging COVID-19 research trends in the field of business and management: A bibliometric analysis approach. *Journal of Business Research*, *118*, 253–261. DOI: 10.1016/j.jbusres.2020.06.057

Vesely, S., & Kim, B. (2024). Survey evidence on public support for AI safety oversight. *Scientific Reports*, *14*(1), 31491. Advance online publication. DOI: 10.1038/s41598-024-82977-5

Vinuesa, R., Azizpour, H., Leite, I., Balaam, M., Dignum, V., Domisch, S., & Nerini, F. F. (2020). The role of artificial intelligence in achieving the Sustainable Development Goals. *Nature Communications*, *11*(1), 233. DOI: 10.1038/s41467-019-14108-y

Wachter, S., Mittelstadt, B., & Floridi, L. (2021). Why a right to explanation of automated decision-making does not exist in the general data protection regulation. *International Data Privacy Law*, *7*(2), 76–99. DOI: 10.1093/idpl/ipx005

Wachter, S., Mittelstadt, B., & Russell, C. (2018). Counterfactual Explanations without Opening the Black Box: Automated Decisions and the GDPR. *ArXiv:1711.00399 [Cs]*. https://arxiv.org/abs/1711.00399

Wagner, S. J., Matek, C., Shetab Boushehri, S., Boxberg, M., Lamm, L., Sadafi, A., Winter, D. J. E., Marr, C., & Peng, T. (2024). Built to Last? Reproducibility and Reusability of Deep Learning Algorithms in Computational Pathology. *Modern Pathology*, *37*(1), 100350. DOI: 10.1016/j.modpat.2023.100350

Wagner, T. L., & Blewer, A. (2019). "The Word Real Is No Longer Real": Deepfakes, Gender, and the Challenges of AI-Altered Video. *Open Information Science*, *3*(1), 32–46. DOI: 10.1515/opis-2019-0003

Walia, H., Chandra, S., & Lal, V. (2024, December 14). Growing concern over deepfakes – CERT-In issues advisory. Available at https://www.khaitanco.com/thought-leadership/Growing-Concern-over-Deepfakes-CERT-In-Issues-Advisory

Wang, W., & Siau, K. (2023). Artificial intelligence, ethics, and public trust: A socio-technical perspective. *Journal of Business Research*, *154*, 113386. DOI: 10.1016/j.jbusres.2022.113386

Watch, A. I. (2025, March 31). Global regulatory tracker - United States. White & Case LLP International Law Firm, Global Law Practice. https://www.whitecase.com/insight-our-thinking/ai-watch-global-regulatory-tracker-united-states

Wen, Y., & Ti, P. (2024). A Study of Legal Judgment Prediction Based on Deep Learning Multi-Fusion Models—Data from China. *SAGE Open, 14*(3), 21582440241257682. DOI: 10.1177/21582440241257682

Wieringa, M. (2020). GDPR compliance and AI: Case studies from the Netherlands. *Journal of Information Privacy and Security, 16*(3), 17–29.

Wilkins, D., & Pillaipakkamnatt, K. (1997, June). The effectiveness of machine learning techniques for predicting time to case disposition. In *Proceedings of the 6th international conference on Artificial intelligence and law* (pp. 106-113). DOI: 10.1145/261618.261642

Williams, R. R. (2017). *Hegel on the proofs and the personhood of God: Studies in Hegel's logic and philosophy of religion.* Oxford University Press. DOI: 10.1093/acprof:oso/9780198795223.001.0001

Wilson, H. J., Daugherty, P. R., & Davenport, T. H. (2021). The future of leadership in the AI-enabled organization. *MIT Sloan Management Review, 62*(3), 1–8. DOI: 10.5437/08956308X6203003

Winfield, A. F. T., Booth, S., Dennis, L. A., Egawa, T., Hastie, H., Jacobs, N., Muttram, R. I., Olszewska, J. I., Rajabiyazdi, F., Theodorou, A., Underwood, M. A., Wortham, R. H., & Watson, E. (2021). IEEE P7001: A proposed standard on transparency. *Frontiers in Robotics and AI, 8*, 665729. Advance online publication. DOI: 10.3389/frobt.2021.665729 PMID: 34381820

Woodward, J. (2024, August 22). *47% of legal professionals are now using AI - and adoption is projected to hit 60+% by next year*. Legal Dive. https://www.legaldive.com/press-release/20240822-47-of-legal-professionals-are-now-using-ai-and-adoption-is-projected-to/

Yale Law School. (2024, November 26). *Yale Law School shapes the future of Artificial Intelligence*. https://law.yale.edu/yls-today/news/yale-law-school-shapes-future-artificial-intelligence

Yin, W., Kann, K., Yu, M., & Schütze, H. (2017). *Comparative Study of CNN and RNN for Natural Language Processing*. ArXiv.org. https://arxiv.org/abs/1702.01923

Zarsky, T. (2016). The Trouble with Algorithmic Decisions: An Analytic Road Map to Examine Efficiency and Fairness in Automated and Opaque Decision Making. *Science, Technology & Human Values*, *41*(1), 118–132. https://www.jstor.org/stable/43671285. DOI: 10.1177/0162243915605575

Zuboff, S. (2019). *The age of surveillance capitalism: The fight for a human future at the New Frontier of Power*. The Age of Surveillance Capitalism: The Fight for a Human Future at the New Frontier of Power - Book - Faculty & Research - Harvard Business School. https://www.hbs.edu/faculty/Pages/item.aspx?num=56791

Zuboff, S. (2019). *The Age of Surveillance Capitalism: The Fight for a Human Future at the New Frontier of Power*. Public Affairs.

Zuboff, S. (2019). *The age of surveillance capitalism: The fight for a human future at the new frontier of power*. PublicAffairs.

About the Contributors

Jerry Luftman's career combines the strengths of CIO/practitioner, management consultant, and academic. Dr. Luftman's proficiency in business-IT alignment and digital trends, 19 books, published research, consulting, coaching/mentoring, and teaching/speaking engagements exemplify his expertise and leadership. After a distinguished 22 year career with IBM (where he was among the strategic leaders of the IBM Palisades Executive Education Center, and CIO), he had an exemplary career for 20 years as Professor, founder, and Associate Dean with the Stevens Institute of Technology Information Systems programs (one of the largest in the world). Driven by the strong demand for a global executive education program focusing on managing the digital transformation, Dr. Luftman has leveraged his experience as a CIO, IT management consultant, and leading academician, with his strong network of prominent academics and IT practitioners, to provide a valuable and innovative set of 35 IT management certificates (over 150 courses) via the Global Institute for IT Management.

Aditya Tomer is presently the Dean, Galgotias University, Greater Noida. He is an academician with varied and interdisciplinary interests. Dr. Tomer has to his credit more than 54 publications including Books, Monographs, Chapters, Research Papers, Articles in Magazine and Newspapers. Some of his books namely are Comparative Reflections on the Constitutional Models of India and Australia, Law Governance and Society-A Developing Socio Legal Developing Nations, Rethinking of Juvenile Perspective in Digital Age, Right to Information Act (2005),

Good governance and Human rights in Developing Nations, Rethinking of juvenile Justice system in India and Gender Discourse and Legal perspectives. Dr. Tomer is a keen researcher and has supervised research leading to the award of Ph.D in Law and also LLM. He has presented more than 30 Research papers in National and International Conferences. As an editor he has improved the quality of law journal like Amity International Journal of Juridical Sciences, and Ami code e-Newsletter of Law Dr. Tomer has also contributed to the development of Law Schools by organizing many National and International Conferences, Workshops, Training programmes with NHRC, NCW, NCPC, SCW-BPR&D etc, FDPâ€™s, Panel Discussions and Moot Court Competitions, Legal Aid Camps etc. of high repute

***

Syed Ibad Ali holds a distinguished academic background with a Bachelor of Engineering in Electronics and Communication Engineering (ECE), a Master of Technology in VLSI Design, and a Ph.D. in Electronics and Communication Engineering. With over 13 years of rich academic and research experience, Dr. Ali has been at the forefront of interdisciplinary innovation, merging traditional ECE principles with cutting-edge advancements in artificial intelligence and data science. Currently serving as an associate professor in the Department of Artificial Intelligence and Data Science at Parul Institute of Engineering and Technology, Parul University, Gujarat, he is recognized for his commitment to fostering analytical thinking and research-led pedagogy. His work often bridges theory with impactful applications, inspiring the next generation of engineers and AI specialists. Dr. Ali's passion lies in advancing transparent and ethical AI systems, a vision that is deeply embedded in the themes of this book.

Andi Asrifan, S.Pd., M.Pd. is a senior lecturer in the Doctoral Program in English Language Education at the Graduate School of Universitas Negeri Makassar (UNM), Indonesia. With a Doctor of Education in English Language Education, he has demonstrated a consistent commitment to advancing research in English as a Foreign Language

(EFL), digital pedagogy, and the integration of artificial intelligence (AI) in language instruction. Dr. Asrifan previously served as Head of the Institute for Cooperation and International Affairs at Universitas Muhammadiyah Sidenreng Rappang and continues to collaborate across academic institutions, both nationally and internationally, actively. Over the past two years, Dr. Asrifan has led several research initiatives focused on AI-driven curriculum development, bilingual education in Southeast Asia, and digital parenting in urban Indonesia. He is frequently invited as a keynote speaker at international conferences and serves as a reviewer and editorial board member for various Scopus-indexed journals. His publications have appeared in high-impact outlets and span the disciplines of education, linguistics, and cultural studies.

Harsh Badaya is a research enthusiast and postgraduate student pursuing a Master of Computer Applications (MCA) at Vellore Institute of Technology (VIT), with a Bachelor of Computer Applications (BCA) from Rajasthan University. Research interests include machine learning, deep learning, and their applications in legal analytics, healthcare, and business intelligence. Co-authored a research paper titled "Enhancing Early Lung Cancer Detection using Deep Learning Techniques," published in IEEE Xplore, and contributed to "Hybrid Ensemble Model for Accurate Legal Case Duration Estimation," submitted for inclusion in Moral and Legal Aspects of Artificial Intelligence: Machine Bias and Rule of Law. Proficient in machine learning frameworks, data preprocessing, and model optimization, with a passion for leveraging artificial intelligence to solve real-world challenges and drive AI-driven innovations.

Vikalp Chaturvedi is a dedicated and versatile educator with over 10 years of teaching experience in physics and mathematics, currently serving as a lecturer at Hare Krishna Gurukul. Demonstrates a strong foundation in electronics, modern physics, and mathematics, with additional industry exposure in the telecom sector and academic experience at the Apex Institute of Engineering & Polytechnic College. Brings an effective combination of technical expertise and classroom engagement, along with proficiency in AutoCAD and C/C++ and familiarity with microprocessors and telecom technologies. Passionate about delivering quality education and mentoring students for academic excellence, especially in grades 11–12 and NEET preparation.

Sanjana Chaturvedi is an Assistant Professor at the Institute of Law, Rabindranath Tagore University, Bhopal, specializing in Constitutional Law. She holds an LL.M in Constitutional Law from Ram Krishna Dharmarth Foundation, Bhopal, and an LL.B (Hons.) from Banaras Hindu University, Varanasi. Her professional journey includes mentoring students, organizing career-enhancement programs, and participating in curriculum development. She has contributed to international research presentations and completed a certificate course in legislative drafting from GLC Mumbai. Her research interests encompass environmental law, cyber terrorism, and the role of indigenous people in climate change. She has actively engaged in faculty development programs on intellectual property rights and the National Education Policy 2020. Additionally, she has played a pivotal role in organizing moot court competitions and has been recognized with awards for her contributions to academic excellence.

Lakshmi Harika Palivela completed her B.Tech in Computer Science and Engineering from Jawaharlal Nehru Technological University Kakinada in 2009, M.Tech in Computer Science and Engineering from Jawaharlal Nehru Technological University Kakinada in 2011, and Ph.D. in the faculty of Information and Communication Engineering MIT Campus, Anna University, Chennai in 2020. She is currently working as an Assistant Professor (Sr.) at Vellore Institute of Technology, Chennai. Her research interests include Machine Learning, Distributed systems, Image processing, Data Analytics and Video Analytics

Ashwani Pant has joined MIT World Peace University, Pune as an Assistant Professor of Law Senior Grade, showcasing exceptional efficiency, productivity, and quality in his roles as a Teacher, Programme Coordinator, and in various administrative capacities, backed by 15 years of academic experience. He possesses extensive knowledge of Criminal and Procedural Law, as well as Environmental and Constitutional Law.

Devendra Singh is a distinguished academician with a rich and diverse background in education, research, and academic leadership. He holds dual doctoral degrees—his first Ph.D. in finance and his second Ph.D. in law, with a specialization in banking and AI laws. His academic qualifications also include B.Com (Hons.), M.Com, LL.B (Hons.), LL.M., and MBA (Finance), reflecting his deep commitment to interdisciplinary learning and scholarly excellence. With over 25 years of professional experience, Prof. Singh has made impactful contributions across the domains of teaching, academic administration, research, consulting, and industry engagement. His core areas of expertise include artificial intelligence laws, banking regulatory laws, and finance. At Amity University, Noida, he is currently a professor and the domain head for business law and finance. Prof. Singh has an extensive portfolio of research publications, has chaired numerous national and international conferences, and continues to contribute meaningfully to academic discourse and policy through his scholarly work.

Sumitra Singh is presently working as Asst. Prof at Amity Law School, NOIDA. She has written 5 Books, 35 Book chapters and has presented Papers in more than 150 National and International Conference. She has both Industry and Academia work experience that makes her very zealous and vibrant . She is in various Committee and Subcommittees in our country 's developmental path. She is the Delhi State President, Higher Education Council for Women's Indian Chamber of Commerce & Industry, Co-Convenor of Legal Awareness and Literacy Committee, Coordinator of 2 Law and society-based radio programs, SAMVIDHAN & SAMADHAN, at Radio Amity 107.8 FM. She has also filed 5 patents in herbal medicine. Also, she is the State Advisor for Uttar Pradesh (Advocate Cell), the largest state in India, for our Hon'ble Prime Minister's 152 developmental campaigns. She is also actively involved in various club committee activities and training and development programs at Amity University.

Index

A

B

C

D

E

G

I

L

M

P

R

S

T

www.ingramcontent.com/pod-product-compliance
Lightning Source LLC
LaVergne TN
LVHW081333300926
849161LV00008B/1964